EMERGENCY NOTIFICATION

**Recent Title in
PSI Business Security**

Information Security: A Manager's Guide to Thwarting Data Thieves
and Hackers
Philip Alexander

EMERGENCY NOTIFICATION

Robert C. Chandler

PSI Business Security
W. Timothy Coombs, Series Editor

 PRAEGER

AN IMPRINT OF ABC-CLIO, LLC
Santa Barbara, California • Denver, Colorado • Oxford, England

Library of Congress Cataloging-in-Publication Data

Chandler, Robert C.
  Emergency notification / Robert C. Chandler.
    p. cm. — (PSI business security)
  Includes bibliographical references and index.
  ISBN 978-0-313-36587-4 (hardcopy : alk. paper) — ISBN 978-0-313-36588-1 (ebook) 1. Emergency communication systems—United States. 2. Emergency management—United States. 3. Emergency communication systems—Technological innovations. I. Title.
  HV551.3.C43   2010
  658.4'7—dc22   2010017648

ISBN: 978-0-313-36587-4
EISBN: 978-0-313-36588-1

14 13 12 11 10   1 2 3 4 5

This book is also available on the World Wide Web as an eBook.
Visit www.abc-clio.com for details.

Praeger
An Imprint of ABC-CLIO, LLC

ABC-CLIO, LLC
130 Cremona Drive, P.O. Box 1911
Santa Barbara, California 93116-1911

This book is printed on acid-free paper ∞

Manufactured in the United States of America

Copyright Acknowledgments

Some text is reprinted with permission from Everbridge.

Some text is reprinted with permission from "Crisis Communication," *Disaster Recovery Journal*.

For Curry, Katey, and Keighley

CONTENTS

Preface   ix

Acknowledgments   xiii

Introduction   1

1. Standards, Requirements, and Expectations   7

2. Emergency Notification Basics   20

3. Communication Challenges   55

4. Communication Planning   84

5. Six Phases of Emergencies   106

6. Automated Notification   120

7. Emergency Messages   154

8. Message Maps   169

Notes   193

Glossary   201

Index   205

PREFACE

The general topic of this book explores the process of issuing more effective warnings during an emergency or crisis situation. The key idea is that it is essential to succeed at communicating with the right people, at the right time, in the right ways during an emergency. Effective communication for emergency notification is important. Security, safety, and business survival are all dependent on effective emergency notification communication.

During an unfolding emergency, it is essential to notify and alert individuals; contact the crisis management team; and manage the command, control, and coordination communication functions essential to respond, mitigate the threat and potentially save lives. The notification of affected or vulnerable individuals is essential whether the emergency is the result of a natural disaster, industrial accident, workplace violence, active shooter, or terrorist incident. Effective emergency notification can also facilitate communication with families and the surrounding community; keep all key processes functioning even when people are displaced from their desks, phones, and usual locations; and distribute timely information about ongoing risks, medical and psychological resources, and human resources and personnel information.

It was the massacre at Virginia Tech University in April 2007 that served as one of the social "tipping points" for widespread interest in emergency notification in the security business continuity, and disaster recovery fields (as well as among senior administrators and executives) across the nation. The role of emergency notification (or lack thereof) was a central aspect of the tragedy that occurred on that campus. It seemed that the expectation for rapid, effective, and targeted individual mass notification of students and campus constituents became the norm in the aftermath of that shooting rampage. In addition, the lack of a simple coordinated and effective means to deliver vital warnings to residents has hindered emergency responses in disasters such as Hurricane Katrina, other college campus shootings (e.g., Northern Illinois University and Louisiana Technical College), incidents of workplace and public violence, and occurrences of devastating weather events.* These crises continued to highlight the need for more effective emergency notification communication. Currently, there are efforts in both the public and private sectors to improve and enhance emergency notification communication capabilities.

Meanwhile, far too many businesses, schools, and organizations still rely on outdated, inefficient, and slow manual efforts despite advances in communication technology. These new technologies range from first-generation reverse 911 systems to a number of next-generation low-cost, Software-as-a-Service (SaaS), Web-enabled, full-service products that include options such as text-to-voice conversion, multiple languages, and SMS (short message service) text messages.

This book is intended for security, business continuity, disaster recovery, and emergency response personnel at all levels and in all industry segments. The book is also intended to provide information and strategies for mangers as well as senior management and executives to recognize, understand, and respond to the demands for emergency notification capabilities. It contains practical information that would be useful for all businesses, agencies, schools, and other organizations both in the private and public sectors.

The purpose of this book is to describe the communication challenges and opportunities during emergencies. It presents a model for the phases of an emergency and how the various warnings and alerts are most effective in the context of effective emergency notification. Each phase is clearly recognizable and serves as a time line for the types of communication strategies, methods, and messages that should be priorities. In the following chapters, you will review the major periods and phases of messaging and communication to widely dispersed target audiences, including high-mobility targets who present emergency notification challenges. In times of crisis, communication lines often fail when they are needed the most.

There are many challenges for communicating effectively during emergency incidents. How do you simultaneously contact all your people when they are geographically dispersed and may be on the move? What should you say, to whom, and when should you say it? How will your audience perceive or interpret these urgent messages and warnings? Certain businesses have unique communication needs for security, scalability, compartmentalization, and integration with enterprise-wide needs. How can emergency notification communication work effectively in such contexts? Businesses may need to rapidly communicate

---

*Nationwide Cell Phone Alert System in the Works, http://www.usatoday.com/money/industries/telecom/2008-04-08-fcc-emergency_N.htm/ (accessed May 1, 2010).

with employees in numerous geographically dispersed buildings and facilities in times of emergency. Recovery or resumption communication is also an important aspect for information dissemination considerations. It is obviously important to be able to notify employees of a crisis situation, but to get back to business as usual also requires comprehensive and effective notification and information dissemination.

The ultimate value of this book lies in its role to lay the groundwork for understanding the functions, purposes, capabilities, advantages, and limitations of automated emergency notification systems. Because not all systems are alike, these chapters will help the reader understand the differences between various notification technologies currently on the market. The common features of automated notification systems were designed to directly address challenges of crisis communication. Some key ideas in using automated notification systems are to make communicating with many as simple and effective as communicating with one; to support business processes that require rapid, accurate, and verified communication; to address the proliferation of networks and devices that make mass communication more complex and less efficient; to communicate quickly, easily, and efficiently with large numbers of people in minutes, not hours; to use all contact paths, especially when the regional or local communication infrastructure is damaged or not working; to ensure two-way communication for better visibility and planning; to reduce miscommunication and misunderstandings by using accurate, consistent messages; to free key personnel to perform critical tasks by automating manual, time-intensive, error-prone processes; and to improve overall communication effectiveness by eliminating any single point of failure.

Finally, this book offers the reader a brief introduction to a process of emergency notification messaging that is called *message mapping*. Message maps are crisis communication tools, blueprints to help simplify complex messages. They are important because message communication in the midst of a crisis is hampered by absentee rates, panic, and lack of planning. Message maps are clear, concise messages that speed communication during chaos. They are appropriate before, during, and after an event, and allow an organization to make better use of information prior to a crisis. Formalized, planned communication eliminates the potential for erroneous messages born of panic and chaos. In creating message maps, employees and constituents are reassured of an organization's ability to handle a disaster. Constituents and stakeholders are now demanding due diligence for creating the optimal emergency notification systems and procedures. This book is a resource for businesses seeking to establish effective emergency notification communication practices. It covers the tools, automation technology, and processes of emergency notification as well as such fundamental aspects as risk communication, message mapping, information loading, audience comprehension and compliance variables, and practical issues such as exercising and testing of emergency notification systems. This book is for every security employee, manager, executive, crisis manager, business continuity planner, emergency manager, and leader in every industry and field. The following pages should help inform you, motivate you, and give you a basic road map toward a dependable and valid system for emergency notification communication.

The following chapters will cover some important informational aspects to help you understand the basic needs, functions, and options for emergency notification communication. Chapter 1, "Standards, Requirements, and Expectations," presents the current regulatory and legal requirements that compel most businesses, schools, hospitals, and agencies to have in place the capability for effective emergency notification communication. Chapter 2, "Emergency Notification Basics," presents a brief history of emergency notification efforts along with a review of all of the currently available communication tools, technology, and various alert systems that are used for emergency notification. Chapter 3, "Communication Challenges," summarizes the primary difficulties and obstacles for effective communication during emergencies, crises, and disasters. Chapter 4, "Communication Planning," offers suggestions and guidelines for preparing an emergency notification communication strategy and plan. Chapter 5, "Six Phases of Emergencies," explores the different aspects of an emergency and offers a framework for organizing communication goals and responses so as to correspond with the unique needs of each phase of an emergency.

Chapter 6, "Automated Notification," offers an introduction to the nuts and bolts of contemporary automated emergency notification system projects that are currently available to help meet the demands for warning capability. Chapter 7, "Emergency Messages," explores the various characteristics of what an emergency message should accomplish, how to construct more effective emergency messages, and also ways that an emergency can impact how an audience reads, understands, and acts on messages during the peak period of an emergency. Finally, Chapter 8, "Message Maps," describes the innovative method developed by the author for premediating emergency notification messages and mapping out a sequence of messages targeting key audiences at key points in an emergency and finally how such message maps can serve as an overall road map for communication during an emergency.

I hope that the reader will successfully learn and apply these important concepts and principles for emergency notification communication contained in the following pages of this book.

Robert C. Chandler, PhD
Orlando, Florida
January 15, 2010

ACKNOWLEDGMENTS

I acknowledge the assistance of Anita Chandler, Jennifer Sawayda, Marc Ladin, Linda Souza, Candi Green, Younjee Kim, O. C. Ferrell, Linda Ferrell, and Tim Coombs, who were valuable in the completion of this project.

I also acknowledge Everbridge and the Tandberg companies, which provided valuable technical information and permission to use material prepared and previously released as white papers, publications, Web content, Webinars, and published essays. I also acknowledge the Centers for Disease Control and Prevention, Department of Health and Human Services, pandemicflu.gov, and the Department of Homeland Security for the public domain materials prepared by the U.S. federal government that appear in this book.

I thank the administrative team at the Nicholson School of Communication at the University of Central Florida, who helps manage the vital tasks so that I can pursue my research and projects such as this book. I also thank Dr. Peter Panousis, dean of the College of Sciences at the University of Central Florida, whose support and encouragement of me to pursue scholarly projects has greatly facilitated the writing of this book.

INTRODUCTION

What is emergency notification and why should you assess and enhance your capabilities to alert and warn people? It is important to understand why business managers should develop and enhance their emergency notification communication capabilities. In addition, you should also consider what basic and fundamental factors are at play in successful notification, what are the available tools and technology available to ensure effective notification, and what are the best practices to ensure consistent emergency notification in all types of situations and contingencies.

In September 2009, officials in the Tavares (Lake County), Florida, water department discovered the presence of fecal coliform, or *Escherichia coli* bacteria, in the city water supply.[1] (These bacteria can make anyone who ingests it sick with diarrhea, cramps, nausea, and headaches. At special risk are infants, young children, and people with severely compromised immune systems.[2]) The citywide water contamination was discovered early on a Saturday morning. City officials were especially concerned with warning people with weakened immune systems and caregivers for children about the contaminated water as quickly as possible. There was a more general need to quickly alert the 13,000 Tavares residents with the urgent warning. Racing against both the clock and the daily routine of residents who would be consuming the water as the day progressed, the city officials hurriedly created a "boil order" notification warning message that was intended to alert residents of the need to boil all water for at least one minute before using or to use bottled water for drinking, cooking, cleaning dishes, making ice, and brushing teeth.[3] (Boiling water kills bacteria and other organisms.) The next challenge that morning was to figure out how to successfully inform all of the residents of the warning and "boil order" before they would next unknowingly turn on the tap.

The city of Tavares used both its Web page (http://www.tavares.org/) and a "reverse 911 calling system" as the primary means of notification (they also alerted the local news media as a secondary notification channel). However, there were many Tavares residents who did not immediately receive the notification. The limitations of Web-posting warnings (essentially waiting for residents to visit the Web site in order to become informed) and using hit-or-miss reverse 911 calling systems (calling only landline telephones but not mobile telephones and not reaching residents who were away from home on a weekend day) were apparent. In fact the TV station WKMG reported that many Tavares residents were notified late on Saturday or not at all by the city's efforts because of coverage and accessibility limits of the reverse 911 system used, as well of their having no reason to visit the city Web page at that time to learn of the situation. A substantial number of residents learned about the boil order from the news media on Saturday evening or even later, and many of them reported that they had consumed and used city water throughout the day, unaware of the contamination.

The general conclusion of many residents and the news media was that the city had failed to adequately alert the residents to the danger in a timely and efficient manner. Residents were upset, confused, and angry; city officials were frustrated; and everyone seemed to agree that there had to be a better way to get these alerts out swiftly, successfully, and satisfactorily. Once again, the need for a functional, fast, efficient, and effective emergency notification solution was illustrated.

One element of emergency preparedness for the responsibility to notify people successfully during an emergency is to have a comprehensive communication plan (and more broadly a comprehensive emergency or crisis or disaster plan). A comprehensive communication plan provides the ability to deliver an accurate, timely, understandable, coordinated, and effective emergency notification message to all selected target constituents as well as to confirm that the messages have been received, understood, and acted on in an appropriate way. Large-scale disasters like Hurricane Katrina and localized emergencies such as university campus shootings have also accelerated the adoption of mass notification technology by businesses, schools, agencies, municipal and governmental units, and organizations both large and small.[4] Many of these tragedies (e.g., Northern Illinois University, Virginia Tech, and far too many other examples of workplace or campus homicide and violence) have also elevated the needs for large-scale, effective, and rapid emergency notification capabilities. How can you, in all hazards, get the word out quickly, accurately, and successfully to the right people at the critical time? How can you increase the odds of reaching the greatest number of people, even if they are highly mobile? How can you enhance the quality of your messages to better ensure that they are understood and generate an appropriate response from the target? How do you know that the messages are working? How can you confirm that your communication is meeting your goals? These are the basic questions that are covered in this book. However, it will also address some bigger issues such as the differences between pure "notification" and more complex forms of communication (two-way, dynamic, and those far more richly meaningful than just notification triggers) as well as the importance of placing notification in the context of premessaging and a long-term view of communicating with constituents.

This book addresses the general topic of emergency notification communication. It briefly reviews the history of contemporary emergency notification systems as well as analyzes the various communication methods and technologies available as communication channels to reach people in the event of an emergency. It also discusses some of the challenges for emergency notification as well as some specific solutions for overcoming those challenges. The book reviews new automated mass notification systems that have been proven effective in delivering warnings and alerts. The book also explores the nature of messages and how perceptions of risks and warnings change during an emergency. Finally, the book presents a method for creating more effective emergency notification messages and creating message maps to enhance the process for issuing effective warning notifications.

The U.S. federal government continues to support and advance new ways to share critical, time-sensitive information in times of crisis with the public.[5] As part of its ongoing efforts, the federal government is developing a nationwide emergency alert system that would send text messages to cell phones and other mobile devices wherever a crisis or emergency occurs. The Federal Communications Commission (FCC) is seeking to establish technical standards and other requirements that for the first time would make such communication possible.[6] Although wireless carriers would not be required to upgrade their networks to accommodate the alerts, those that agree to participate would have to implement the new FCC-mandated standards for a national cellular phone–text message alert system.[7] Four national cellular phone providers—AT&T, Verizon Wireless, Sprint Nextel, and T-Mobile—have each said they almost certainly will take part if the FCC adopts an advisory committee's recommendations on how the system would work.[8] If approved, the proposal would initially enable warnings (in English) of 90 characters in length for each alert message.

The FCC action stems from a 2006 federal law that ordered sweeping upgrades in the way emergency alerts are sent to mobile devices, landline phones, and broadcast TV stations.[9] Currently, many local government and law enforcement agencies can send warnings to mobile devices, but receiving these messages is voluntary and individuals must sign up for the service.[10] The failing is that people will receive such alerts even if they are not in the affected zones, whereas those who did not register but are in the danger zones will not receive the alerts.[11] Another limitation is that the current systems are sequential delivery mechanisms in which a separate text must be sent to each registered person, which can create a bottleneck in the wireless network and often results in delays in the delivery of the warnings. The newly proposed nationwide system would enable a local, state, or federal agency to send an alert by means of a still-to-be-determined federal office that would serve as the centralized communication source for the alert messages. It is the responsibility of that office to relay the alert to participating wireless carriers, to be transmitted to all of their customers in the targeted areas.[12]

The Federal Emergency Management Agency (FEMA) is currently analyzing available technology, and the FCC is working with wireless telephone and data carriers to study the feasibility of a national comprehensive emergency notification system. However, such a federal government–backed warning or alert system, even if deemed feasible, is years away from design, testing, and implementation. It is unclear how accessible or practical such a system would be for a given local community, or more pointedly a business, school, or hospital.

On the other hand, it is imprudent to simply depend on local or national government agencies to ultimately meet the needs for emergency notification. Emergencies impact us on local levels. A national notification system would probably be impractical for local agencies and businesses. When an emergency will threaten the people and facilities at your manufacturing plant, office, school, or establishment, the first duty for notification will most likely fall upon local shoulders. Wider scale emergencies would need levels of notification from municipal, county, or state levels. In fact, some emergencies are not sufficiently significant or widespread to trigger national or state government alert systems. Yet even a localized emergency may nonetheless threaten business operations and personal safety or even create life-and-death situations. In many emergencies the sole source of warning alerts falls on local officials and private-sector security managers in schools, manufacturing plants, or businesses. Every organization should be prepared to get urgent notifications out to the right people at the right time to save businesses, reputations, and lives.

Despite this obvious need, still far too many local governments, businesses, schools, and private-sector and not-for-profit organizations lack demonstrated capabilities for effective emergency notification. Even though communication technology has rapidly evolved in the past decades, disappointingly the planning and preparation for utilizing these new tools and the essential focus on the fundamentals of effective messages and communication processes has lagged. Large-scale disasters like Hurricane Katrina and localized emergencies such as university campus shootings have also accelerated the demand for accurate and specific knowledge resources about effective emergency notification communication.

In the private sector, a number of vendors are offering next-generation, fully integrated automatic emergency notification solutions that enable near-instant notification via a wide range of contact paths. These systems can deliver voice, text, graphical, or multimedia emergency notification messages to targeted audiences both small and large.

Many government agencies and authorities are also bringing new emergency notification capabilities online. However, the government systems are inherently inadequate for the wide range and scope of emergency communication needs. Every workplace, school, church, not-for-profit agency, sports stadium, commercial landlord, retail establishment, hospital, and countless other organizations will at some point need to quickly and effectively notify their own people about an urgent situation, danger, or threat. So while it is important to be consistent with the government notification and warning efforts, it is the primary responsibility to be prepared to communicate with those to whom one is accountable during the next emergency.

An automated notification system also provides organizations with the ability to notify customers proactively and efficiently about a variety of time-sensitive offers, such as upcoming sales, promotions, and special deals. For example, a mass notification system can be used to notify customers about a 48-hour sale on a certain item and allow the customer to place an order simply by responding to the notice. Companies can also use a mass notification system to remind customers of service or warranty expirations and to allow them to renew the service for another year.

There are three fundamental benefits of automated notification in the context of customer service management:

- Mass notification can increase revenue for an organization by proactively notifying customers.
- Costs are reduced by enabling a single individual to send out and manage the responses to a notification campaign.
- Mass notification can build "stickiness" for a company or brand by allowing frequent, low-impact interactions with customers.

Mass notification offers many benefits in the context of informing employees about routine events, such as meetings, annual sign-up periods for health benefits plans, and notifications about new corporate policies. The use of a mass notification system can significantly increase the response rate for these events, inform management about who needs more detailed information about an issue, improve overall employee productivity by making sure that employees stay on schedule, and reduce the overall costs associated with informing employees about important events. In order to make the most of emergency communication planning, it is of the utmost importance to consider several key background factors involved in your organization.

Obviously, such mass automated notification solutions also play a central role for emergency notification. The communication technology needed to instantaneously deliver messages to all key target audiences is only part of the emergency notification communication challenge. Thirty-second telephone messages, SMS text messages, e-mails, instant messages, 1–800-Call Center recordings, and all forms of messages have to be carefully constructed and created to have the maximum effect at the critical moments that they reach the target audiences. This book addresses the aspects of the specific written and spoken emergency notification messages. It reviews aspects such as warning messages and perceptual filters along with the nature of message effectiveness (perception, attention, understanding, comprehension, and [behavioral] response). Also covered are issues such as information adequacy (load), readability, comprehension, and new emerging lexigraphical multimedia emergency messages and warnings: the future of emergency notification.

During a crisis, it is imperative for a business to have a written plan for when that crisis happens. Message maps help organizations communicate clearly during a crisis. A message map should be created prior to a crisis, so that organizations have the time and resources to explore all possible scenarios. Planned communication ensures messages are understood by the widest possible audience.

It is important to understand why business managers should develop and enhance their emergency notification communication capabilities, what basic and fundamental factors are at play in successful notification, what are the available tools and technology available to ensure effective notification, and what are the best practices to ensure consistent emergency notification in all types of situations and contingencies. The book starts with a review of legal mandates and requirements for emergency notification capabilities.

This is an important and timely topic for all business security personnel, as well as managers, executives, leaders, administrators, and officials charged with the task of designing, implementing, and ensuring efficacy of delivering widespread warning messages to the right people at the right time during an emergency. There are a number of positive developments in improving emergency notification capabilities in both the private and public sections. This book introduces some of these efforts to you, so that when the next emergency arises, whether it is a water contamination issue or an active shooter incident, emergency notification can occur swiftly and successfully.

CHAPTER 1

STANDARDS, REQUIREMENTS, AND EXPECTATIONS

Recent catastrophic events have shaped new legislation, calls for industry standards, public expectations, and insistence from stakeholders for effective emergency notification. This chapter reviews a number of legal requirements that compel steps for emergency notification communication including Public Law (PL) 110-53 [Title IX] and the National Emergency Communications Plan (NECP) as well as U.S. presidential executive orders.

There are a number of emerging specific definitions of industry standards for emergency notification capabilities, but all include the requirement to demonstrate the ability for quick, effective, and successful emergency notification of those at risk during emergencies. The chapter reviews capabilities, requirements, expectations for preparation, and performance norms for emergency notification communication that emerge from both legal mandates and expectations of stakeholders and the general public.

REASONS TO PREPARE FOR EMERGENCY NOTIFICATION COMMUNICATION

At the most basic level, emergency communication pertains to the alerts, warnings, and notifications that should be issued to responders, key personnel, people at risk, and in many cases the general public during an emergency incident. Such emergency notification processes include the tools, techniques, systems, and messages that are used to ensure that they are able to contact the right people at the right time with the right message and to enable an appropriate behavioral response. Effective notification communication is certainly worthwhile and it makes a lot of common sense to ensure that you can effectively alert and warn people during an emergency. In addition, there are a number of regulatory and legal mandates that require due diligence efforts to ensure the capacity for emergency notification. In most cases there is both a business rationale as well as the requirements to prepare for effective emergency notification communication.

Emergencies are sudden, nonroutine situations that contain inherent threats and require an immediate response. Emergencies are a result of natural disasters, accidents, deliberate criminal and malevolent acts, or malfunctions of safety systems and devices. The dangers posed by emergencies include fire, flood, disease, violent weather, earthquakes, product safety issues, violent attacks, and terrorism.

This communication must come from both public and private sectors, at the federal, state, tribal, territorial, regional, and local levels. At the crux of that response is the capability of every business, school, agency, or public-sector body to have in place a comprehensive emergency communication plan. Numerous "after-action" reports throughout the history of emergency management have cited "communication difficulties" among the major failings and challenges to effectiveness in emergency response. It is now recognized that a successful response to a major emergency incident—either a terrorist attack, industrial accident, criminal event, or natural disaster—requires a coordinated, interoperable response by the public safety, public health, and the emergency management community.

Diligent businesses, schools, agencies, and companies have a formal plan for emergency preparedness, business continuity, and disaster recovery. Although there are many important components of such plans, it is widely acknowledged that the backbone for any effective notification implementation is a well-designed and tested communication plan. Part of any comprehensive communication plan is to (1) have the sustained capability to alert and notify critical target audiences of immediate dangers, (2) provide instructions, and (3) verify that these warnings are being heeded. Recent regulatory requirements have added a sense of urgency to the need to create sustainable emergency communication capabilities.

Every day in cities and towns across the nation, security and emergency response personnel respond to incidents of varying scope and magnitude. The ability of security and emergency responders to communicate with each other in real time is critical to establishing command and control at the scene of an emergency.[1] Equally important is the capability to warn and alert people to emerging or impending dangers so that they can safely stay out of harm's way. In fact, it is imperative to have the capability to alert and warn people during a wide range of local or regional events such as weather conditions, traffic issues, illness, fire, industrial accidents, workplace disruptions, altered schedules, school closures, or other contingencies. However, it has been the major catastrophic events that have driven home the vital role of emergency notification in successfully alerting and warning the public.

On September 11, 2001, in the aftermath of the terror attacks in New York, the public address system mistakenly notified twin tower occupants to stay where they were, including many who had both the time and access to evacuate the building. Other messages produced more confusion and delayed behavioral response until it was too late for many. In the midst of smoke and confusion, the emergency responders marched up the stairs of the Twin Towers doing what they were supposed to do, and when their communication system failed (radio frequency repeaters and other communication devices), many of the heroes of 9/11 never received the warnings about the structural failures of the buildings and directions to evacuate. Many of those responders were still heading up higher in the towers when the buildings fell. Effective communication is a life-and-death matter in emergency situations. It is critically important to get the right message to the right people no matter the circumstances.

"The 911 Commission Report" documents (among other shortcomings) multiple failures in the content, dissemination, and distribution of messages during the emergency notification process. These failures ranged from insufficient and inaccurate instructions and information disseminated over the public address systems inside the World Trade Center towers to the inadequate performance of the radio "repeaters," which hindered effective notification of emergency responders. In short, some people were wrongly instructed to stay in place when they should have been instructed to evacuate, and many never received any communication whatsoever when they should have been notified of the need to evacuate. Perhaps most telling in the report was the general lack of emergency communication planning evidenced by the absence of procedures, systems, technology, and training for emergency communication as the events unfolded. Furthermore, the report documents the misunderstandings, inoperable equipment, lack of redundant systems, and failure to confirm both understanding and behavioral compliance in the emergency response operations at the World Trade Center. One lesson that emerged is the importance and fragility of sustaining communication during disastrous emergency situations. It is incumbent to plan to avoid the inevitable breakdowns and disruptions of an emergency.

Emergency communication also proved problematic during Hurricane Katrina. Hurricane Katrina was the most destructive natural disaster in U.S. history.[2] The efforts to inform and notify the residents of New Orleans during the onset of the storm were largely nonexistent.

Thousands of residents received no instructions or directions about seeking shelter and safety. There was no effective evacuation messaging. There was no centralized means of alerting or contacting people. Both landlines and cellular telephone systems were down. People were literally "in the dark" as well as in the dark in regard to receiving urgently needed information. After the storm passed, and as chaos unfolded, the information dissemination mechanisms in the city and parishes simply disappeared.

Katrina is regarded as a case study for a poor emergency response. It is also an excellent case study of widespread misinformation, a poorly informed population, and failure to provide timely, accurate, or sufficient emergency warnings to select populations and locations for ultimate relief. Katrina shows a near-worst-case example of the absence of successful emergency notification. Residents were uninformed or misinformed about evacuation options, availability, and location of shelters. Furthermore, the storm crippled 38 911 call centers, disrupting local emergency services and knocking out more than three million customer phone lines in Louisiana, Mississippi, and Alabama. Mass media broadcasts were likewise severely affected, as 50 percent of area radio stations and 44 percent of area television stations went off the air, according to a 2006 White House Report.

THE FEDERAL RESPONSE TO KATRINA: LESSONS LEARNED[3]

The private-sector companies as well as schools and other agencies also failed to adequately communicate with their people in the hours leading up to the storm's landfall and throughout the disaster.[4] There were widespread complaints and ongoing dissatisfaction with both public- and private-sector sources for the failures to successfully communicate during the emergency.

In addition to the "life-or-death" urgency to notify people during an emergency event, there is the emerging or rising expectations of a right to be informed. The public expectation is that entities have an obligation to quickly inform or alert them to emergency situations. This was made clear in the aftermath of the Virginia Tech campus shooting. One clear consensus from the Virginia Tech massacre is that constituents and stakeholders expect (demand) rapid, accurate, and reliable emergency notification communication during these disastrous events. Increasingly, senior management and security personnel are being held directly accountable for sustaining effective emergency notification communication. It is well past the time when managers can reasonably say that such emergency notification needs were "unanticipated" or not within the scope of their security and emergency planning efforts. Due diligence demands that modern threats be met with planning and testing the use of modern communication methods, tools, and techniques in order to ensure that emergency notification occurs swiftly, accurately, and effectively. Having valid and reliable emergency notification capabilities is not only the due diligence thing to do; new regulations have mandated such systems for both the public and private sectors.

In response to the 9/11 and Katrina events, new legislation has been enacted such as PL 110-53, which includes "Implementing Recommendations of the 9/11 Commission Act of 2007" and "Improving Emergency Communications Act of 2007." These new laws call for enhanced emergency preparedness in both the public and private sectors. They also call for minimum standards for emergency notification communication systems. The new public-sector requirements go beyond a mandate to simply buy new equipment over the next three years, to also assess the operable and interoperable emergency communication on a nationwide scale. The new requirements emphasize the human element and cross-jurisdictional cooperation of emergency communication.

Toward this objective, the U.S. Department of Homeland Security (DHS) has announced the formation of the NECP to address gaps and determine solutions so that emergency response personnel at all levels of government and across all disciplines can communicate as needed, on demand, and as authorized.[5] The NECP is the first national strategic plan aimed to improve emergency response communication, and complements overarching homeland security and emergency communications legislation, strategies, and initiatives.[6] While the NECP enhances governance, planning, technology, training and exercises, and disaster communication capabilities with recommendations and milestones for emergency responders and relevant government officials, it largely leaves to the private sector the responsibility for emergency notification communication.[7]

The NECP is designed to drive measurable and sustainable improvements consistent with the *National Response Framework*, National Incident Management System, National Preparedness Guidelines, and the Target Capabilities List. NECP goals, along with these other department strategies, will improve nationwide response efforts and bolster situational awareness, information sharing, and command and control operations.[8] The DHS's Office of Emergency Communications developed the NECP in cooperation with more than 150 public- and private-sector emergency communications officials. The department's new Interoperable Emergency Communications Grant Program is available to assist in achieving communication enhancements consistent with the NECP.[9]

EXECUTIVE ORDER: PUBLIC ALERT AND WARNING SYSTEM

In 2006, the president issued an executive order stating that U.S. policy is "to have an effective, reliable, integrated, flexible, and comprehensive system to alert and warn the American people. . . ."[10] To achieve this policy, the president set out a list of required communication capabilities for the secretary of the DHS to meet that respond to the recommendations of experts in the field. In short, these requirements cover the following[11]:

- evaluating existing resources
- adopting common protocols, standards, and other procedures to enable interoperability
- delivering alerts on criteria such as location or risk
- accommodating disabilities and language needs
- supporting necessary communication facilities
- conducting training, testing, and exercises
- ensuring public education about emergency warnings
- coordinating and cooperating with the private sector and government at all levels administering the existing Emergency Alert System as a component of the broader system ensuring that the president can alert and warn the American people

THE WARN ACT

The Warning, Alert, and Response Network Act (WARN Act), as signed into law as Title VI of PL 109-347, required the establishment of a Commercial Mobile Service Alert Advisory Committee by the FCC.[12] Following the signing of the act into law, the FCC assembled the committee, as required, with members from state, local, and tribal governments, from industry and associations, and with representatives of persons with special needs. This committee, within a year of formation, was charged with providing the FCC with recommendations on technical requirements, standards, regulations, and other matters needed to support the transmittal of emergency alerts by commercial mobile service providers to their subscribers.[13]

The digital broadcasting capacity of public television stations are to be used to "enable the distribution of geographically targeted alerts by commercial mobile service providers," based on recommendations from the committee.[14] These provisions are to ensure the development of a new national warning system at the federal level, to be used for presidential alerts, and to support development of alerts to commercial mobile devices.[15] The WARN Act also included provisions for commercial wireless service providers to opt in or out of the emergency alert service, with requirements for informing consumers. Chapter 2 will provide a more comprehensive review of the existing emergency notification efforts in both the public and private sectors. However, there is a clear mandate at the federal level for more effective emergency notification communication.

NEW EMERGENCY NOTIFICATION REQUIREMENTS

PL 110-53 [Title IX] specifically addresses private-sector preparedness and defines important business continuity provisions to be carried out by the DHS.[16] The combined results of these various requirements will be to eventually establish an "Accreditation and Certification Program" for private-sector preparedness.[17] The Accreditation and Certification Program is intended to provide businesses and organizations with a clear road map for strengthening preparedness, response, recovery, and ability to continue operations. In addition, Title IX also requires mutual cooperation between DHS and qualified private-sector entities to develop appropriate "best practices" for risk identification, hazard mitigation, and voluntary standards that address sector-specific and small business concerns, including emergency communication.

The responsibilities of the private sector, including those pertaining to emergency notification communication systems, are stipulated in PL 110-53 [Title IX]. These suggestions include necessary emergency preparedness, managing, and response resources.[18] These steps include the following:

- establishing emergency communication
- developing and maintaining emergency preparedness, response plans, and associated operational procedures that include emergency notification
- developing and conducting training and exercises to support and evaluate emergency preparedness, response plans, and operational procedures
- developing and conducting training programs for security guards to implement emergency preparedness, communication, and response plans, and operational procedures
- developing emergency communication procedures to provide vital information to those at risk
- responding to requests for information from the media and/or the public

The law also stipulated the need for compliance and accreditation standards for all aspects of disaster and emergency preparedness. Although there is not yet a universal set of standards, there are a number of different voluntary standards for the private sector that have come forward in response to PL 110-53.[19] Some of these standards apply directly to the role of emergency communication preparedness for private-sector companies. In the very near future, there will be specific standards for which every organization will have to demonstrate compliance. We already see sufficient draft versions of these standards circulating that give us the basic checklist of what certification might require. Some of the common features of these minimum due diligence standards for emergency communication include (1) demonstrated redundancy, (2) sustainable internal communication, (3) emergency notification, (4) documentation, (5) a communication center, (6) a comprehensive communication plan, (7) advanced planning for emergency communication, and (8) validation of the system and message for ensured effectiveness.[20] These important factors warrant further attention.

Redundancy

Routine communication systems and modalities are usually inadequate for emergency communication needs. Often in disasters or emergencies they are unavailable or inaccessible. Sometimes they experience overcapacity or are physically damaged by a sudden emergency or disaster. Thus, it follows that there should be a redundant layer of reliable communication technology that serves as a backup to the primary means of communication. Most proposed industry standards include items such as the provision, delineation, and testing of feasible backup systems. Thus, if landline telephone service were unavailable in an emergency situation, what is the stipulated backup emergency communication method? The recommendation of the proposed standards is that there should be a planned pattern of fail-safe communication tools, technology, and systems that complements existing communication resources. These planned redundancies should take into account the next generation of sophisticated emergency notification communication resources. To ensure that you have adequate redundancy (using a standard such as the point of diminishing return) requires an examination of the crisis communication capabilities and particularly the needs of specific operations and target audiences.

Procedures

The recommendation is that you should establish, implement, and maintain procedures to swiftly and accurately disseminate alerts, information, and notifications to targeted audiences. This would include procedures for gathering and processing information as well as indelible operating steps to ensure that messages are created, transmitted, received, understood, and result in an appropriate behavioral response.

This would include an information policy (which governs information that can or cannot be released) as well as job duties and procedural steps to ensure that you rapidly respond to requests for (1) preincident, (2) incident or disruption, and (3) postincident information needs. This should also include procedures to provide information to internal and external audiences, stakeholders, and constituents (including clients, customers, and the news media). Additionally, it should include procedures to appropriately respond to stakeholder questions and requests for information.

Dependable Internal Communication

The suggestion is that you will have reliable internal communication between the various levels and functions of the organization and with your partners. This would include a comprehensive system to ensure uninterrupted exchanges of receiving, documenting, and responding to relevant communication from those within your command, control, and coordination as well as to appropriate external partners.

In some cases it might be necessary to demonstrate that your message system is compatible and integrated with other systems (mechanical interoperability issues) and that you should utilize recognizable communication code systems that are consistent with external risk or threat advisory systems (or the equivalent). Achieving this goal would require not only extensive planning, but also training, testing, and validation efforts. The goal is to prepare sufficiently in order to demonstrate that no matter the contingencies of the emergency circumstances, you have the ability to sustain communication with the right people at the right time with the right tools and the right language.

Emergency Notification

One core capability that should be demonstrated is the swift and decisive warning of people who are potentially impacted by an actual or impending emergency. This would include directive messages (such as seek shelter or evacuate) as well as disclosure or informational messages. Notification of employees, families, neighbors, vendors, customers, clients, providers, stakeholders, and other relevant constituents (depending on your unique circumstances) would have to be accomplished. In addition, the effectiveness (comprehension) of your notification messages would depend on whether the words, language, codes, and other alert signals are meaningful for audience members who may be under stress, distress, or even duress.

Emergency notification includes facilitating communication with emergency responders and notifying the appropriate authorities at the right time during an emergency. The achievement of this expectation depends on two factors. First, the right message containing the right amount of information would have to be delivered successfully at the right time. Second, the targeted recipient would actually have to read, understand, and act on the message. The proposed standard would expect demonstration that an emergency notification system is capable of achieving that proficiency.

As mentioned before, the recommendations are that one should demonstrate ensured availability of the communication means, with emphasis on functionality during a crisis situation. This means that the principle of redundancy applies to your emergency notification communication processes for all audiences. Additionally, in order to comply with these recommendations, your system would have to ensure the interoperability of communication tools used by multiple responding organizations and personnel.

Documentation

One emerging recommendation is that you document basic aspects pertaining to your emergency notification communication. This means that in an after-action review, the goal is to be able to document when you knew what, the specific steps you took, what language and messages you used, and what means you used to attempt to notify audiences. There is likely to be both second-guessing and demands for tight accountability for the types of information disclosure decisions you made and how quickly. Also, you would have to record what due diligent efforts were made to communicate risks, dangers, and advisories to audiences during the emergencies.

In light of these recommendations, there is a growing recognition that emergency notification communication should include a systematic and complete recording of vital information about the incident, actions taken, and decisions made. Some of the newer automated notification systems build these documentation recording capabilities into the automated system to produce a thorough log sufficient for after-action review as part of their systems. The automatic capture of key actions and time lines appears to be a fundamental expectation.

Communication Center

The emerging standards discourage ad hoc or "floating" communication management. In fact, almost all of them emphasize the suggestion for a central contact facility or communication hub for emergency communication. The important role of emergency communication is underscored by the recommendation that personnel, physical space, and virtual operations are assigned and dedicated for emergency communication functions. Some organizations have space set aside in an Emergency Operations Center (EOC) for emergency communication functions, whereas others repurpose routine communication centers for emergency purposes. Either approach can work; however, it is important that the communication functions are fully integrated, interactive, and proxemal to the overall emergency command operations. These functions are central—not peripheral—to all emergency management. They need to be at the center of the process and not isolated.

Comprehensive Communication Plan

You have to have a comprehensive communication plan to handle emergencies. This includes outlining basic decisions, priorities based on life and safety, and in consultation with stakeholders about whether to communicate externally about significant risks and threats. Other questions that must be resolved include the following: (1) what will be communicated (and things not to be communicated), (2) when, (3) how, (4) to whom, and (5) how these messages fit the overall policy and plan for emergency management. Such plans should be developed for handling risk communication before, during, and after an incident.

You should determine who has the authority to approve and disseminate messages or specific information. Are there messages that can be "preapproved" so as to avoid unnecessary delays during an emergency situation? It is also important to document all such decisions and to record how that documented policy was followed during the emergency. The advantage of developing such policies in advance is that all of the relevant input can be brought to bear on the decision (e.g., senior management, legal, public relations, human resources).

In instances when there is a decision to communicate and notify audiences of risks and circumstances, the organization should establish and implement specific methods for this external communication, including alerts and warnings. Obviously, such messages should preserve the integrity of sensitive information, but also serve as honest disclosures of risks and display transparency in efforts made to warn.

Advance Planning for Emergency Communication

Hand in hand with the decisions about what types of warning and emergency notifications that you are willing to provide in various circumstances, it is also important to create, test, strategize, and revise a communication strategy, specific tactics, and a game plan for how you are going to implement your warning messages to the audiences that you have targeted.

Prior to an emergency you should develop a communications strategy based on your determination of a list of various questions you compile in your message-planning analysis. This would include sample questions such as the following:

- who needs information
- what information is wanted but not necessarily needed
- what information is needed or required
- when is the information needed
- what means would best transit the required information
- where might your audience be located at the time of the emergency
- what channels or devices might be unavailable or most available
- what constraints exist or who should be the "source" for certain emergency messages

A comprehensive plan will include both push-and-pull communication methods, have a designated spokesperson, identify a vocabulary of key words and terms, have more effective messages and media relations, and have a proactive misinformation and rumor response plan. Communication plans need to be proactive (not reactive). The plan needs to identify the message, the means, the audience, the source, the timing, and measurable objectives for each step along the way in the emergency communication time line.

Validation of the System and Message Effectiveness

Scholarly consensus points to developing messages for release at specific stages of an emergency well before an incident unfolds. These messages can be tested and validated before they are used. Messages should be carefully developed following methods and models for constructing messages. These developed message templates can be drawn upon during the hurried and hectic environment of an emergency to ensure higher quality messaging as opposed to attempts to construct and write coherent and meaningful messages in the context of an urgent crisis. In addition, like all aspects of a security or emergency response system, the emergency notification system itself needs to be tested periodically to demonstrate its reliability and effectiveness.

Emergency communication investments are among the most significant, substantial, and long-lasting capital investments that businesses make. Therefore, it is an important topic that should be considered as a fundamental aspect for doing business operations. In addition, technological innovations, research findings, and best practice norms for emergency notification communication are constantly evolving at a rapid pace. Hence, it is both worthwhile and necessary to stop and examine the status of your emergency notification communication plans.

PROACTIVE STEPS TO ENSURE NOTIFICATION REQUIRED

Demonstrating that you have emergency notification capabilities is not an "optional" activity. Due diligence requires that you make such capabilities a strategic priority. In addition to the regulatory and accreditation mandates, stakeholders now hold an expectation that you will have the capacity to effectively alert your people and those within your span of operational parameters to dangers or threats. It is not a question of "if" the next emergency will occur, but rather "when." The time to begin preparing is *now*, because if you wait to start contemplating how you will alert people and warn them once an emergency is underway, then it is already too late.

SUMMARY OF KEY POINTS

- Major catastrophes such as 9/11, Katrina, and Virginia Tech have shaped legislation, industry standards, private company requirements, public expectations, and stakeholder demands for emergency notification.
- New government-sponsored notification systems are coming online but may be inadequate for emergency notification needs of business, education, and local communities.
- New emergency notification technology provides opportunities for more effective emergency notification effectiveness. In particular, automated notification solutions may be particularly useful to meet the need and expectation for notification.
- There is a critical need for proactive emergency communication planning, in advance of an emergency situation, including creating messages, maps for message sequences, and procedures for notification.
- It is important to validate messages and test communication systems and to confirm message effectiveness.
- Demonstrating that you have emergency notification capabilities is not an "optional" activity. Due diligence requires that you make such capabilities a strategic priority.

CHAPTER 2

EMERGENCY NOTIFICATION BASICS

This chapter reviews the recent history of emergency notification efforts and describes a number of different types and categories of emergency notification. It also covers the various delivery channels (modalities) that can play a role in contemporary notification programs, including the relative strengths and weaknesses of the main tools used today to quickly alert people in the event of an emergency.

ALERTS AND WARNINGS

Early humans probably adapted warning calls and cries to alert one another of potential dangers (e.g., predators or natural disasters) once they banded together in social groups, much like other species of mammals still do to this day. Over the next tens of thousands of years, humans have persisted in the efforts to warn and alert others to the dangerous events that can suddenly threaten life, health, and safety. Over the centuries humans have utilized technology such as bells, flags, fires or smoke, horns, and warning symbols to better alert and notify others of looming dangers. In the past 100 years, these efforts have increasingly become more sophisticated as technological advances have enabled more effective and specific emergency notification delivery. It is on this most recent period in the history of warning communication that this chapter is focused.

EMERGENCY NOTIFICATION MODALITIES

There are many types of mechanical alarms in use to alert people to various threats or dangers. One familiar example is buildings equipped with fire or hazardous material alarms to signal for an evacuation. Even the computer on which this book was written is capable of issuing a warning message about a "danger" that might threaten the program system and, perhaps, more menacing threats such as a potential computer virus, worm, Trojan attack, or breach in the system's firewall. Although these are all important and useful subjects related to the topic of emergency notification, this book is focused more specifically on the communication tasks of notifying a specific audience—the general populace and/or specific individuals in targeted categories or geographical regions—about threats to their health, safety, and well-being. This chapter provides an overview of recent and current types of emergency notification mechanisms. Perhaps the place to start our discussion would be with one of the more dramatic of these types of alert devices, the public warning siren.

Public Warning Sirens

The civil defense siren (also called an air raid siren, tornado siren, tsunami siren, or outdoor warning siren) has been used for more than a century. These audible sirens have been used to warn civilian populations during times of war or natural disaster threats.

Sirens were widely used during World War II by both the allies and the axis governments with the advent of the military use of bombardment and rockets launched against both military and civilian targets. In the peacetime context, audible sirens have been used to warn of natural and man-made disasters, including weather threats and industrial accidents.

Sirens were incorporated into the National Emergency Alert System, which also utilized broadcasting stations. Many in my generation can recall the regular tests of the Emergency Broadcast System that always seemed to interrupt our favorite programs on television and radio. In fact, these tests were so regular that the distinctive tone announcing each test of the EBS system was subsequently followed by words that entered both popular culture and the lexicon of a generation: "This has been a test of the emergency broadcast system. Had this been an actual emergency you would have been advised where to tune for additional information for your local area."

Using various audible tones, horns, and sirens as the primary medium for an emergency warning "message" obviously has limitations on how much specific or detailed information can be conveyed.

Siren Warning Signals

Because of the limited communication (information) content that warning sirens can convey, this book does not include a detailed analysis of the communication effectiveness for emergency notification of various audible alarms, alert tones, or sirens. In addition, other than local "tests" of these sirens in communities, there is frequently little or no systematic effort to train the population as to the "vocabulary" of potential meanings for the different tones that are used in a given area. There are other uses of sirens and tone signals in various communities across the country. The purposes, intended meanings, and behavioral responses sought from the target audiences who hear such signals are fragmented, inconsistent, and unpredictable. Although there are clearly some situational contexts when a siren warning is functional, the limitations and lack of specific information content severely limit their utility. Although there are specialized warning needs for clearly identified threats (with a specific and clear behavioral request such as take shelter or evacuate) such as train derailments, tornados, hurricanes, volcanic eruptions, or tsunamis, there are limits to such systems serving as an effective general hazard emergency notification system.

Alarms

Sirens are typically an outdoor device to signal an emergency situation, and alarms are most commonly designed to alert the occupants within a structure or building. An alarm typically uses sounds, lights, or other signals to alert people to a dangerous threat. Such alarms are among the oldest of the modern mechanical emergency communication modalities.

The message sent out by an alarm is usually a single or dual-dimension communication channel (whether bell, tone, and/or lights). Hence the message that is transmitted by an alarm is at best an attention-grabbing device (assuming that it is heard or seen) and has limited capacity to deliver complex information. Although the amount of "information" that can be communicated is inherently limited, nonetheless an alarm for a specific hazard or context (e.g., fire in a building) can be effective at gaining attention and alerting people for taking a specific action (e.g., evacuation).

Alarms, even when they are working properly, are a rather obtuse and unsophisticated communication medium. They can get our attention and alert us to possible danger, but they can't communicate specific details or even contingency information. For example, unless a complex vocabulary of alarms is developed (such as the various signals for the siren systems), an alarm may trigger an evacuation of a building along prescribed routes. In situations when one or more of these exit routes leads to or through an area where the hazard has occurred or is occurring, alarms cannot communicate the need to take an alternative exit path. Even with a planned vocabulary of alarm signals, there is a limit to how much information can be communicated via this medium. Even though such alarms are severely limited by how much information they can communicate, there are still important uses for alarms in localized settings.

Using a vocabulary of different tones and patterns (also called "alarm coding") can enhance the emergency communication potential for alarms. However, it is necessary to train personnel to recognize and respond to the signal in order to interpret and understand the emergency message (because there are limits to how much instructional information can be provided by the alarm system).

The classic communication model for alarms depends on prior instruction and training as to what an alarm "signals." Recognizing that the alarm signals danger, the desired behavioral response should motivate people to take the actions for which they have been previously instructed (e.g., evacuate a building). Experience with fire drills indicates that one of the main problems with even this simple process is that they don't work all that well. In some cases, alarms are not heard or even are ignored. Common reasons for the disregard of alarms include assumptions that the alarm is a false alarm or that it is merely a test or drill that is presumed less important than completing routine tasks.

There are new alarm systems on the market that attempt to address the information capacity limits with traditional alarms. Recently, alarms have evolved to include audible, visible, tactile, or digital signage text to alert people. Ringing bells are still common, but new alarm systems include public address systems, which can provide supplemental live or prerecorded instructions to people during the alarm. Trained emergency and security personnel can discontinue the replay of automated messages in order to provide real-time voice instructions. Alarm systems, particularly next-generation systems, still play an important role for emergency notification.

"HAZARD-SPECIFIC" EMERGENCY WARNING SIRENS AND ALARMS

There are some regional or localized hazard-specific emergency warning systems. These typically focus on a single threat and have specific and highly specialized emergency warning content and behavioral instructions.

Dam failure sirens and alarms provide notification for people living and working within a specific geographical area in the event of a dam failure danger. These alarms and sirens provide emergency notification to businesses, schools, government agencies, and private individuals.

These alarms can provide an alert to trigger an evacuation and to adjust utilities and other systems so that the impact of a dam failure can be minimized. Likewise, earthquake sirens and alarms provide for notification of people living and working within a specific geographical region that may be threatened by an earthquake or its aftershocks. Using very specific, sophisticated scientific equipment and high-speed computers, it is now possible to provide an alarm for an entire region to go out just in advance of an earthquake or aftershock. Although the advance warning times are still very short (even in the best of systems a 20-second advance warning alarm is considered a major achievement), these warnings nonetheless have the potential to give those most at risk time to seek cover or safer areas inside homes, schools, shops, and workplaces.

The dangers of severe weather (including tornados, thunderstorms, tropical storms, and winter storms) have led to the creation of numerous world, regional, and local warning siren and alarm systems. There are many such alarm and siren systems in place all across the United States.

In recent years, the threats from tsunamis have led to the establishment of new warning alarm networks, an example of which is the Indian Ocean Tsunami Warning System (IOTWS) that was established to alert at-risk populations. The IOTWS was created after the 2004 Indian Ocean earthquake and resulting tsunami, which left some 230,000 people dead or missing.[1] Many analysts claimed that the disaster would have been mitigated if there had been an effective warning system in place, citing the Pacific Tsunami Warning Center that operates in the Pacific Ocean.[2] Currently, at least one not-for-profit operation is offering voluntary emergency notification using mobile short message service (SMS) as a delivery channel for tsunami warning messages. Integrated Tsunami Watcher Service (ITWS) offers a free 24/7 SMS service for tsunami warnings to subscribers.[3]

Beyond sirens, alarms, or warning tones, there have emerged other contemporary methods to issue a warning and rapidly inform targeted audiences. Perhaps the most basic and widely utilized is the telephone.

COMMUNICATION CHANNELS

There are a number of communication technologies that enable far richer and more complex communication than a simple horn, siren, or whistle. One characteristic that distinguishes these rich media forms of distance communication from the lean forms is that these tools provide the means of exchanging complex symbolic and interpretive messages between people, over great distances. Communication researchers typically categorize these various modalities as different communication "channels." Of course, some channels have the capacity for more information and message quality (e.g., telephone compared with e-mail) than others. Some of these richer media options even create the potential for two-way or interactive communication in real-time exchanges. The following section reviews the basic list of channels that are commonly used for emergency notification communication purposes.

Telephones

Alerting contacts via the telephone has been used in differing forms for emergency notification since shortly after telephone usage became widespread. Telephone service has been, for decades, a widely available means of delivering notifications. Key advances include answering devices to receive and record a message (although with limited means to verify that a message has been heard) and mobile phones that expand the range of reaching targeted audiences. However, trying to contact a lengthy list of individuals is a resource-intensive, time-consuming, fairly inefficient, and unreliable notification process. There are a number of reasons why a dependence on contact directories and dialing is an inherently inadequate basis for an emergency notification solution.

The widespread use of mobile telephones in the 1980s and 1990s has increased the usefulness of the telephone as an emergency notification medium. Most contemporary notification systems deployed today make use of telecommunications as part of the contact pathways for communicating alerts. Furthermore, mobile telephones have in recent years given way to personal digital assistant (PDA) devices and smart phones so that in all practical terms mobile telephone users are able to use every communication option that someone sitting at a workstation enjoys, including communication accessible by telephone, computer, Internet, e-mail, social networks, and Web-based applications.

Telephones: Telephone Calling Trees

As telephones became ubiquitous in the 1930s and 1940s, many businesses, schools, agencies, churches, and other organizations developed the telephone calling tree as a means of urgent notification or message dissemination. The basic concept of the telephone calling tree was that an emergency notification message could be sequentially delivered to a limited number of people (e.g., five individuals), who would in turn then each call five more people based on a specified calling list, and each of those individuals would in turn each call five more individuals. In this way, a manual sequential process, using telephones and a compound calling factor should (theoretically) enable the message to be disseminated to all persons on the calling list in a relatively shorter period of time (compared with the primary caller trying to reach everyone on the cumulative list).

In reality, telephone calling trees have some fundamental flaws as an emergency notification system. First, not everyone was consistently available to receive the inbound call (particularly in the age before answering machines). Each missed call in this system had a multiplier effect, because all the subsequent "descendant" calls that that person would have theoretically made would not go forward. Second, the more extended the calling "chain" of links, the greater the likelihood that the relayed messages would become distorted, key information omitted, or even extraneous bits of information would randomly be added—sometimes with serious consequences. An example of this could be seen in watching a sequence of people passing along some instructions: persons in the chain might emphasize one aspect over others, forget to pass along every detail (deeming something irrelevant), or follow the natural tendency to make the message "whole" or complete by supplying details, rationales, and possible implications that make sense to them but were not part of the message that they were instructed to pass along. Although answering machines, mobile phones, call forwarding technology, and other new tools have prolonged the use of telephone calling trees by many businesses, schools, and other groups, the general verdict is that the inherent limitations of such a system are too often overlooked and that the effectiveness of such an emergency warning system is dangerously diminished.

Despite these shortcomings, according to a 2007 U.S. DHS survey, approximately 62 percent of companies still maintain a telephone calling tree as their primary emergency notification system for emergencies and disasters.

Telephones: Reverse 911

Reverse 911 is a communication method that allows emergency coordinators to quickly contact listed telephone (landline) numbers using centralized dispatch callers or an automated recorded message. The term reverse 911 simply indicates that rather than an individual calling the authorities (911 dispatchers) to report an emergency in this case, the authorities are calling the individual members of the community to alert them about the emergency. Some of these systems use auto-dialer technology (probably better known as robo-sales calling) in order to ring as many numbers as possible as quickly as possible. The basic concept of a reverse 911 system is to allow emergency services to do the reverse of a traditional 911 call and to inform the public of a known hazard. Reverse 911 is designed to target geographical areas or designated list-based calling with either a dispatcher or a recorded message. Reverse 911 is now used in many communities, counties, and municipalities.

Although often rudimentary, reverse 911 systems are widely used for both mass notification and resource callout purposes. Typically these systems utilize phone numbers provided by telephone companies segregated by area code, LATA (local access and transport area) code, or geographical prefix numbers. There are a number of commercial vendors who can provide the tools and technologies to establish an auto-dial system that can be used for emergency notification. These systems can play a role in emergency notification communication. Some of these systems offer limited types of interactive capabilities.

Telephones: Telephone Hotlines and Call Centers

One use of telephones for emergency notification is the telephone hotline. Audience members are provided a toll-free number (in advance of an emergency and reiterated during and after an emergency) that they can call to get information or additional information. These calls may be directed to a call center, which would be activated at the onset of an emergency or perhaps staffed 24/7 with routine work and then quickly reassigned to the emergency situation if the event warranted. Alternatively, the hotline can play a recorded message, which can be frequently updated during emergencies. Having callers contacting you is considered a pull method of emergency notification, and this type of approach can be effective with a motivated and informed target audience.

Telephones: In Case of Emergency (ICE)

One interesting side note to our discussion of emergency communication and telephones is the idea of having your mobile phone capable of being used for emergency contacts even if you are incapacitated. The In Case of Emergency (ICE) campaign has gained momentum in recent years. "The idea is to store the word 'ICE' in the address book of mobile phones with the name and phone number of the person that should be contacted in the event that the cell phone owner is injured and unable to communicate this information. For more than one contact name and priority, use ICE1, ICE2, ICE3, etc. It's that simple."[4]

According to Grand Traverse County Michigan Emergency Management and Homeland Security Department, research shows that more than 75 percent of people carry no details of whom they would like contacted following a serious accident. "With 'ICE' first responders and hospital staff will turn to a victim's mobile phone address book and know immediately who to contact. When seconds matter, this information may be vital. For example, the emergency contact may be able to provide critical information about the victim's medical history. Research also suggests people may recover more quickly from the psychological effects of their loved one's injury if they are involved at an earlier stage in the emergency."[5]

One should carefully consider a number of factors when designating the ICE contact (especially when children may be involved), because this person may be asked to provide consent for emergency medical treatment. Make sure that the person whose name and number you are giving has agreed to be your ICE contact and that your ICE partner has a list of people to contact on your behalf—including your place of work.[6]

According to the Grand Traverse County (Michigan) Emergency Management Department:

The original concept, conceived by Cambridge paramedic Bob Brotchie, involved putting the acronym ICE in front of your designated emergency contact. Follow these hints to get the best out of ICE: Make sure the person whose name and number you are giving has agreed to be your ICE partner. Make sure your ICE partner has a list of people they should contact on your behalf—including your place of work. Make sure your ICE person's number is one that's easy to contact, for example a home number could be useless in an emergency if the person works full time. Make sure your ICE partner knows about any medical conditions that could affect your emergency treatment—for example allergies or current medication. Make sure if you are under 18, your ICE partner is a parent or guardian authorized to make decisions on your behalf—for example if you need a life or death operation. Should your preferred contact be deaf, then type ICETEXT then the name of your contact before saving the number.[7]

Make sure your ICE person's number is the one that's most likely to make contact. For example, a home number could be useless in an emergency if the person works full time, so you many want to have several alternative numbers (such as ICE1, ICE2, ICE3, . . .), which indicates a sequence of emergency contacts.[8] Your ICE contact should know about any medical conditions that could affect your emergency treatment—for example allergies or current medication.[9] If the person is under 18 years of age, their ICE contact should be a parent or guardian who is authorized to make decisions on their behalf. If a contact is hearing impaired, then consider using an address such as ICETEXT and then the name of your contact before saving the number.[10] To avoid problems with some phones that won't display duplicate names for the same number (e.g., when "mom" and "ICE" are the same number), you can add an asterisk after the number for your ICE contact. The phone will treat this as a distinct telephone number, and the call should go through even with the "*" added to the number.[11]

Digital Signage

Digital signage is increasingly used as means of emergency notification communication. Digital signs (such as those displayed as LCD, LED, plasma, or projected images) can be deployed as emergency warning systems that incorporate orthographic (textual) messages that are conveyed by means of electronic displays that can be quickly updated as the emergency situation develops. "Communication content" in the context of digital signage can be much more than just text-based messages. These displays offer the ability to show images, graphics, and video (and audio), and some even allow for two-way communication.

The disadvantages of digital signage for emergency notification are readily apparent. Signs are in a fixed location and depend on the target audience passing by, being attentive, and selecting to read and understand the messages. There are a finite number of display locations and capacity limits for how much information can be successfully communicated in this manner.

SMS and Text Messaging

Available on a wide range of networks, SMS is more commonly known as text messaging. Text messaging allows for the exchange of brief textual, word messages via mobile telephones. SMS text messaging is the most widely used data application. SMS is often used to describe any text message.

Most mobile or cellular telephone networks were obviously designed primarily for telephone conversations. SMS came about by taking advantage of the signaling paths needed to control the telephone calls during time periods when no telephone call signaling traffic was occurring. In this way underused capacity in the phone network could be used to transport messages. This piggybacking mode was in part the reason why the length of the messages was limited, so that the messages could fit into the existing signaling formats (hence the name *short message service*).

One advantage for emergency communication that this utilization of capacity gaps in cellular phone service enables is that text messages frequently can be sent to or from areas where the cellular signal is too poor to successfully make or receive a telephone call. These short messages require a minimally sufficient signal, even if it is only available intermittently or is very weak. Another advantage for emergency communication applications is that mobile device-originated SMS messages can also be used for two-way communication and for functions such as SMS polling or voting.

SMS may also play a role in the new cellular phone alert messaging services that the federal government is currently moving toward developing. The Federal Communications Commission (FCC) envisions a nationwide emergency text-messaging emergency alert system. Consumers with mobile phones capable of receiving text messages would receive these alerts unless they specifically chose to be excluded from receiving them. The FCC envisions that such a system would be used for a variety of emergencies: natural disasters, criminal or terrorist incidents, industrial disasters, or even instances of child abduction. The message could be targeted to all wireless customers in a specific geographical area, from a specific cellular phone tower up to a nationwide alert to every cellular phone customer in the nation, within a matter of minutes.

Pagers

Prior to the widespread use of mobile phones in the 1990s, pagers (or beepers) were the most widespread tool for mobile communication. Some pagers only receive a minimal message of a handful of characters (typically a phone number that receivers understand that they are to call). More sophisticated pagers can send or receive SMS messages and can enable the creation or reading of e-mail. Although no longer a widely dispersed communication device, pagers still are used in very narrow and specific target audiences (including first responders, emergency management, hospital workers, and information technology). Pagers tend to continue to work in times of emergency and are more widely deployed where mobile phone networks are limited.

E-mail

E-mail is a ubiquitous method of exchanging textual messages (as well as graphical, audio, and multimedia content) to Internet-connected computers, PDAs, or smart telephone devices.

Emergency communication advantages of e-mail include its widespread accessibility and the ability to provide extensive textual information and to incorporate online links and images in the message. Disadvantages include the increased size of the e-mail, the tendency for quick-glance reading (or recipients ignoring the message entirely), misinterpretation and misunderstanding, as well as security and privacy concerns. Nonetheless, e-mail is a major backbone communication channel and appears to be destined to play a central role in any contemporary emergency notification communication system.

E-mail has changed the way people communicate in a short period of time and has displaced other communication media as a means of interaction. E-mail has significantly displaced face-to-face communication, telephone calls, and written exchanges (e.g., hard copy or snail mail). As part of a next generation of computer-mediated communication, e-mail has changed the expectations for communication. A number of intrinsic communication problems have been identified with e-mail. One of these is "e-mail overload" (also known as e-mail fatigue). E-mail overload occurs when a recipient ignores e-mail messages because of a large volume of inbound communication and/or a high percentage of unsolicited and unimportant e-mail traffic (also known as spam).

E-mail messages often lack contextual and interpretive clues that usually accompany face-face or even telephone conversations that can result in more frequent misunderstandings about tone and implications of messages. Information in context is much easier and faster to understand than unedited and sometimes unrelated fragments of information. Communicating in context can only be achieved when both the message creator and the receiver have a full understanding of the context and issue in question.

It is useful to remember that e-mail is a push communication method—that is, the sender controls who receives the information, and that information is launched to a targeted audience via this delivery path. Not everyone has 24/7 access to e-mail, and there are challenges for reaching target audiences during high mobility. It is also an asynchronous method of communication (synchronous communication is an interaction that includes real-time message-response opportunity such as a face-to-face conversation or a telephone conversation, whereas asynchronous communication is an interaction that has an inherent "delay" that may be unpredictable, such as sending an e-mail and awaiting a reply) that provides an undependable method for feedback, questions and answers, or two-way interaction. Therefore, e-mail alone rarely provides a comprehensive emergency notification platform and should be used in conjunction with other push methods along with pull communication methods to provide a comprehensive emergency notification solution. On the other hand, e-mail has become one of the most widely used methods of communication. It would be hard to envision a modern emergency notification system that did not incorporate the use of e-mail for communication.

It is also useful to note that just because a targeted recipient's system receives e-mail messages does not automatically or inherently mean that the person has read and understood the message and is acting appropriately in response to the message. Nonetheless, many modern systems can at least provide "delivery status notifications." However, these are not universally compatible across platforms. They also require time that may be in short supply. Additionally, there is no way to confirm that the underlying communication was successful. Yet e-mail is a popular option for emergency notification when documentation of emergency communication is required, because it is possible to save a record of the e-mail exchange for later reference.

The use of e-mail messages as one of the primary means to provide emergency notification communication was a much analyzed centerpiece of the after-action review of the tragedy at Virginia Tech, given the use of e-mail as the primary means of disseminating alert and notification messages. E-mail alerts have been used by other universities and schools, companies, agencies, and local governments in a number of different situations. There are some advantages for e-mail messages for certain audiences and situations, but there are also clear-cut limitations. E-mail as a communication means is also incorporated into a number of the automated emergency notification systems that are currently being implemented.

Instant Messaging

Instant messaging (IM) is a synchronous communication modality that allows communicators to send and receive text messages. The messages are composed and sent via computer software. IM is a form of primarily (perceived) synchronous communication between two or more people using (for the most part) typed text. IM actually predates the Internet; the ubiquitous Internet has certainly contributed to the widespread access and usage of IM. IM is a different modality from e-mail and SMS text messages. It also functions somewhat differently from an "interactive" standpoint because of the perceived synchronicity of the interaction. In popular terms an IM exchange is often called a chat, and communicating via this media is called chatting. Internetwide, messaging clients include systems such as ICQ, AOL Instant Messenger, MSN Messenger, Google Talk, Yahoo Messenger, Excite-Messenger, and Same Time instant messenger.

IM's real-time interaction capability means that it can serve as a useful platform for emergency alerts. IM has already been deployed by the National Weather Service (NWS) sending enhanced notification messages and real-time chat interaction with individuals, the media, and constituents.[12] IM has been used for emergency communication because it provides an effective and efficient means for transmitting alerts that permit immediate receipt acknowledgment and/or reply. IM is also popular when documentation of emergency communication is required in that, like e-mail, it is possible to save a conversation log for later reference.

   The rise of mobile instant messaging (MIM) has also been a boon to emergency notification because of the mobility that the IM systems afford by allowing access from computers, PDAs, smart phones, and other connectivity devices. IM is also useful for emergency notification communication because of the ease with which clarification questions and a quick reply can be accomplished. For example, one study reports that IM users see IM as a preferred medium for quick, semi-permanent "flashes" that require a near-immediate response.

   One additional emergency notification use for IM is the auto responder and auto-answer technology. You can provide automated responses that reply to incoming messages with detailed information. For example, a dedicated IM address could be distributed in advance of an emergency or included along with alerts in all formats. This IM address could be set up to have a message or series of messages (prepared in advance) that provide detailed information for a number of common hazards. There are some sophisticated programs (most used in marketing and advertising efforts) that transmit answers to questions that simulate an actual person responding. This information would be available at the convenience of the audience and would not pull key personnel away from other duties at critical times. This would be a complementary way to make additional information accessible along with a Web page.

   The widespread use of IM has increased the usefulness of IM as an emergency notification medium. Most contemporary notification systems deployed today make use of IM as one of the contact pathways for communicating alerts.

Meebo Technical Box

One system that allows connectivity between all of the different instant messaging (IM) systems has recently been introduced. Meebo IM enables users to access contacts on all the major IM networks (including AIM, Yahoo!, MSN, Google Talk, ICQ, and Jabber) using a single contact list and an Internet browser. Meebo is a new communication and media company that has a product with the potential to break down the barriers that have thus far prevented IM from being a ubiquitous communication channel like the telephone or a short message service. Meebo claims to provide IM and group chat to more than 40 million users at meebo.com and with their partner Web sites.[1]

Meebo enables communication on any IM network, on social networking systems (such as Gmail, MySpace, and Facebook Chat), and with people in Meebo Rooms. Meebo also enables live communication integrated into any Web site with Meebo Rooms, Meebo Community IM, and Meebo Me.

---

[1]About Meebo: Instant Messaging Everywhere, Company Web site, http://www.meebo.com/about/.

Meebo is a live communication platform—IM from absolutely anywhere. Integrative platforms such as this may eventually offer another primary pathway for emergency notification communication.[2]

_____

[2]Ibid.

Web Page

A Web page is a rich media text and image document accessible via the Internet. Because the Internet provides ubiquitous access to Web pages from multiple portals and modalities, it has rapidly replaced broadcasting as the means to swiftly make information available to the widest possible audience. It also has the advantage of continuous messaging (you can log in and read the information at any time, compared with situations when you may have missed a broadcast warning). In addition, it provides documentation for the information that is disseminated.

A Web page, as a rich communication medium, can contain numerous types of information that can be seen, read, or heard or can provide interaction opportunities. The basic formats include text in a number of different formats: nontextual information (including 2D images, graphics, maps, and drawings), animated images, audio features, videos, and interactive functions (including hyperlinked text, click-to-play, buttons, tabs, forms, polls, surveys, and access to other resources including databases), and lexigraphical representations (e.g., a 3D evacuation map). The Web page can also contain software programs to collect data from those who access the Web page. These features may all be useful in emergency notification communication applications. It seems obvious that Web pages are another foundational communication modality for emergency notification communication applications. The Pepperdine Application Box provides an extended example.

Pepperdine Application Box

Web pages can be used for advance education and training for emergencies as well as a means of communicating alert or notification messages. For example, Pepperdine University (Malibu, California) maintains a dedicated Web page (http://emergency.pepperdine.edu/) specifically for emergencies, which provides background information, instructions for emergencies, alerts, and status updates, where visitors can check on current conditions at various campuses and locations during an emergency.[1] During an emergency, the

_____

[1]http://emergency.pepperdine.edu/emergency-communication/ (accessed March 4, 2010).

latest updates and decisions of the University's Emergency Operations Committee, such as class cancelations, campus closures, and any instructions to the university community, are posted and updated regularly.[2] The site also lists disaster awareness information that provides instructions as to how the university community should respond in various emergency situations. The online system on this site adds the entered enrollees to the list for sending automatic messages, delivered to the contact paths that each individual selects as his or her preferred medium. Pepperdine considers the Web page and the automated notification system as part of the emergency notification solution to get information out to the most people quickly, accurately, and efficiently, and in formats that are adapted for each audience.

Visitors can choose to get emergency update information by selecting the affected campus locations. In addition, the Web page provides detailed information for a number of emergencies, disasters, and crisis events including active shooters, brush fires, crimes in progress, earthquakes, floods, hazardous materials, power outages, severe winds, structure fires, terrorist attacks, or accidents. The Web site also offers additional information and resources on topics such as personal preparedness, relocation of persons with disabilities, and the "shelter-in-place" program that the university utilizes rather than an evacuation plan for the main campus in Malibu, California.

Students, residents, faculty, staff, and other community members can also register on the Web site for the Everbridge Aware automated notification system that Pepperdine uses for push notification messages.[3] This adds them to the list for automatic messages delivered to the contact paths that each individual selects as his or her preferred medium. Pepperdine considers the Web page and the automated notification system as part of the emergency notification solution to get information out to the most people quickly, accurately, and efficiently, and in formats that are adapted for each audience.[4]

Everbridge Aware is Pepperdine University's automated notification system. The system allows the university to send a message to the cell, office, or home phones of university faculty, staff, and students, as well as SMS/text messages and e-mail. The system is only used during emergencies and for testing. The system is programmed to use the personal contact information provided by each individual in the Web page portal.

Pepperdine's emergency Web page encourages members of the university community to actively seek the latest information from the university's resources. These include the Pepperdine toll-free emergency hotline (it uses a frequently updated recorded message), the emergency Web page itself, and other contacts (mostly toll-free telephone numbers or other Web sites) for information on topics ranging from a class cancelation hotline, area road conditions, or law enforcement and health care provider contact information).[5]

---

[2]Ibid.
[3]Ibid.
[4]Ibid.
[5]Ibid.

Although the Internet and Web pages play a role in emergency notification, using the Web site as a sole source of emergency information is not feasible. Web pages require viewers to reach out to seek the information as opposed to having it delivered to them automatically. One permutation in this regard has been the increasing use of providing "links" to such Web sites along with other push emergency notification messages that provide a means, for those wishing to know more, to quickly access and retrieve information. "Pulling" your audience to your Web page in such a fashion is certainly a useful strategy for an overall emergency notification solution.

Social Networking Services

A social network is a "new media" means of exchanging messages. Typically, these networks are composed of people who share interests and/or activities. There are millions of people who participate in social networks.

The basic model for a social exchange network allows users to create a profile for themselves on Web sites such as MySpace and Facebook. There are also internal social networks that are closed/private communities built from an identified and targeted group of people. Users can control settings that allow postings from others to appear (and in some cases with additional notification that the message has been posted) within their domain area. When these communication channels are unabated, it can be an additional contact path for alerting some targeted audiences.

Mobile social networking has recently enjoyed increasingly widespread usage. Although not yet fully developed, there appears to be potential for applications of emergency notification communication using social networking connections. One such social networking and microblogging service where this can already be demonstrated is Twitter.

Twitter

Twitter is a social networking and microblogging medium in which participants can send and read updates (known as tweets). Tweets are short text-based messages. Users can send and receive tweets via the Twitter Internet Web site, and alternative SMS applications. There is a limit of 40 characters for Twitter "tweets."

The 2007 Southern California Wildfire Application Box illustrates the potential notification value of Twitter.

Regardless of design, it appears that communication media such as Twitter will increasingly play a greater role in swift dissemination of

2007 Southern California Wildfire Application Box[1]

In October 2007, when wildfires ravaged Southern California (and threatened my own home), local residents exchanged alerts and notifications through a number of online "social media" tools such as blogs, annotatable maps, photo sites, and instant messaging services. Although geographically isolated and displaced, they were still able to gather and disseminate emergency information on, for example, the progress of the fire, the location of evacuation areas and shelters, and which schools and businesses were closed. They received this information when it was unavailable and not forthcoming through traditional notification channels.

There is some research to suggest that blogs, maps, photo sites, and instant messaging systems like Twitter do a better job of getting information out rapidly during emergencies, such as the shootings at Virginia Tech, than either the traditional news media or existing government emergency mass notification efforts. The study, performed by researchers at the University of Colorado, also found that those using Twitter during the fires in California in October 2007 kept their followers (who were often friends and neighbors) informed of their whereabouts and of the location of various fires minute by minute. Organizations that support relief efforts are also using Twitter. The American Red Cross has used Twitter to exchange minute-to-minute information about local disasters, including statistics and directions.[2]

"Another example of Twitter being used as an emergency notification tool is during the 2008 Mumbai attacks. During the attacks, eyewitnesses sent an estimated 80 tweets every five seconds as the tragedy unfolded. Twitter users on the scene helped in compiling a list of the dead and injured. In addition, Twitter users sent out vital information such as emergency phone numbers and the location of hospitals that needed blood donations.[3]

"The use of Twitter by victims, bystanders, and the public to gather news and coordinate responses to the November 2008 Mumbai siege led CNN to call it 'the day that social media appeared to come of age.'"[4]

"In February 2009, the Australian Country Fire Authority used Twitter to send out notification alerts and information updates regarding the 2009 Victorian bushfires. During this time the Australian prime minister, Kevin Rudd, used his Twitter account to send out information on the fires, how to donate money and blood, and where to seek emergency help."[5]

---

[1]J. Palmer, "Emergency 2.0 Is Coming to a Website Near You," New Scientist (May 2008), 60. http://www.newscientist.com/article/mg19826545.900-emergency-20-is-coming-to-a-website-near-you.html. (accessed February 6, 2010).

[2]Ibid.

[3]Tweeting the terror: How social media reacted to Mumbai. CNN. http://edition.cnn.com/2008/WORLD/asiapcf/11/27/mumbai.twitter/index.html. accessed on February 6, 2010.

[4]Ibid.

[5]Ibid.

emergency alerts and information. It seems quite reasonable to suggest that emergency managers should actively seek to find ways for communication networks such as Twitter to become a major part of their comprehensive emergency notification communication plans.

COMMON ALERTING PROTOCOL (CAP)

According to the Congressional Research Service: Common Alerting Protocol (CAP) is a standardized format that has been developed for use in all types of alert message formats. CAP has received widespread support from the public safety community and has been accepted as a standard by the international Organization for the Advancement of Structured Information Standards (OASIS). One of its key benefits is that it can be used as a single input to activate multiple warning systems. It is being used as a standard for new, digitized alert networks using multiple technologies. The Emergency Interoperability Consortium (EIC) has a memorandum of understanding with DHS to improve and expand the use of CAP and other XML (Extensible Markup Language) standards in emergency alerts.[13]

CAP is a data format for exchanging public warnings and emergencies between alerting technologies . . . [that] allows a warning message to be consistently disseminated simultaneously over many warning systems to many applications. CAP increases overall warning effectiveness and simplifies the task of activating a warning for responsible officials.[14]

According to the Congressional Research Service, "CAP is compatible with systems that offer the following items:

- flexible geographical targeting using latitude/longitude boxes and other geospatial representations in three dimensions
- multilingual and multiaudience messaging
- phased and delayed effective times and expirations
- enhanced message update and cancelation features
- template support for framing complete and effective warning messages
- digital encryption and signature capability
- facility for digital images, audio, and video"[15]

BRIEF HISTORY OF MASS NOTIFICATION SYSTEMS

It may be helpful to briefly review the recent history of attempts to create successful emergency communication systems. This provides a good context to understand contemporary efforts to create variations of such systems. In addition, these efforts provide an excellent learning opportunity to understand what does and what does not tend to work effectively with such effort.

The following section provides a brief general review of the major efforts for creating alert systems over the past century for a number of different threats and using various communication technologies as they were available.

Emergency Broadcast System

The Emergency Broadcast System (EBS) was created by the U.S. federal government as a method of communicating with the public in the event of an emergency. The primary objective of the EBS was to provide emergency notification to the public in the event of a nuclear attack. The EBS system replaced and superseded earlier procedures and systems that had been in place since World War II. It relied on an activation of tonal warnings similar to the categories established for outdoor sirens. These tonal warnings would interrupt programming and provide instructions to the public to listen to a predesignated list of mass media outlets (television and radio) as the source for official government announcements and instructions.

A nationwide activation of the EBS was called an Emergency Action Notification (EAN). Broadcast stations were required to activate their EAN. Although the EBS was never intentionally activated by the president of the United States for a legitimate national emergency or nuclear attack, the EBS was implemented more than 20,000 times between 1976 and 1996 to broadcast civil emergency messages and warnings of severe weather hazards.

Emergency Alert System

The Emergency Alert System (EAS) was created in 1997, replacing the EBS, used for more than three decades. The EAS relies on delivering emergency notification messages via private-sector (largely commercial) mass media broadcasting technology. It is very comprehensive, covering both AM and FM radio and cable television, including low-power stations, digital satellite and cable television providers, and satellite radio providers.

The current EAS would deliver an audio-only message that is one way (without feedback or asking questions). It would have no real way to measure who (if anyone) is listening, whether they understand the information, and how they might be responding to the message that they had just heard. It is not clear whether in today's 24/7 news media environment the EAS system would be capable of providing emergency information that CNN or other news channels would not have already reported.

The EBS was originally developed in the 1950s when TV and radio broadcasting was the primary means for communicating emergency messages to the general public. Today, the EAS has additional communication options available as a means of communicating emergency messages to more targeted audiences. Today the Federal Emergency Management Agency (FEMA) jointly administers EAS with the FCC in cooperation with the NWS, an organization within the National Oceanic and Atmospheric Administration (NOAA).[16]

The Department of Homeland Security is introducing a program that should be able to disseminate emergency message broadcasts using satellite and public TV broadcast towers. Legislation was passed at the end of the 109th Congress (the Warning, Alert, and Response Network Act, or WARN Act, as signed into law as Title VI of Public Law [PL] 109-347) to ensure funding to public television stations for installing digital equipment to handle national alerts. "[T]his law also required the establishment of a committee to provide the FCC with recommendations regarding the transmittal of emergency alerts by commercial mobile service providers to their subscribers."[17]

According to the Congressional Research Service, several initiatives are underway within the federal government to improve, expand, and integrate existing warning systems. The most important of these—in terms of using, testing and developing leading-edge technology—is the Integrated Public Alert and Warning System (IPAWS), a public–private partnership in which the Department of Homeland Security (DHS) has a leadership role. In the meantime, many communities are installing local alert systems that send voice, text messages, and e-mail.[18]

The National Response Framework emphasizes the separate roles of state and local agencies and other nonfederal entities in disseminating alerts. The different responsibilities of federal agencies and those of state and local agencies has led to problems with coordination and to uneven effectiveness of EAS utilization. This differentiation has produced an apparent obstruction to the implementation of a new program that would expand notification beyond broadcasting channels to include transmitting alerts over cell phones and other modern communication technologies.

The FCC is currently working with commercial mobile phone service providers to create a Commercial Mobile Alert System (CMAS) in response to requirements in the Warning, Alert, and Response Network (WARN) Act, as signed into law (Title VI of PL 109-347).[19] Once implemented, this could result in the capability to disseminate emergency notifications via cell phones. Unfortunately, FEMA, which is the lead agency for EAS, has stated that it does not currently have the authority to manage services deemed necessary for the successful operation of CMAS and that there is a need for additional administrative and legislative action before CMAS will be a reality.[20] Implementation of CMAS is on hold until a federal agency can be identified to take on the role of receiving, verifying, and transmitting nonfederal alerts to cell phone operators.

Many aspects of the EAS, summarized earlier, are discussed in detail in a 2007 report from the Government Accountability Office (GAO).[21] The GAO initiated a study of the functioning of EAS from the perspective of emergency preparedness in government operations. On the basis of its findings, the GAO has made recommendations to FEMA and the FCC for additional planning and greater involvement with stakeholders.[22] The report identified problems such as gaps in disaster planning and insufficient redundancy to ensure uninterrupted broadcasting nationwide.[23]

The report provides an important observation about the capabilities of new communication technology. Digitized signal technology for EAS is the same as that used for the NOAA Weather Radio (NWR). Widely recognized as the backbone of public warning systems, NWR broadcasts weather forecasts and all-hazard warnings for natural and man-made events. The compatibility of the signals makes it possible for EAS equipment used by the media to receive and decode NWR messages automatically. Weather radios can be tuned directly to NWR channels. Many can be programmed to receive only specific types of messages (e.g., civil emergencies) and at specific locations, using Specific Area Message Encoding (SAME).

Standardized SAME codes can be used in almost any device with a radio receiver. These can sound an alarm or set off a flashing light. Similar technology is available to provide NWR messages by satellite TV and over the Internet as messages or as e-mail. Therefore, although EAS and NWR are broadcast technologies set up to operate on a one-to-many basis, these broadcasts can be screened and decoded to provide customized alerts.[24]

There are several more advanced systems currently being used in the public sector that include new emergency communication channels, technology, and computerized automation capabilities.

Public-Sector All-Hazard Warning Efforts

Given the advanced state of other communication technologies, especially the Internet and wireless devices, the reliance on delivering EAS warnings by radio and television broadcasting is increasingly out-of-date and means that much of the public may remain out of touch during an emergency.[25] Some states and communities are pioneering alert systems that utilize other infrastructures. In particular, many communities participate in programs with e-mail or Internet alerts, and some issue mass alerts by telephone.[26]

Call Centers

Some of the technological solutions for disseminating alerts and providing information rely on call centers, including 911 emergency call centers (also referred to as Public Safety Answering Points, or PSAPs). The 9/11 Commission Report describes[27] the often inadequate response of 911 call centers serving New York City during the September 2001 terrorist attacks. The report's analysis of the 911 response suggests the following solution: "In planning for future disasters, it is important to integrate those taking 911 calls into the emergency response team and to involve them in providing up-to-date information and assistance to the public."[28] Such a solution would require a common infrastructure that would support a number of communications and warning needs. Many recommendations have encouraged the development of greater end-to-end connectivity among all types of emergency services.[29]

DEPARTMENT OF HOMELAND SECURITY

In recent years, the new DHS has also pushed for new public notification capabilities.[30] DHS has also sought to coordinate with existing public-sector notification efforts.[31] In 2004, NOAA and DHS's Information Analysis and Infrastructure Protection Directorate signed an agreement that allows DHS to send critical all-hazards alerts and warnings, including those related to terrorism, directly through the NWR All-Hazards Network.[32] Under the agreement, operational procedures were established to develop warning and alert messages that will be sent to NWR for entry into EAS and for broadcast to radios and other communication devices equipped with SAME technology.[33]

DIGITAL EMERGENCY ALERT SYSTEM

According to the 2008 Congressional Research Service report "Emergency Communications: The Emergency Alert (EAS) and All-Hazard Warnings," the DHS has also completed two successful pilot tests of a digital technologies and network alert system called the Digital Emergency Alert System (DEAS).[34] DEAS uses the additional capacity that digital technology provides for broadcasting to send digitized alerts to almost any communications device, including wireless.[35] The rollout of DEAS is part of IPAWS. Development of IPAWS is under the leadership of FEMA's National Continuity Programs Directorate.[36] It will use digital media—including digital TV—to send emergency alert data over telephones, cable, wireless devices, broadcast media, and other networks.[37] The program will provide the base for a national federal public safety alert and warning system using digital technology.[38] Another joint program under the IPAWS umbrella is a pilot project with NOAA to test a geo-targeted alert system using a type of reverse 911. (Reverse 911 is a term sometimes used to describe any calling system that places calls generated by a public safety call center to a specific audience.)

PROPOSALS AND POSSIBLE FUTURE PROGRAMS

Advocates of all-hazard warning systems are seeking interoperability among warning systems, standardized terminology, and operating procedures in order to provide emergency alerts and information that reach the right people, in a timely manner, in a way that is meaningful and understood by all.[39] In 1999, FEMA and the U.S. Departments of Commerce and Agriculture took the lead in a multiagency working group to explore ways to create an all-hazard emergency warning network.[40] According to a 2008 Congressional Research Service report their recommendations included using NWR as the backbone for a national all-hazard warning system and the establishment of a permanent group to promote improvements in warning systems.[41] The following year, the National Science and Technology Council at the White House sponsored a report that explored the types of technologies and systems that are used or could be used for emergency alerts.[42]

The following is a short list of the report's recommendations[43]:

- the creation of a public–private partnership that would bring all stakeholders together
- one or more working groups to address issues such as terminology, technology, location-specific identifiers, and cost-effective warning systems
- system standardization
- increasing the number of communications channel for warnings

The report concluded that substantial improvements in early warning systems could be achieved through coordination, adoption, and better use of existing emergency communication technologies by both public- and private-sector organizations.

In 2000, a public–private multidisciplinary group was organized as the Partnership for Public Warning (PPW).[44] In 2002, this group received funding[45] in order to convene meetings and prepare comments regarding the Homeland Security Advisory System (HSAS). Workshop findings were later expanded into recommendations in "A National Strategy for Integrated Public Warning Policy and Capability." The purpose of the document was to "develop a national vision and goals" for improving all-hazard warning systems at the federal, state, and local levels.[46] PPW suggested that DHS take the lead in developing a national public warning capability. The PPW discussed the role of an alert system in public safety and homeland security, and concluded that current procedures are "ineffective." PPW's recommendations centered on developing multiple, redundant systems using various technologies with common standards that would be "backward compatible" with EAS (including AMBER Alert codes) and NWS technologies.[47]

SPECIALIZED ALERT SYSTEMS

Given the widespread availability of rapid advancing communication technology, it is not surprising that there are a growing number of specialized alert efforts for various contexts and situations. It may be useful to note just a few of these to get an idea of where and how such specialized and narrow targeted alert systems are changing the landscape for emergency notification.

Health Alert Network

The Health Alert Network (HAN) is a program under the Centers for Disease Control and Prevention (CDC), an agency of the U.S. Department of Health and Human Services. According to its Web page, the HAN system is intended to "ensure that each community has rapid and timely access to emergent health information; a cadre of highly trained professional personnel; and evidence-based practices and procedures for effective public health preparedness, response, and service on a 24/7 basis."[48]

Currently, the HAN Messaging System directly and indirectly transmits health alerts, advisories, and updates to over one million recipients. The CDC wants HAN to become a national program, providing health information and the infrastructure to support the dissemination of that information at the state and local levels.[49] Many of the existing state-based HAN programs have more than 90 percent of their population covered under the umbrella of HAN, although some of that is with indirect and mediated messages.[50]

J-ALERT System

According to Reuters, Japan introduced a national emergency notification warning system in early 2007 called the ALERT System.[51] The J-ALERT public emergency notification system transmits alerts about dangers such as earthquakes, terrorism, tsunamis, and even the threat of North Korean missiles.[52] The system uses satellites to activate public address speakers in public places.[53] Once the system is fully operational and is deployed across all of Japan, it should provide a means for emergency notification.[54] Unfortunately, many provincial and municipal authorities have been slow to adopt the J-ALERT system, and it is unclear whether it will ever achieve its goal for comprehensive national coverage of public spaces for alerts.

Active Shooter Warnings

An active shooter is customarily defined as "an armed person who has used deadly physical force on other persons and continues to do so while having unrestricted access to additional victims."[55] This definition includes "snipers" and workplace invasions by gangs of criminals or terrorists. The campus shootings at universities such as Virginia Tech have caused a paradigm shift in expectations for emergency notification, especially on multibuilding campuses or facilities. The challenges of warning students, faculty, staff, visitors, vendors, and members of the local community have motivated a number of campus-specific efforts for emergency alert systems. Many of these active shooter alert systems rely on variations of existing modalities including loudspeakers, sirens, bells, e-mail alerts, text messages, digital signage, Web page updates, landline telephones in classrooms, telephone calling trees, mass media alerts, and cable television interruptions, among other options. Some campuses have adopted fully integrated automated emergency notification systems (which is what Virginia Tech has done) to coordinate emergency notification in these situations.

By the time an active shooter begins an assault, there is little time to recognize the threat, activate a response, and begin emergency notification to save the lives of people in the immediate "killing zone." The need for urgent emergency notification capabilities is glaringly obvious in instances of active shooters on campuses, workplaces, or public spaces. The fact is that in many active shooter incidents, innocent lives may be lost within the first few minutes of the incident. In these situations, this reality dictates the need to rapidly assess the situation and act quickly to alert a highly mobile audience who may be in danger in order to effectively save lives.[56]

AMBER Alerts

An AMBER Alert is a child abduction alert bulletin in the United States and Canada, as well as other countries, issued upon the suspected abduction of a child.[57] AMBER is officially an acronym for America's Missing: Broadcasting Emergency Response but was originally named for Amber Hagerman, a nine-year-old child who was abducted and murdered in Arlington, Texas, in 1996.[58] Exceptions are in Georgia, where it is called Levi's Call[59]; Hawaii, where it is called a Maile Amber Alert[60];

and Arkansas, where it is called a Morgan Nick Amber Alert.[61] Those plans were named after children who were abducted in those states.

When a child has been abducted, authorities can send an AMBER Alert that notifies broadcasters and activates digital signage.[62] AMBER Alerts can also be automatically printed on lottery tickets, delivered to wireless devices, and posted on Web pages.[63]

Silver Alerts

Several states, including the state of Florida have created a Silver Alert system for emergency notification purposes.[64] Similar to AMBER Alerts, the Silver Alert is designed to create a widespread notification, asking citizens to be on the lookout for seniors who become lost.[65] The Silver Alert emergency notification system was created after Mary Lallucci's mother checked herself out of a Pinellas County, Florida, nursing home and accidentally drove into the intracoastal waterway where she drowned.[66] The impetus for the Silver Alert stems from the fact that Florida's elderly population is growing, and the state is committed to putting in place tools and technologies to ensure their safety and protection. The Silver Alert is a standardized and coordinated law enforcement and state agency response system that shares information with the public to improve the chances of a safe recovery.[67]

For a Silver Alert to be issued, the missing person must be 60 years or older, and there must be a clear indication that the individual has an irreversible deterioration of intellectual faculties (i.e., dementia). This must be verified by law enforcement but can be waived under extraordinary circumstances.[68] When notified, the public can play an important role in the rescue of missing elderly persons with a cognitive impairment. According to the Alzheimer's Association, 95 percent of persons who are missing in these situations are found within a quarter mile from their place of residence or last known location.[69] When members of the public hear about a Silver Alert in their area, they should actively make note of the description of the person and any additional information provided. If the public encounters or believes they see the vehicle or the missing person, they should immediately call 911 or *FHP (347) to respond. They should make note of the person's whereabouts and if applicable, the vehicle tag, direction of travel, and location observation (highway/street, city, and county).[70]

Media outlets have the option of whether to broadcast Silver Alert information. Large audiences can be reached through the media, thereby enhancing everyone's efforts in safely recovering a cognitively impaired missing person. On the other hand, there is little effort made to communicate with specific geographical or targeted audiences.

Unlike cases of child abduction, the EAS is not used for Silver Alerts. However, just as with missing child alerts, television and radio stations will be notified, and the information can be broadcasted to the viewing or listening public. The local law enforcement agency is responsible for contacting their local and regional media outlets. The dynamic digital signage message signs will be activated regionally or statewide to alert the general public.[71]

TARGETED NOTIFICATION SYSTEMS

As communication technology has evolved (e.g., computerized auto-dial/call centers, cell phones, pagers, PDAs, e-mail, and high-mobility communication devices) during the past several decades, there has emerged a next generation of emergency notification tools. Rather than "mass" notification of the general public via the mass broadcast media, signage, or sirens, these new systems allow the specific targeting of groups or individuals. These next-generation emergency notification systems have enabled more specific message targeting, delivery confirmation, measurement of audience response, and even two-way communication. Just as significantly, these new emergency notification tools have expanded the capacity for both messages and information content compared with a multitone siren or alarm system. This advantage has created new opportunities for more specialized and effective emergency notification communication.

INTEGRATED EMERGENCY NOTIFICATION IN THE PUBLIC SECTOR

The U.S. federal government is developing a national emergency text-messaging capability. The FCC is currently working to set minimal requirements that could make such a system feasible. Although wireless carriers would not be required to upgrade their networks to accommodate the alerts, those that agree to participate would have to implement the FCC's standards. Four major national cellular telephone service providers—AT&T, Verizon, Sprint Nextel, and T-Mobile—will most likely participate if the FCC adopts such a new national integrated emergency notification system.[72] It appears that the initial parameters of such a system would limit warnings to the English language and 90 characters in length. This new network is expected to be up and running within the next few years.[73]

According to Paul Davidson: [T]he FCC action is rooted in a 2006 federal law that mandated upgrades in the way emergency alerts are sent to mobile devices, land-line phones, and broadcast TV stations. Local, regional, and law enforcement agencies can send warnings to mobile devices, but residents must sign up for the service. Plus, those who enlist receive alerts even if they're out of the affected area, while visitors who haven't joined don't get the news. Also, a separate missive must be sent to each resident, clogging the network and delaying the arrival of many alerts.[74] One conceptualization of the proposed system would also allow a designated county, state, or federal first responder to activate an alert to a controlling authority that would review, filter, edit, or amend the alert and then create the message for distribution.[75] Activating the new notification system would relay the alert to participating wireless carriers who would then contact all the cellular and mobile telephones in the specified zone(s) with the 90-character text message.[76] The messages would be broadcast to many users in the targeted region. Consumers with text message-capable phones would receive alerts unless they opt out. The proposed system could conceivably be used for a variety of crises, and messages could be targeted to a specific geographical region or an entire state, or could even become a national alert.[77]

The proposed system does not address the more fundamental questions about how those 90-character text warnings should be worded and what senders might expect in terms of behavioral compliance. The ultimate effectiveness of such systems will still depend on the messages (and message maps utilized), the comprehension and understanding of the message recipients, and the degree to which such warnings result in appropriate behavioral compliance of those warned so as to ensure the safety and well-being of those audiences.

REGIONAL ALERT SYSTEMS

Some county and municipal government agencies have created local all-hazards alert systems. The various systems that have been adopted include those that issue e-mails, text messages, and cell phone calls for all types of events and hazards, ranging from traffic delays to tornados.

In an effort to provide swift real-time notification during emergencies, even the small village of Manhattan, Illinois, uses a Web page, e-mail alerts, and text messaging to issue free alerts to residents during emergencies ranging from gas leak evacuations to "suspicious persons in a neighborhood who have approached a child."[78] On the other hand, many regions and municipal governments still use outmoded approaches to hazard alerts. Lubbock, Texas, is a representative example of such "last-generation" approaches to emergency notification.[79] Their emergency notification plan relies on citizens (somehow) "becoming aware of an emergency" (presumably by hearing sirens or information transmitted by radio and television broadcasters) and in turn offers general instructions to citizens, directing them to "turn your radio on and tune it to one of the emergency alert stations, KFYO-AM, AM 790, or KZII, FM 102.5."[80] The city also promises that "official information may also be transmitted from local TV stations and local cable stations" and that the "City of Lubbock cable channel (Suddenlink channel 2) will provide information direct from the City of Lubbock Public Information Office."[81] Sadly, Lubbock, Texas, is not the only municipality to use a "crossed-fingers" approach to alerting their residents and visitors during an urgent emergency situation. There are some positive indications that these outdated approaches to emergency notification are slowly giving way to new next-generation approaches to all-hazard alert systems.

Other communities have also experienced problems with different types of noncomprehensive notification systems and wireless-only systems or with notification efforts managed quasi-manually under the direction of law enforcement agencies, telephone authorities, or reverse 911 alerting plans. Fort Collins, Colorado, experienced emergency notification difficulties in June 2009, when attempts to notify residents of a tornado report via cell phones and e-mail messages were unsuccessful in alerting nearly 100,000 targeted residents. It is common for some of these providers to charge per message sent. In cases with unlimited messaging/calling the service fees can top $100,000 annually whether you utilize the system or not. The city of Houston, Texas, has been delaying implementing an emergency notification system offered by wireless providers mainly because of the expensive price tag and service limitations offered.

On the other hand, a number of municipalities have adopted comprehensive, multichannel automated emergency notification solutions that appear to be quite effective. For example, Fairfax County Virginia's voluntary (opt-in model) Community Emergency Alert Network (CEAN) transmits emergency alerts, notifications, and updates during a major crisis or emergency, in addition to day-to-day notices about weather and traffic.[82] The CEAN system will send notification messages to all devices that a resident registers, including e-mail, mobile phones, text pagers, satellite phones, or wireless PDA devices.[83] The CEAN system allows individuals or businesses to register for the notification service and has categories for those with special needs, both physical and social. In addition to the push notification messages, CEAN maintains a Web page that provides a wide range of supplemental and additional information that a resident can access to learn more about the alert.[84]

Likewise the District of Columbia has a voluntary (opt-in model) called Alert DC.[85] The Alert DC system provides rapid text notification and update information during a major crisis or emergency. This system delivers important emergency alerts, notifications, and updates on a range of devices including e-mail, cell phone, pager, BlackBerry, or wireless PDA.[86] When an incident or emergency occurs, authorized D.C. Homeland Security & Emergency Management personnel can rapidly notify registered residents using this community alert system. Alert DC is a connection to real-time updates that includes instructions on where to go, what to do or what not to do, who to contact, and other important information.[87] Alert DC is available to citizens of the District of Columbia as well as to individuals traveling to or working in the District. In addition to the push notification messages, Alert DC maintains a Web page that provides a wide range of supplemental and additional information that a resident can access to learn more about the alert.[88]

Government-provided notification systems still have significant functionality gaps (not likely to close for at least several more years), and many of the single-channel (e.g., wireless providers) notification plans are both expensive and have significant limitations. The best options for emergency notification capabilities can be found in the automated emergency notification solution products. Such automated notification systems would seem like a good choice for businesses, schools, hospitals, and other private- and public-sector agencies.

Concurrent with the emergence of such systems as these, there is a growing number of private-sector-oriented, all-hazards-capable emergency notification products and vendors on the market. Although the basic goals and functions of these services are similar, there are some important differences. It can be quite helpful to have a basic understanding of the different options available on the market.

PRIVATE-SECTOR-INTEGRATED (ALL-HAZARDS) EMERGENCY NOTIFICATION SYSTEMS

In the past few years there have been a number of private market vendors who have created hardware- and software-based products designed specifically to be utilized for emergency notification. These products can be found under some different monikers, such as Mass Notification, Automated Notification, or Emergency Notification Systems. Different systems offer different features, and some of them are more useful for certain tasks than are others. There are certainly differences in these options. However, all of them seek the same general objective of allowing one or a small team of your crisis communication managers to coordinate and disseminate a large number of rapid message transmissions with efficiency, lower costs, and minimal staff. The next sections will look at some of the various features, advantages/disadvantages, and options available in these systems.

Automated emergency notification systems empower organizations to maximize their communication effectiveness. With such systems one person can communicate with tens, hundreds, or thousands of people anywhere, anytime, via any communication method, including phone (landline, mobile, and satellite), e-mail, IM, text messaging (native SMS), fax, BlackBerry, PDA, pager, and more. The better automated emergency notification systems will even continue to cycle through each and every communication device available until the message is delivered and confirmed by the recipient. Automated emergency notification systems multiply your ability to communicate exponentially. Given the available tools that exist today, it is inadequate to rely on old-fashioned, slow, incomplete contact information and error-prone manual telephone calling trees.

Automated Notification

Crisis management, disaster recovery planning, and business continuity are fast-growing and rapidly changing fields in the business, education, and government sectors. Analysis of past crises and disasters has shown that communication breakdowns and gaps are a major limiting factor in effective response, management, and recovery. There are many reasons why communication failures might occur during emergencies; however, one of the more significant areas is the contact paths, channels, and communication technology tools used to interact and reach key target audiences at critical points in time.

During an emergency, crisis, or disaster, organizations must communicate quickly, clearly, and efficiently with employees, constituents, stakeholders, clients, and customers to protect lives, limit economic loss, and prevent the spread of misinformation. As should be clear by this point in the book, communication is a critical component of successful crisis management, business continuity, and disaster recovery. An organization's lack of communication preparation in the face of a major crisis, natural disaster, or terrorist attack can lead to thousands—even millions—of dollars in lost revenue and can put people at risk. Poor performance during an emergency also damages customer, stakeholder, and community confidence.

Communication is critical in other disruptions even if they do not rise to the level of a full-blown crisis. Whether a business interruption is something as temporary as a telephone service outage or as serious as a shutdown of facilities and services, planners must be prepared to respond to such interruptions quickly and effectively to continue operations while minimizing the impact to the organization. Getting the word out to the right people at the right time (particularly when normal and routine communication channels are impacted) is a sign of a superior organization. However, the need to ensure and sustain effective communication in more serious crises and disasters is even more imperative. Regrettably, too often communication is left to old habits or even to chance, without thorough preparation.

There are a number of automated emergency notification solutions currently on the market. These are covered in more detail in a subsequent chapter of this book. Most of these systems provide integration of notification messages using multiple contact paths to reach the targeted audiences. Some automated systems are internally maintained by the organization. Sometimes called free-standing or box systems, these usually require the organization to build, maintain, and control the audience's phone numbers and activate the system using their own computer services. There are both technological challenges as well as the most pressing issue of keeping information and contact databases current.

Next-Generation Interactive Automated Notification Systems

Other automated systems utilize external servers accessed by a Web application. The challenge of gathering phone numbers has been increased with the interest in SMS/text messaging because this service is available on most mobile phones.

ACT-SaaS Service

Some automated notification solutions provide notification-proprietary ACT-SaaS service, an advanced Software-as-a-Service (SaaS) delivery model with multiple data centers in an active–active configuration— the only mass notification provider to offer this level of security, performance, and availability. A more detailed discussion of automated notification systems is contained in a subsequent chapter of this book; however, one technological innovation that deserves mention in this discussion of notification techniques is the ACT-SaaS service.

The ACT-SaaS service provides scalability, availability and security, lower implementation and maintenance costs, free upgrades, delivered maintenance, and fast implementation. ACT-SaaS enables customers to access powerful software over the Internet at maximum performance levels without purchasing or maintaining hardware, software, or telecommunications equipment. Unlike some Application Service Provider (ASP)-based mass notification systems, an ACT-SaaS notification system focuses more on what the customer wants rather than on what solution the provider can deliver. With superior performance, scalability, and lower total cost of ownership (TCO), an ACT-SaaS notification system is the number-one choice of large organizations over ASP, on-premise, and simple SaaS solutions as a direct reflection of the change in business requirements and demands by organizations.

An ACT-SaaS mass notification system provides dedicated availability plus access to additional communication resources across multiple data centers, ensuring the highest level of message throughput—several times faster than on-premise or ASP solutions, which are limited by port capacity or server access in a single data center. The vendor maintains all aspects of the system infrastructure, avoiding problems caused by notification solutions that depend on third-party technology to deliver messages. ACT-SaaS enables everyone—employees, customers, and more—to log in to the system from anywhere, anytime. These systems employ multiple data centers in the United States and Canada using a proprietary ACT-SaaS active–active configuration—the only mass notification provider to offer this level of performance, availability, and security—so the system is always available when it is needed.

With ACT-SaaS, data resides on advanced infrastructures, not on third-party-leased equipment. Built-in redundancy ensures continual access regardless of the situation. On-premise software requires an expensive up-front purchase of perpetual licenses and annual maintenance fees in addition to the internal resources necessary to manage the equipment, telecommunication lines, backup power, data backup, redundant networks, and more. ASPs require restrictive ports-of-capacity purchases, resulting in a dramatically higher TCO than ACT-SaaS at a much lower capacity. All ACT-SaaS costs are included in one annual subscription agreement, requiring less capital upfront and delivering considerable cost savings over time.

Companies tend to choose ACT-SaaS for its security, cost savings, and ability to scale as needs increase; smaller companies find ACT-SaaS to be the logical choice because of the flexibility of its pay-as-you-grow structure. ACT-SaaS is scalable and extensible; as an organization grows, so can its notification solution. ACT-SaaS offers dramatically faster implementation times. Rolling out an ACT-SaaS solution to all or part of your organization is easy: no additional hardware or software to buy and no time spent installing applications or training staff. Implementations are measured in days and weeks versus other solutions that require several months or more to deploy. When message delivery time, system availability, and security are the key criteria for your notification system, the only practical, cost-effective solution that organizations large and small are turning to are ACT-SaaS notification solutions. With significantly shorter implementation times, fewer budget overruns, and unparalleled reliability, ACT-SaaS is quickly becoming the best-practice solution for every organization. Such a notification system delivers the highest levels of performance, security, reliability, and scalability to meet the stringent emergency communication requirements of some of the world's most sophisticated and security-conscious organizations.

These applications and all its components are stored in highly secure, globally dispersed data centers accessible only to approved company employees. One such vendor, Everbridge, provides the automated notification system via its proprietary ACT-SaaS, an SaaS delivery model with multiple data centers in an active–active configuration—the only mass notification provider to offer this level of security, performance, and availability. With active–active data centers, data are continuously replicated between data center locations. If service is disrupted at a data center location, all traffic is dynamically rerouted to a different site so that the systems remain continuously available with none of the time delays associated with notification solutions that fail over and over again.

SUMMARY OF KEY POINTS

- As humans have evolved, so too have the means of warning others about dangers and threats.
- As modern communication technology has developed, so too the use of such technology for warning and alert systems has incorporated these devices in various warning efforts both generally and hazard specific.
- There are many recent and current types of emergency notification efforts, including public warning sirens, horns, and alarms; civil defense (both in the United States and the United Kingdom); tonal warning systems; alarms; and hazard- or context-specific warning efforts.
- There are many communication channels (modalities) or technologies currently available for emergency notification.
- The rise of automated and comprehensive emergency notification solutions developed in the past decade has offered communities and private-sector organizations a useful new tool for emergency notification.

CHAPTER 3

COMMUNICATION CHALLENGES

This chapter reviews the common communication challenges, breakdowns, and bottlenecks that occur during emergency and disruptive situations. In addition, the chapter reviews the impact (psychological and physical) of emergencies on people (both those who create and receive emergency messages). The chapter examines first messages as well as messages on day one and beyond of a crisis. Finally, the chapter looks at the challenges for a crisis management team (CMT), crisis communication roles, and the crisis communication team.

THINGS THAT CAN GO WRONG—USUALLY DO

There are several key aspects of what makes an emergency message effective and successful. This includes recognizing management and communication challenges, analyzing your audience, and looking at ways to improve your crisis communication plan in order to make your messages convey what is needed.

The occurrence of an emergency simultaneously creates communication challenges. Simply put, a crisis creates the expectation for communication from the organization to a wide range of different audiences. These needs include informational, financial, safety, responsibility, causation, consequences and effects, and projections for recovery and return to normal operations. Although it is helpful to group the various audiences into specific categories in order to fully understand what their expectations or agendas might be, it is also important to remember that there are no discrete boundaries of membership between these categories in your audience. Every business has an important and unique set of key stakeholders who expect communication during crises. These stakeholders are important and must be addressed with information if the crisis communication is to be successful. Failure to adequately address key stakeholders may threaten the long-term survival of both people and the company.

There are many different types of communication challenges ranging from logistical and technological to psychological and contextual variables. It may be helpful to mention a few of these challenges in order to help with your own brainstorming and planning processes.

COMMON EMERGENCY COMMUNICATION CHALLENGES

The following is a sample list of common challenges faced during a crisis:

- anticipating communication needs
- taking the initiative to communicate
- breakdowns of communication systems and technologies
- high levels of stress placed on individuals and teams
- rapidly occurring events and changing information
- aggressive demands for information
- critical analysis from the media and public
- poor information-gathering capacities
- lack of sustainable communication systems with rapid feedback
- inability to convey accurate meaning (explicit and implicit)
- collaboration issues
- challenges of geographical dispersion

Crises require cross-communication among groups that are not in the same physical location and may not interact on a regular basis. Government agencies, businesses, health officials, external experts, and the public all need to share information in order to respond effectively to a large-scale crisis. These groups may not have in-person meetings with each other often. They are made up of people who may not know each other well and may not have developed an understanding of the nonverbal cues that comes from frequent face-to-face contact.

In place of face-to-face meetings, most organizations tend to rely on communication tools such as radio, telephone, and e-mail, which do not easily allow for rich, real-time interactivity. These tools hinder the natural communication process and require users to guess at some of the information, or the context, of what is being shared. These technologies are known as lean communication channels.

For everyday situations, lean channels may be sufficient because there is time to confirm and reconfirm information. In a crisis, however, lean channels may not allow for all of the information essential for a response to be communicated. At the same time, in a crisis, users are under a significant amount of emotional stress. They need to gather and decipher information quickly, while potentially facing physical harm. The lean communication tools are simply not robust enough to avoid the misinterpretation that can result from stress. Rich, natural communication is required.

UNIQUE CHALLENGES OF COMMUNICATION IN EMERGENCIES

Crises present unique challenges to the management of communication. One unique aspect of crisis situations is the breakdown of communication systems. We rely on a great amount of supporting infrastructure (e.g., people, technology, locations, routines, and informational resources) during ordinary times. Hence, we are surprised and profoundly frustrated when these presumed "reliable, dependable, and available" resources suddenly prove not to be reliable, dependable, or available. The loss of telephone or e-mail contact, the loss of facilities or access to facilities, the loss of routine schedules or meetings, the absence or loss of key personnel, the loss of coordination assets, the loss of reliable and consistent communication technology, and the loss of information resources all contribute to unique (often unanticipated) challenges of effective communication during crises.

A second unique aspect of crisis situations is the extraordinarily high levels of stress that crises produce on individuals, teams, and even leaders. Crisis communication management can be very stressful. Those who do not manage stress successfully often fail during these situations. Emotional and mental stability is a prerequisite for effective crisis communication leadership. During emergencies and crises, the demands on their skills are tremendous. Research indicates that crisis experiences produce both physiological and psychological impacts on individuals. It is not uncommon to learn of reports where key individuals "froze up" or failed to respond (or respond fast enough) because of the stress and pressure of a crisis situation. Decisions to activate crisis plans, order evacuations, and take action to save lives must be made under very trying conditions and circumstances.

A third aspect of crisis situations is that events occur rapidly. Communication choices about messages, target audiences, methods, channels, strategies, frequency, or redundancy must be reached under severe time constraints and with limited information resources. It is imperative that decision-making skills be honed to provide for the best decisions and notification as rapidly as possible under some of the most challenging and demanding circumstances. Crisis work must be done during periods of high personal anxiety. Prudent planners must consider the impact of such events on personnel, responders, managers, and crisis team members.

A fourth aspect of crisis situations is aggressive demands for information and analysis from the media and the public. To be effective, emergency notification communication must have an appropriate message that reaches the targeted audience at the optimal time and can be understood and acted upon regardless of the circumstances. It is not just what you say and how you say it, although those aspects are important—but it is the attention, perception, needs, and cognitive abilities of people in the midst of a crisis and how they will understand and react to your messages that ultimately determine how effective will be your emergency communication.

Every communication situation during a crisis must be approached with consideration of many dynamics. Therefore, communicated messages are complex and ambiguous at the same time. Successful public communication seeks to balance the needs and expectations of all of these diverse audiences and speak to each of them while not miscommunicating to the remainder. During crisis situations companies will want to provide timely, accurate, and relevant information to constituents through the process of emergency notification. During a crisis, there are common informational needs that the media and public will expect. These include details, the chronology of events and information about policies or procedures in place to mitigate, respond, investigate, or recover. All of these information needs can be aided by emergency notification messages.

FIRST MESSAGES IN AN EMERGENCY

During an emergency situation, people want to know the facts, how serious the situation could become, some recommendations for what they should do in response, and the means to either respond or seek out additional information that they might need. First messages should strive to set the necessary tone, get the facts right, repeat them or update them in a consistent way, and tell people what they should do. Consistent messages are vital. There are several considerations when creating emergency communication to an audience. As a general rule for emergency notification, messages should be brief and precise. Emergency situations frequently produce apprehension and anxiety and provide a number of psychological distractions that diminish many people's ability to focus, concentrate, and process information. It is a safe assumption that during the context of an emergency or high-anxiety event most of your audience will process the first 30 seconds or about 30 words of a message. As messages proceed beyond these compact boundaries, an increasing number of potential audience members stop reading or listening or stop understanding what they are reading or hearing. Your message should be front-loaded with the relevant information at the time of a critical event.

Crisis communication challenges can be segmented into four main categories. One of these categories is participation barriers, which hamper all key members of the crisis communication response from completely participating. These can also include issues concerned with the other categories, because failures in multiple areas tend to have reaching impacts on other failures and can affect participation in the emergency response. Another category is known as the C-3 inefficiencies: command, control, and coordination operations within the organization that are flawed during a crisis. A third category deals specifically with information quality and communication during a crisis. Finally, collaboration issues can plague a crisis response team with the potential for groupthink, divisiveness, and personality conflicts. (Groupthink is a dysfunctional process within a team where no one challenges the sense of the majority of the group and decisions are reached by uncritical consensus and can result in poor or weak outcomes.) Each of these challenges can lead to disastrous results if not handled correctly.

PARTICIPATION BARRIERS

One important communication factor is that it is essential to ensure that all of your key people are fully participating (they are mentally and actively engaged) in the decision-making process as well as the crisis management process. This requires active listening, appropriative communication response, and overcoming apprehension about "speaking out" at critical times. There are some typical barriers to optimal participation in these processes. The following list summarizes some of the more common barriers to sustain ongoing active participation:

- relational and liaison barriers
- motivation, morale, and stress issues
- lack of participation of all key stakeholders
- inherent communication technology weaknesses
- command, control, coordination (C-3) inefficiencies
- lack of sustained authority
- inability to ensure suitable behavioral compliance
- incorrect resource deployment
- breakdown in logistics maintenance
- time pressures

C-3 Inefficiencies

C-3 operations are difficult to orchestrate in the midst of an emergency situation and are often the most challenging aspect of a crisis. Focus tends to be placed on sending commands, but pitfalls related to receiving and understanding information are often left unaddressed. C-3 failures can result in dire consequences, particularly when subordinates do not receive, understand, or obey instructions from superiors.

The reverse is also dangerous. Superiors can exhibit a similar lack of understanding of information presented from the field, often resulting in poor decision making.

Although command and control may imply a top-down hierarchical view of operations management, rarely are C-3 activities executed in a meaningful way by individuals wielding unique authority. They are almost always the product of a high-quality team communicating and coordinating effectively. Therefore, C-3 operations can benefit from clear communication rules, such as turn-taking and clarification of roles and responsibilities.

Information Quality

Ineffective crisis teams can suffer from inadequate information exchange. This may be the result of poor reconnaissance or information-gathering capacities, either due to human error or technology limitations in reaching the information source. They may lack sustainable communication systems with rapid feedback. Without a feedback loop, it is difficult for teams to identify relevant information and discard irrelevant information.[1] Teams need to practice gathering and sorting through information prior to any crisis in order to quickly identify what is the most essential.

Collaboration Issues

High success rates in crisis response have traditionally been associated with team response rather than with individual response.[2] Coordination, trust, and diversity of information all can contribute either to a team's success or to its failure during a crisis event. The effective team is the one that "optimizes the processes for getting, storing, retrieving, allocating, manipulating, interpreting, and discarding information."[3]

Teams, however, have additional coordination overhead that cannot be ignored. Among the most predictable challenges in sustaining effective team communication are (1) distributed personnel, including decision makers and actors; (2) distributed decision-making processes; (3) distributed information exchange networks; and (4) overlapping systems requiring coordination.[4]

Geographically distributed personnel, including decision makers and actors, creates a challenge of distance and timing barriers to exchange information and ideas, and to generate creative solutions. In addition, basic prob lems of accessibility and availability routinely plague dispersed personnel during disasters and emergencies. It always seems like somebody is out of position and/or unavailable at the critical time when you most need to communicate with them. It is also far more difficult for a team to make effective decisions when they are distributed in different locations—even if your conference call is functional and you were able to reach every one. The decision-making processes during an emergency are easily interrupted and derailed. The wider the reach required for gathering and distributing information, the more vulnerable such processes are during emergencies. Distributed information exchange networks are difficult to sustain during crises and disruptions. Finally, the more complex the total number of overlapping organizations systems requiring coordination, the greater the challenge for sustaining effective processes during an emergency situation. These challenges make it extremely difficult for a distributed or localized team to come to a fully informed decision that involves all of the key stakeholders at the critical moments of an unfolding emergency.

In crisis situations, teams may be even more widely distributed than usual. Travel disruptions may occur at the very time when rich and extensive face-to-face interaction is most imperative to manage the situation. During a pandemic, for example, quarantines may keep people inside their houses. Natural disasters may make roads or public transportation inaccessible. Such distribution can lead to confusion and ineffective crisis response.

Various factors have been found to impact team effectiveness negatively.[5] Such factors include insufficient time, lack of information resources, procedural conflict, poor group leadership, uninterested and unmotivated members, no organizational assistance, no financial compensation, and changing organizational expectations.[6] The normal checks and balances that are provided by more time, routine meetings, less stress, and extended face-to-face interaction are often missing in crises, leading to poor team performance. Even the most experienced teams can display divisiveness, groupthink, personality dominance, inaccurate group perceptions, and poor information disclosure.[7]

The strength of teams is found in the input of different points of views, challenges, and even disagreements that provoke the team toward better decisions and actions. Diversity of perspectives can be utilized as a powerful resource.[8] On the other hand, teams need to be focused on common objectives and work together closely to ensure that fragmentation does not derail them. In order to avoid unhealthy divisiveness, a common understanding of the problem and procedures is necessary for effective crisis management.[9] One key factor in avoiding the divisiveness problem is trust. Trust has long been associated with what makes work in organizations possible.[10]

Among the goals for teamwork during crises is to achieve the optimal level of interaction so that the team sustains its cohesion and coordination.[11] However, the team must also retain the "tension" of challenging different points of view, critically assess proposed decisions, and maintain a healthy sensibility about the limitations of the team itself.

While cohesion can make a group strong, it can also increase a tendency to slip into groupthink, whereby proposals are uncritically accepted by team members who do not want to "rock the boat" by challenging the prevailing opinion. Team cohesion is often substituted for a more rational decision process afforded by more diverse views.[12]

The very nature of crisis situations makes them conducive to groupthink. High stress levels, time pressures, a team's need for sustained high levels of cohesiveness, the urgency for a solution to problems, and the use of only lean communication tools can limit a team's interaction and healthy disagreements among its members. Many debriefing sessions of poor decision-making groups uncover individuals who were silent (while disagreeing) because they did not want to appear to "break up" the harmony of the team. This silence could be caused by self-censorship of personal opinions or the vetting of critical information from outside sources. These characteristics increase the danger of groupthink during crises.[13]

In addition to divisiveness and groupthink, teams can also suffer from the personality dominance of certain individuals. When a single member or subset of the group becomes too dominant, information may not be fully disclosed and false assumptions may be made. An overreliance on personal judgment and reduced contributions of team input will cause some leaders, using directed leadership styles, to fail to recognize that what appears to be consensus among the team is in fact merely fragmented silence.[14]

COMMUNICATION BREAKDOWNS

Communication can fail during emergencies for a variety of reasons. The following paragraphs attempt to explain some common reasons for communication failures. A communications failure has a tendency to make the crisis even worse. Keep reading and you will find hope for your organization's crisis communication practices.

The things that can go wrong when you are trying to communicate to the right people at the right time can generally be organized into three broad categories. The three common categories for emergency communication failures and breakdowns are (1) people, (2) processes, and (3) technology.

People

People aren't machines. We have to interpret the world around us to find order and make sense of it. We frequently make mistakes and misunderstand seemingly simple messages. We make assumptions (all too often wrong) and attribute a wide range of things to both messages and other people when we communicate with them. There are enough different "issues" involved with routine communication problems, mistakes, misunderstandings, and breakdowns to address in a completely separate book. However, these tendencies do not magically disappear once we find ourselves caught up in an emergency. On the contrary, the flaws and foibles that interfere with human communication tend to become more pronounced and problematic as the tension, stress, and anxiety of an emergency are brought to bear on each of us. This tendency is true for you and your team as well as the people whom you are attempting to notify during an emergency.

Communication does not involve pure information exchange. Communication is always mediated to some degree, some to a greater extent than others. We communicate through messages that we must construct. As we construct messages, we choose how and in what ways we will "say something." Word choices, tone, and implicit aspects abound in even seemingly simple messages. This requires the receivers of a message to interpret and make sense of what they think the sender is saying. This mediation effect creates another problem with communication that involves people. The more complicated and leaner the mediation between sender and receiver of a message, the more possible it is for effective communication to misfire.

Far too often we end up with misunderstandings or "misunderstood meanings." The fact of the matter is that "understanding" is an interpretative process that requires the active involvement of the message recipient in order for there to be any meaning. In this sense, the old cliché is quite true: Meanings are in people, not words. Understanding intended messages is a complex process that requires multiple cues.

There are important differences between various individuals within a target audience. Most of these variables can be identified by means of different demographics, including culture, ethnicity, age, gender, and native languages. Emergency communication must adapt to the varied demographics and backgrounds of your target audiences. It is essential to conduct a thorough audience analysis prior to crafting messages and certainly before sending out alerts. You should customize the alerts on the basis of geographical location, languages, and economic resources of your target population. Typically, failing to take these factors into account leads to reputation damage because of what is interpreted as being inappropriate or insensitive. However, sometimes this omission can put the safety and well-being of people in jeopardy. Somewhat obviously, alert messages must be written in the recipient's language (spoken and written). Less obvious is that in certain critical situations people have tendencies to revert to thinking and understanding in their native languages, even if they are competent in secondary languages. This means that for some targeted audiences, even though you communicate with them routinely in one language, it may be best for you to send multilingual or foreign language alerts to them during emergency situations. This tendency for native language reversion is frequently overlooked as a communication challenge for emergency and disaster communication. It is also essential that all messages be coordinated and consistent across all levels, from all sources, and in all media (including different languages).

You should also take cultural, ethnic, and other community factors into account when designing emergency alerts. This includes but goes beyond word choices. Implicit assumptions, cultural values, traditions and customs, religious assumptions, and issues of identity should also be taken into account.

There are also differences in how individuals perceive situational risk. Unknown or uncommon risks are commonly perceived to be more risky than are familiar or risks to which people are routinely exposed (even if the "mundane" risks are probabilistically more threatening than the uncommon risks). Communicating risk is one of the more complex but important tasks during an emergency. Risk perception is a social scientific field of study that investigates the subjective judgment that people make about the dangerousness (how likely is the threat and how bad could the threat be to well-being) of a particular risk. A number of social scientific–based reasons have been put forward that seek to explain why different people make different estimates of the danger of various situations. Some individuals may overestimate the risks and react inappropriately in ways that could create additional problems. On the other hand, some individuals may perceive the risks of the threat as so low or remote that they do not act at all upon receipt of an alert warning. It is important to recognize that different individuals will perceive the risks associated with your notification differently. Therefore, it is important to provide clarification and meta-messages to communicate an appropriate sense of urgency.

I learned the term situational awareness, which pilots use to describe a necessary condition for safe flying. I found the concept helpful while designing warning notification messages for those who are in the midst of an emergency situation. Situational awareness is often described as "knowing what is going on so you can figure out what to do next." Different individuals have different degrees of situational awareness. This is an important consideration of how your notification messages may be perceived by some in the audience. You must assess the status of your people, the problem, the situation, and the courses of response, taking into account that some people may not understand the threats or may not take them seriously. This requires multiple communication cues, messages, and interaction.

Selective perception and selective attention also play a role in the human factors that are involved in how people understand and process warning messages. Selective perception and selective attention limit what people notice and remember during an emergency. This is a process by which people let in or screen out messages they receive or have an opportunity to see or hear. They do so because of their attitudes, beliefs, usage preferences and habits, conditioning, and distractions that cause them to focus their attention elsewhere. This is also a filter and screen through which individuals read notification messages. Inattentional blindness (also called perceptual blind spots) is the term given to the process of overlooking or not paying attention to stimuli in one's perceptual field. This research often is used when critiquing the observations of an "eye witness" who did not "see" or "hear" something when others testified that it had occurred. This notion of people who are not able to see things that are actually there is helpful to us as we try to create messages that fall into the realm of those to which people pay attention, recognize and perceive, and process in a way that leads to a change in awareness and behavior.

Inattentional blindness can be a result of limits in the human brain's ability to have a wide perceptual field of focus (e.g., one's focus on object A involves an inherent and necessary lack of focus on object B) or the result of mental distractions (e.g., thinking about a complex problem or situation). Inattentional blindness possibly can be caused by the lack of an internal frame of reference to contextualize and make sense out of what we are seeing (e.g., seeing something for the very first time can be disorienting and often it is difficult to describe it or know what it was). It is important to note (for emergency notification communication) that humans have a finite capacity for attention perception and message processing that seems to diminish during highly stressful and anxious moments. Therefore, the amount of message information that can be processed typically decreases at times of crisis and during emergencies. Important aspects of messages may be overlooked or not recognized. Your words may fall on "deaf brains" if the recipient's attention lies elsewhere at the moment that they "hear" or "read" the emergency message. It is frustrating to recognize that the barriers to successful communication may reside in the mind of the intended target audience member.

Finally, there are just basic differences in human reaction time to messages and alerts. There appear to be a number of factors that affect reaction time including differences in recognition ability, choices, the number of stimuli, fatigue, reasoning, remembering, imagining, and past learning.

Obviously, people are affected strongly by emergencies. Both your team and your various targeted audiences are impacted by emergencies, which in turn affects our reactions to them. In some instances, there will be heightened anxiety, stress, or perhaps fear (for safety or perhaps for loved ones). Many people have described the various cognitive distortions that are commonly experienced during emergencies. For some, perceptions of time slow down and for others perceptions of time speed up. In some cases, there is a lack of ability to focus, whereas others report heightened sensations of unitary or extraordinary focus. In many cases, those who are caught up in a true emergency find that their ability to think clearly may be impaired. These tendencies are made worse when you add in contextual distractions such as noise, situational confusion, lights or sirens, and vivid images of the unfolding emergency.

It is in this context that people's ability to comprehend messages, imperfect in the best of situations, is usually further impaired by the physical and cognitive effects of experiencing an emergency. The role of selective perception, limited attention, cognitive noise and distractions, and both physiological and psychological stressors tend to exacerbate tendencies to misinterpret, misunderstand, and exhibit attention blindness and deafness.

Imagine the change in thoughts and priorities at the instant that a person receives an alert (sometimes even with a test message) that there is a fire, explosive device, or armed active shooter loose in the building. A robust combination of emotions, uncertainty, and anxiety floods the higher order cognitive processes. It is in this emergency context—not experienced in the routine workplace environment—that your audience will be trying to focus to read, comprehend, understand, and respond to your emergency notification message.

Additional Dimensions of the Cognitive Impact of Emergencies

My field experience and measurements indicate that verbal comprehension drops with an increase in distractions, cognitive noise, and stressors experienced during emergencies. This includes corresponding decreases in the ability to read complex instructions or directions. At peak periods (most frequently in the response and management phases) this diminished cognitive capacity can cause disorientation and losses in cognitive functioning. Sometimes described as "brain fog," the impaired mental functioning during periods of high stimulation, stressors, and distractions associated with an emergency situation can, for the untrained and unprepared, cause surprising difficulty in performing simple tasks such as focusing, reading, listening, reflecting, thinking, and making decisions. In addition, concurrent manifestations include reports of confusion, forgetfulness, and physical manifestations such as auditory and visual impairment, trembling, and loss of coordination and high-order motor control.

These situational variables must be taken into account when crafting notification messages that are to be delivered at potentially peak periods of cognitive impairment. My field experience and measurements indicate that verbal comprehension drops an average of approximately four grade levels during these peak periods. This means that verbal or written messages that would normally be easily read and understood might prove to be too confusing, overcomplicated, or simply not understandable by someone who is experiencing the effects of an emergency on his or her thinking abilities.

Some have compared the cognitive impairment experienced during peak stress times of an emergency to the cognitive capacity diminishment experienced in high-altitude, low-oxygen environments. Research indicates that the average reading level among the general (literate) public in the United States is approximately at the 10th-grade reading level; thus, on average for general population audiences, we might assume that our emergency notification messages should be written at least at the sixth-grade reading level or lower to ensure the widest possible range of comprehension and understanding of our alert.

In addition to the changes in cognitive processing capabilities that the stress, distress, and duress of an emergency environment can create, there are also other changes among people experiencing an emergency that message writers should take into consideration. These include the following factors:

- changes in assessments of perceived risk changes
- information-loading reductions (lower cognitive limits on how much or how many things we can think about)
- attitude–behavioral consistency interaction and uncertainty anxiety effects
- changes in situational awareness perception
- selective attention (including attention blindness), reaction time changes (in most cases these changes result in slowed reaction times)
- diminished cognitive processing that involves thinking, reasoning, remembering, imagining, or learning

In most people the cognitive abilities typically decrease as crisis stress increases (peaks). Unless there is a lingering traumatic stress syndrome, these abilities return to normal levels relatively quickly. However, it is useful to remember that people possess different cognitive abilities and limitations, which in turn affects decision-making capabilities in a crisis in different ways and to different degrees.

One's ability to comprehend messages changes from low- to high-stress contexts. Typically individuals can, on average, process about seven distinctive issue or information features in a single message unit during low-stress contexts. As mentioned previously, the average reading level among the general (literate) public in the United States is approximately the 10th-grade reading level during routine and non-stressful measurements. When receiving instructions and directions, the average North American focuses on the competence, expertise, and knowledge of the message source.

In high-stress contexts, recipients are only able to process on average three distinctive issue or information features in a single message unit. Thus, there is on average a greater than 50 percent decrease in one's cognitive abilities to grasp various message factors. This is also true when measuring the recognition of the subtleties and nuances in messages (the highly stressed individuals had a diminished capacity to do so). Furthermore, as previously mentioned, delete (untrained) individuals drop on average about four grade levels in their reading and verbal comprehension abilities during peak periods of high-stress situations. Finally, even the evaluation standard used for receiving instructions and directions changes. During high-stress contexts the average North American no longer critically focuses on the competence, expertise, and knowledge of the message source. This foreshadows a problem because misinformation and rumors can create unwanted behavioral responses during emergencies.

In these situations, the audience is likely to pay more attention to those whom they perceive as trustworthy, honest, and without motives to mislead or deceive them. In addition, studies suggest that message sources perceived as more oriented toward compassionate listening that is caring and empathic and are rewarded with higher levels of attributed credibility and corresponding message acceptance. High levels of identification with the source of the message (e.g., "they are like me" or "we have things in common") will lower the threshold for accepting and acting on a behavioral request. In fact, the only other stronger variable is when the source of the message is personally known by the receiver (which is why emergency notification messages need to have as a source or sender someone who is personally known by the receiver to gain the strongest likelihood of attention, perception, and compliance).

Communication processing shifts in low- to high-stress situations. Emergency and crisis stress (distress/duress) negatively affects the cognitive process. Therefore, emergency notification messages must balance ideas, information, and words in the context of a crisis. You should create messages that are accurate, consistent, and simple, and that reinforce each other. Since confusion is easily achieved during an emergency, try as much as possible to avoid mixed or erroneous messages that will only add to the confusion and make your better written messages more likely to be lost in the chatter.

Processes

The routine processes of writing messages, gaining approval, deciding on a delivery modality, and taking the time to send messages are typically disrupted by emergencies. You will be pressed for time and people during an emergency. If you customarily rely on message approval processes, you may find the procedures are unworkable during the emergency. You will have compressed time lines and immediate deadlines. In addition, you should anticipate that the people involved in the processes will themselves be disrupted and hampered.

There are always challenges of obtaining accurate and current information during an emergency. Recognizance is a key part of an effective notification process. You can't inform and notify people of things that you don't know yourself. Also, having wrong, inaccurate, incomplete, or constantly changing information does not make for a great alert message foundation. This means that the quality of your outbound information is directly dependent on the quality of your inbound information. You must have a process in place that enables gathering, retrieving, analyzing, processing, using, and ultimately discarding information. Such a process may not be the first thing to come to mind when one thinks of improving emergency notification communication, yet it is critical for effective notification communication.

Because inbound information is critical (and communication plays a key role), you should look at the communication connections between you and your information sources just as closely as you look at the connection between you and those whom you seek to alert and notify in an emergency. Your goal should be, in every message you send: Be First, Be Right, Be Credible.

In fact, the communication processes among your own internal team have a direct and immediate effect on the quality of emergency notification messages. This interaction includes the communication exchanges in which you conduct the assessment and risk analysis. Faulty or wrong conclusions in these deliberations can result in dangerously wrong outbound alert messages. You should review the communication processes, procedures, and training to ensure diligent and vigilant decision making. Quality communication does not just happen automatically without planning, training, and preparation.

Ensure that your processes will work during the peak periods of the emergency. Test and validate messages as well as channels and procedures well in advance of an emergency. Any communication scholar would recognize that successful or effective communication is a complex process with many variables. Among these variables are the important roles that messages, delivery channels, and receiver perception and interpretation play in the communicating process. There are also contextual factors, information issues, missed connections, technological breakdowns, and compressed times that impact the overall success of communication. When one considers emergency notification communication, it is critically important that one does not make simplistic assumptions about rote "transfers of information" or mistakenly assume that language and words are objective and neutral mechanisms of conveying mere information. Emergency notification communication is about much more than just information that is transmitted and delivered via some device. Too often the discussion of emergency notification communication centers on few aspects beyond delivery devices and technology. Although reliable telecommunications equipment and delivery modalities are an important aspect of emergency notification communication, they are only one of the major variables that must be considered.

Sequential Communication Breakdowns

There is another communication problem that manifests itself during emergencies. This is the tendency for failures, breakdowns, and problems to occur during a communication sequence. Researchers have long confirmed that when we pass a message (or information) along via a sequence of mediating points (e.g., people), the message tends to change. These changes (errors) occur almost predictably in the forms of distortions, omissions, and additions. This communication phenomenon is also the basis for the entertaining and educational "telephone game," which most of us participated in during our primary school days. The telephone game in its most common form is played by having participants sit in a circle or semi-circle, and a message (e.g., narrative, story, or information) is whispered to the first person who in turn whispers the message to the next person, and then each in turn passes the message along to each person in the sequence. At the end of the process, the last person to hear the story shares it with the entire group. Invariably, the message is distorted from its original state, typically with omissions, additions, and changes to key parts and aspects of the message.

During emergencies, whenever we have information or messages that are relayed or "passed along," we have to assume that there is an intrinsic tendency for errors to occur. This tendency increases proportionally to the number of links in the sequence and the degree to which specific corrective measures are in place to double-check, reconfirm, and verify information. In general, my recommendation is that lengthy communication sequences should be avoided during emergency communication. Wherever possible, communication should be as a direct connection (with no or minimal links) between the originator and the ultimate targeted receiver. This is another reason why automated direct notification systems offer an advantage of reduced sequential communication errors when compared with other approaches with far more links in the communication chain.

Technology

The communication tools you rely on are frequently unavailable or nonfunctional during emergencies. Network theory tells us that networks can usually survive random faults and outages, but that they will collapse when even a small percentage of the largest hubs are damaged or removed. Communications depend on two types of networks: the lines and switches that carry communications signals and the electric power grid. If major hubs for either of these networks are disabled, a systemic communications failure may result.

Some organizations are now trying to ensure themselves against systemic failures by building their own redundant systems. Examples include contracting with multiple wire line and wireless telephone carriers and Internet service providers, constructing in-house cellular antennas, and arranging for calls to be rerouted to an alternate site if necessary. There are two problems with this approach: (1) it is expensive and (2) it addresses only one end of the communication link. Being able to make telephone calls is of little use if the people you are trying to reach can't receive them.

Even when there is no systemic damage, localized problems may interfere with communications. The point of failure can often be individual pagers, cell phones, or radios. Power requirements for these devices are much greater when they're under heavy use. Also, because they are useful only when they are left on, conserving battery power in a crisis is not an option. A cell phone battery may last for two days or more when it is used intermittently, but in the continuous use brought on by an emergency it will last only a few hours, rendering it useless in the long run.

Overloading can occur when there is unusually high traffic or damage to parts of the system. When disaster strikes, people immediately pick up the telephone to find out whether their friends and relatives are safe, to rearrange their plans, or just to find someone who knows more than they do about the situation. These calls may so overload the system that most calls just get busy signals. So even when there is no damage to the telephone system or equipment, it may be impossible to make the calls needed to arrange disaster response. If portions of the system are damaged in the disaster, the situation is even worse. When traffic is shifted to the undamaged portions, these may quickly become overloaded and may even shut down. The more nodes become unavailable, the more overloaded and vulnerable the remaining nodes become. Network theorists call this a cascading failure.

Overloading can also occur at the level of the organization, either because local telephone equipment such as a PBX (private branch exchange) is overloaded or because not enough staff is available to answer telephone calls. The volume of calls coming in to a company or government agency may block urgent calls that are needed to arrange disaster response.

Radios, especially older models or radios on older networks, are vulnerable to interference and channel conflicts. Emergency responders sometimes find themselves trying to talk at the same time or even dealing with "bleed over" from nearby channels. Communication intended for specific individuals or groups must be broadcast to everyone on the radio network, and their simultaneous responses further clutter the channel.

First responders to emergencies frequently rely on handheld radios for on-the-scene communications. However, when emergency responders arrive on the scene of an incident, their radio communications are often on different frequency bands, making it difficult to coordinate. Technical solutions to this problem exist, but they are often expensive and cumbersome to install. In addition to these logistical problems, having multiple responders on scene can create other communication problems. For example, the 2003 California wildfires spread so quickly through so many jurisdictions—more than 50 in San Diego County alone—that agencies effectively stopped communicating and focused on their own geographical areas.

In an emergency or a disaster, important buildings may be destroyed, damaged, or made otherwise inaccessible (e.g., if buildings all around them are burning). If the disaster recovery plan is dependent on access to a particular site (for example, if the only link or the only information database is in that location), then coordinating the disaster response can be extremely difficult.

During an emergency, people move around. Trained personnel may head for the disaster site, thinking that they can help. People who are already at the site, but are not in a position to help, try to go home. If transportation problems keep people from arriving where they intended to go, disaster coordinators may not know where to find them. A critical aspect of business or government continuity planning is maintaining up-to-date contact information for everyone who must be notified or summoned in an emergency. Searching for phone numbers during an emergency wastes precious time, sometimes with life-and-death consequences.

Contacting all of the key people during a critical event is a challenge and can be a time-consuming process. The time it takes to call them or find them in person can hamper disaster response and recovery. Personnel are also distracted from other tasks by having to spend time trying to contact people. Sometimes the time-consuming nature of one-on-one communication leads emergency coordinators to make decisions they might otherwise not have made.

Communication is an essential aspect of organizing your emergency response and incident management. This communication should be real-time, two-way, and integrated. Your communication relies on having up-to-date and comprehensive information ready at hand. This information is not always easy to obtain during an emergency, so advance planning is vital. A report on the 1998 Florida wildfires concluded that miscommunication heightens during a crisis and can be exaggerated by half-truths, distortions, or negative perceptions. During this crisis, officials relied on media to tell the public what was occurring and how they could protect themselves. However, local governments did not always centralize communications, and many reporters complained that other news organizations were receiving more information or better information than they were. Similarly, during the 2002 anthrax attacks, the Centers for Disease Control and Prevention (CDC) came under severe criticism for releasing incomplete and inconsistent information about the attacks. Local officials stated that they had to obtain information from the news media instead of from the CDC. Inconsistent communications can confuse the public about the degree of danger they are in and the precautions they need to take.

In the modern workplace, another major challenge is the high mobility of target audiences. For example, notification that relies on fixed landline telephones would not seem to be a primary means of contacting employees who are highly mobile. Furthermore, all individuals probably have preferred (best contact) communication channels at different times of the day or days of the week. It is important to be able to reach everyone on the best and most preferred contact pathway at that point in time during an emergency.

During an emergency, key communication personnel may be unavailable or the communication tools are overloaded. If the emergency has made one of your key communication personnel suddenly unavailable, you might find yourself with a gap in communication (unless you carefully plan in advance for redundancies in personnel or automate the process).

All of these factors represent challenges to communication that must be overcome by advance planning and preparation. Some challenges are particularly acute during the first minutes or hours of an unfolding emergency. The following section focuses in on some the challenges that are particularly problematic on day one of an emergency.

COMMUNICATION CHALLENGES OF THE FIRST DAY

There are many challenges that might be experienced on the first day of an emergency or crisis. These challenges must be kept in mind when designing an emergency notification plan and dealt with appropriately when the crisis strikes. Listed here are some examples that have been adapted from the National Education Association (NEA) Crisis Communications Guide and Toolkit.[15]

Rumor Control

Rumors are a common occurrence when information is lacking. There is a tendency to create rumors to fill the gap of lacking information. Be proactive in disseminating information and craft a reputation for honesty and credibility. It helps to ensure that your communication is timely and accurate.[16]

Phone Line Jams and Loss of Internet Access

Crises can create environments that will no longer support common modes of communication. Use a combination of sources and establish duplicate avenues such as multiple lines and services.[17]

Media Intrusion

The media interfering with an established organizational emergency plan can lead to confusion and often is harder on the victims because they can be bullied by media. Have an established identification system in place that will clearly mark which information is a part of the business and which is part of the media.[18]

Scattering of Personnel

In the face of a disaster or immediate crisis, the natural instinct is to flee the danger. Unfortunately, this instinct makes ensuring the safety and making an accurate account of those involved more difficult. Establishing predetermined locations that individuals can retreat to and educating employees on predetermined channels of communication may help in reporting their whereabouts or other safety issues.[19]

Media Mistakes

Accuracy is often sacrificed for haste in the media. This situation is where trust from preestablished relationships come into play. Incorrect information should also be immediately dispelled and replaced with correct information.[20]

CHALLENGES AFTER THE FIRST DAY

Many challenges will continue on the second day of a crisis or emergency. Challenges and suggested responses from the NEA Crisis Communications Guide and Toolkit are provided in this section.[21]

Potential for Eroded Credibility

The past actions and reputation of a business will greatly determine the expectations placed on its responses to a crisis. If current behaviors do not meet or exceed the stakeholders' expectations, a loss of credibility will occur. Your communication should be consistent, reliable, reassuring, and trustworthy. The NEA guide recommends that you should take the following necessary actions to maintain credibility[22]:

1. Provide advance information.
2. Ask for input from all stakeholders, and even perceived opponents.
3. Listen carefully.
4. Demonstrate that you've heard their concerns, and then adjust actions accordingly.
5. Stay in touch.
6. Speak in plain language.
7. Bring victims/involuntary participants into the decision-making process.[23]

The constant need for information from employees, the community, the media, and the general public develops in all stages of a crisis. Emotions are running high and patience is lacking in such an environment. Immediate implementation of information channels that are accessible to all members of the community, the media, and most important, all employees is best during the development and implementation of an emergency notification plan.

Panic and Alienation

When a routine is broken and normal operations are disrupted, anxieties will increase and those affected may begin to feel alienated and anxious. Centers or avenues for receiving information, assistance, counseling, and contact with others should be made available to those affected.[24]

The Continuation of Media Feeding Frenzies

The media in their zealousness for achieving new information may resort to creative means of gaining access to information sources. Using a system for responding to media and setting parameters for coverage may help.[25]

CHALLENGES OF THE RETURN TO OPERATIONS

Though the crisis may be over, emergency notification plans must keep in mind the return to normal organizational functioning.[26] This is the time when communication is especially important in adjusting all organizational members back to normal, as well as the greater community that was impacted by your company when it was in a crisis.[27]

Community Feelings

Bitterness and blame from stakeholders may erupt and cause further divisiveness. Avoid the natural tendency to blame or offer simplistic solutions to the crisis. Instead, open communication to all those affected by the crisis (e.g., victims, employees, consumers, media, and the general public) and follow with consistency and action.[28]

Victims' Feelings

Anxiety, frustration, and anger may hamper the ability to move on. The perception of a victim is different and more emotionally raw than that of a bystander. The business must understand the difference and exhibit patience during this time.[29]

Divisiveness

Lawsuits and media coverage of legal disputes often create the taking of sides. A company should not allow legal threats to inhibit continued, effective, honest, and open communication with all stakeholders. Leave the legal considerations to the legal department.[30]

PRIORITIES IN A CRISIS FOR EFFECTIVE EMERGENCY COMMUNICATION

Though it may sound like there are an insurmountable number of challenges to think about when dealing with a crisis and subsequent emergency notification messages, you don't need to worry! These challenges will not pose a problem if your organization has considered the following priorities and has designed a thorough means of dealing with crises through communication. Preparation is essential. For example, Robert Zito, the executive vice president of communications for the New York Stock Exchange after 9/11 noted: "Until the crisis comes, in whatever form, you don't really understand how valuable all the preparation was."[31]

Preparing for Emergency Communication Success

One of the most crucial priorities to be handled before the crisis strikes is knowing how to manage the crisis and to prepare to communicate with the right people at the right time with the right message in the right way. Your top priority for effective emergency communication is to make sure your business is prepared for disaster long before it strikes. This means having materials and information premade and prepositioned. During a crisis, if people in your business are not able to properly communicate with one another, even the best emergency communication plan is useless. Thus, it is important to create a crisis communication plan in addition to a crisis management plan. Effective communication among organizational members can save you from stress and disorganization when a crisis strikes. The goal is to create synergy. Your organization should consist of a cohesive, knowledgeable, and capable group of people who are properly prepared to take on crises. Here, the priority is to assess your company. A good way to get started in this planning process is to talk, brainstorm, or do whiteboard exercises with key people. Just talking about crises and the emergency communication issues during each stage of a crisis raises awareness and creates a positive ripple effect among the members of your company.

The Crisis Communication Plan

Effective command, coordination, and control during and after disasters are only achievable to the extent that you have a sound and workable plan for communicating. It is imperative to compose a complete communication plan to use during and after a disaster or emergency. This plan should detail how the organization plans to communicate with employees, families, customers, the local community, emergency responders, government authorities, and the news media during and in the aftermath of a disaster. Employees will need to be alerted to the occurrence of an emergency, and receive evacuation or shelter-in-place instructions. People will need to know when, if, and how to report to work when business operations resume. This emergency notification may involve the use of an automated notification system, a secure page on the company Web site, an automated telephone calling system, recorded messages available at an 800 telephone number, or a variety of other techniques and devices. Obviously, all of these must be planned out well in advance of the onset of a disaster. Crisis managers will need immediate and reliable intelligence during critical events in order to make the emergency notification communications effective. They will provide feedback to senior management along with accessing and utilizing all relevant information needed for protecting personnel and business operations and communicating with all stakeholders. The public, especially the news media, will certainly have informational needs that they will expect to be satisfied during and after such crises. It is important to communicate frequently with the public through the news media. Furthermore, customers, investors, and other stakeholders will have questions about the impact of any disaster to ongoing operations. The bottom line is that a well-thought out and detailed communication plan is essential to managing both a crisis and the consequences of a crisis for any organization.

The Crisis Management Team

It is important to establish or reevaluate the CMT. This team might include, but is not limited to, key personnel from the following departments:

- operations
- security
- legal
- public information communication (public relations)
- management (chief executive officer and other top executives)
- finance

Members of the CMT should be able to identify one another and should also be easily identifiable by others. Wearing brightly colored jackets with simple identification on the back is a good way to make CMT members more easily recognizable. It is also important to be prepared to care for the CMT, as well as employees, in case of an emergency. Your entire staff might be detained on premises, so it is vital to have an emergency supply of water, food, blankets, medical supplies, and other supplies. Caring for the crisis team entails not just meeting these needs, but also includes providing places to sleep and rotation schedules. The CMT should have an emergency operations center both on and off premises where they can meet and prepare information. There should always be an updated list of emergency information for employees, families of employees, key community members (e.g., fire departments, police, and health care providers), news media contacts, and shareholders.

The Crisis Communication Team

The communication sector of the CMT is incredibly valuable. This part of the team will develop a comprehensive communication plan and carry it out. The crisis communication team consists of spokespersons, receptionists who will take calls in times of crisis, and anyone else who will act as a liaison between the public and the business. There may need to be more than one spokesperson who will communicate with the media. In this case, it is imperative to have cohesion among spokespersons to unify the message related to constituents. It is also advisable to have spokespersons practice speaking in front of a camera. This process can increase their comfort level in front of the media and can be reviewed for flaws in the spokespersons' presentations.

Organizational Members

In addition to creating a CMT, an effective manager makes sure all employees from managers to custodial staff know key information about the business. First, employees should be aware of the business's mission. What does the business stand for? What are the important values and goals held by employees? What is the purpose of the business? Also, employees should know how to respond in crisis situations. What is their role? Where can they receive information during a crisis? Who is their spokesperson and how can they refer the media to that person? Orientation is a great place to start this training. Make sure every employee is aware of escape routes, what to do if a crisis occurs when they are on or off the premises, and how they or their families can access pertinent information in case of an emergency. Making sure that all organizational members are aware of the emergency notification communication plan, challenges, and priorities during this time of crisis will help your company handle a crisis much more effectively and safely.

External Relations

In addition to making improvements within the business, there must also be an effort to improve relationships with outside contacts in order for the emergency notification plan to work most effectively. If the business already has contacts at the nearby fire and police stations, make sure to keep those lines of communication open. Does the business need to seek outside help? Do you need outside consultants to come in for certain types of disasters? Will the organization need assistance from certain groups or specialized people when a crisis strikes? Are key community members aware of the organization's disaster plans, and do they know their role in the plans?

Media and Constituents

The media is an important outlet to stay in contact with. Who are the main contacts at the local news stations? Do you have an area specifically set aside for media access? In times of crisis, it will be important to be proactive in providing media with information, allowing the media a certain level of access, and providing them with the necessary equipment (e.g., outlets) so they can get the necessary information out to the public.

Be aware that the organization has a multiple-identity audience. Members of this audience might include, but are not limited to, the following people:

- all business members (including employees, managers, accountants, and others)
- consumers
- employee family members
- shareholders
- media/news persons
- key members of the community (e.g., fire departments, police departments, hospitals, and government)
- all who have a genuine interest and concern for those affected by the emergency

It is important to tailor the emergency notification messages to address all of these audiences, to keep all constituents informed of progress in improving disaster plans, and to inform them of the role they play in the business. Some of this risk communication is mandated by law. If people live in close proximity to buildings, what crisis information should they be aware of, if any? One nuclear power plant sent out pamphlets to nearby neighborhoods outlining the risks involved in living near the plant. This pamphlet also explained their role during a time of crisis, how they would be notified of the crisis, numbers they could refer to for information, and the procedures they should follow once they learned of a crisis.

FIVE COMMUNICATION STEPS FOR SUCCESS

As a way of summary,[32] communication is the most essential aspect for a business in a crisis, but the very nature of a crisis hampers effective communication. This chapter has served as an introduction to being aware of common challenges and ways to overcome those challenges. The following are five recommendations for successful crisis and emergency communication prepared by Barbara Reynolds of the CDC.[33]

Execute a Solid Communication Plan

Working from a communication plan is as important in a crisis as working from a logistics plan. This book does not focus on the development of a crisis communication plan, but there are several books on the subject that will serve as a helpful starting point for your organization. The speed and consistency of communication notification can make a difference in a company's credibility.[34]

Be the First Source for Information

There are two important reasons to strive to be the first source of information in a crisis. First, the public uses the speed of information flow in a crisis as a marker for your preparedness. Living in the information age means being expected to not only fix the crisis, but also to be able to tell people *while* it's happening that you are fixing the crisis. The second reason is a psychological reality. When a person is seeking information about something they do not know, the first message they receive carries more weight. Therefore, getting the right message out first means that later incorrect messages will have to bounce up against the right message.[35]

Express Empathy Early

A sincere expression of empathy is essential. The public won't be open to you until you express empathy. In its best form, empathy is talking from the heart and relating to fellow human beings as fellow human beings—not victims, not casualties, not evacuees or refugees or the public, but as people who, in a crisis, are hurting perhaps physically but especially emotionally. Research shows that an expression of empathy should be given in the first 30 seconds of starting your message. A sincere expression of empathy early in your notification will allow people to settle down and actually hear what you have to say.[36]

Show Competence and Expertise

If you have a title and are part of the official response to a crisis, the public will assume you are competent until you prove otherwise. According to the research, most people believe that a person holds a professional position because they are experienced and competent.[37]

Remain Honest and Open

Research has shown that most people have several ideas regarding communication. Generally, people feel that (1) *any* information is empowering, (2) uncertainty is more difficult to deal with than knowing a bad thing, and (3) people are prepared to go to multiple sources for information. There is absolute consensus among professionals that the faster you give people bad news the better, because holding back implies guilt and arrogance. Without question, for very good reasons, some information must be withheld. When that is the case, respectfully tell the public that you are withholding information and *why*.[38]

A complete copy of "Crisis and Emergency Risk Communication: By Leaders for Leaders" can be downloaded at http://www.bt.cdc.gov/erc/leaders.pdf. In addition, the "Public Officials Guide to Disasters," includes these steps for communication success, and the related STARCC Principle for successful crisis and risk communication is also available from the Be Ready Utah Web site.[39]

SUMMARY OF KEY POINTS

- Crises or emergency situations have common communication challenges that must be anticipated in planning for successful emergency notification communication.
- Common communication challenges for crises and emergency situations include breakdowns in communication systems and tools; high levels of stress; time demands; vital information needs among audiences; participation barriers; command, control, and coordination issues; limited information availability and poor information quality; collaboration barriers; geographically dispersed personnel; disruptions to teamwork; sequential communication breakdowns; message loading problems; and personnel shortages.
- Emergencies that produce high-stress environments can impact people by creating cognitive processing difficulties. These typically include reduced reaction time, perception and attention disruptions, decision-making diminishment, information processing limitations, mental focus and comprehension losses, inattentiveness, and diminished communication capacity.
- Communication planning should address these challenges for both the "first-day" messages and ongoing communication.

Priorities for overcoming communication challenges should include advanced planning for preparedness and readiness; creation and testing of a communication plan; ensuring communication as a priority for the crisis management team; and designating crisis communication functions and responsibility, as well as preplanning to work with external constituents, stakeholders, the general public, and the news media.

CHAPTER 4

COMMUNICATION PLANNING

This chapter reviews the process of planning for emergency communication as well as the creation of a document that will guide emergency communication, often called "the communication plan." The chapter also reviews various factors important to the planning process including information management issues, managing the core messages, planning for different types of notification, and message-planning tools.

YOU'VE GOT TO HAVE A PLAN

The main theme of this chapter describes the essentials for planning an effective emergency notification process. As discussed in the previous chapter, crisis communication planning is crucial to effective handling of any crisis. Emergency notification planning is a large aspect of this planning and must be looked at as a separate yet connected function of the broader crisis communication plan. Important background factors to consider include building an emergency contact database, and dealing with information and legal policies. Actual planning of the emergency notification plan includes planning the emergency message (down to the details of what you need to say and when), deciding on a communication tool (such as an automated system), training and educating people on the system, testing the system, and making sure the system continues to meet the needs of the organization. Throughout this process, managing your information and translating it to your organization's message is of crucial importance.

The planning for emergency notification communication starts with an organization's decisions on communication in a given incident, what should be communicated, to whom communication should be targeted, when to communicate, and how to communicate. Every organization needs to develop specific protocols and policies for notification. Ideally these procedures should be reviewed for legal obligations and liability issues. This planning should ideally include lines of command and control, notification priorities, communication modalities, messages, and protocol of notification activities. Once such planning has the approval (sign-off) of senior management, then these communication plans should serve as the "playbook" for what should happen and when during a critical incident.

To translate motivation and good intentions for creating sustainable emergency notification communication it is essential, to craft a specific and written plan to document the processes, messages, timing, and targeted audiences for such communication. In short, it is necessary to establish a detailed plan. A communication plan should not be pulled together once an emergency begins to unfold. In fact, the plan should be written, tested, assessed, and validated periodically before its first implementation. Prudent planning practices would suggest that communication plans are always subject to revision, improvements, and updates.

ESTABLISH AN EMERGENCY NOTIFICATION PLAN

An emergency notification plan will facilitate effective emergency communication and help make communication an integrated and deliberate consideration of emergency management preparedness. Otherwise, communication breakdowns are likely to occur, which could threaten operations as well as the health and safety of people. A plan establishes emergency notification as a routine and expected emergency management function and defines the tasks associated with emergency notification as an opportunity and management strategy rather than as a burden or nuisance. The emergency notification plan should be incorporated in the emergency management plan and not be treated as an afterthought or secondary issue. Effective emergency notification *is* emergency management.

Emergency communication is more complicated than just choosing which medium to use. What words and messages you send and the meta-communication aspects may be far more important than the type of communication solution, system, device, or program that you use. Focusing solely on technical software or electronic hardware "solutions" to the neglect of planning for messages, processes, and human factors is insufficient planning. Comprehensive communication planning must include consideration of messages, timing, and people factors. In fact, the nature of your emergency communication plans (what, how, and when you send emergency notices) will also say a lot about your organization's values, priorities, and character.

DELEGATE RESPONSIBILITY AND AUTHORITY
FOR EMERGENCY COMMUNICATION

Notification messages are challenging to create and can generate controversy (and occasionally opposition) from different voices in the organization (e.g., legal and senior management). Although there are planning steps listed in this book that include "vetting" messages, language, and timing with all quarters across the organization (it should have wide-ranging input and feedback from a wide range of people in your organization), the most effective plans are those that are implemented by people who have both the responsibility and authority for disseminating the messages. Best practice norms suggest that you have senior management participate at the outset of developing a notification plan and involve them at relevant points throughout the planning process. Their sign-off and buy-in is an important aspect of an effective plan. This should all be worked out in advance. A plan is *only potential* until it is effectively implemented, and you should anticipate potential obstacles that might impede that execution. However, there needs to be a core group that takes responsibility for creating, revising, and testing the emergency notification messages. They will need substantial work time and resources to prepare, revise, and validate the messages. It is often helpful to bring in an external expert to assist the team in this work. A comprehensive plan will require that target audience members receive advance instruction and training about notification messages. They should learn what to expect, what notices mean, and what they should do when they receive such notices. You also should educate them on what you will be doing at that moment to manage and respond to the emergency (assuming that everything is following the plan).

The role of an information policy is covered elsewhere in this book. However, it is useful to point out at this juncture that organizations have a legitimate interest in controlling the release of some types of information, confidential information that is protected by law from such release, and statements that inadvertently harm the organization, its employees, or the public. It is common to have internal restrictions and limitations on who is allowed to issue communication for a company. When sending emergency notices, the appropriate personnel need to have sufficient authority and a priori approval of the message manuscripts. Such authority allows for the swift dispatch of alerts without any unnecessary delay such as awaiting senior management sign-off on the wording in the message.

Finally, it is often helpful to collaborate with employees and the local community as appropriate when developing notification messages. At the very least, you can use such interactions as an opportunity to build support for, and involvement in, the emergency notification plan.

INFORMATION MANAGEMENT

During a crisis, information will need to be managed in order to effectively utilize emergency communication strategies. Database access and information gathering is very important in order to ensure that your communication is accurate and up to date. On the other hand, it is easy to be overwhelmed by information, particularly during an emergency, so it is essential to be able to successfully wade through all of that information and data to find the facts that you need and cut through the clutter of the rest. In addition, you have to be able to document what information was accessible, which was actively used, and what choices were made about the information that was at hand.

During an emergency you will be preoccupied with other tasks and chores, experience distractions, find yourself short-handed, and face short deadlines. Therefore, your information management policy should be simple and practical; provide means of collecting, considering, and discarding information efficiently; cross-reference different categories of information to other needs and purposes; have a real-time means for validation of information; have a process to vet and disseminate information rapidly, efficiently, and accurately; and track all of the information so that the documentation trail is available for after-action review.

Effective information management tools can help emergency managers create and implement their communication plans. Information management is essential for communication. Adequacy of information can help achieve compliance and sustain two-way communication with both your sources of information as well as those who are dependent on you for accurate, up-to-date, and appropriate information. This is where the ease and reliability of using an automated emergency notification system may come in handy.

MANAGING THE MESSAGE

Obviously it is important to get a response-phase message out quickly. Your notification message in an emergency should be crafted, coordinated, and communicated in a variety of channels. Notification messages need to be appropriately timed and delivered in order to reach the right people at the right time. The message created should be consistent and coordinated in order to avoid miscommunication problems and unnecessary panic. Messages need to be managed just as much as crisis operations need to be managed. As emphasized, make an effort to understand the expectations and information needs of all stakeholders. Don't underestimate their general need to know and be reassured that the organization is acting ethically and with professionalism. Within the constraints of legal requirements and proprietary business concerns, the message should be as forthright and honest as prudently possible. Even if the news reported is negative, it is always better for stakeholders to learn negative information directly rather than to have it "discovered" and presented in the news media under the implication of concealment or evasion. In such cases, the negative impact of the information is amplified by the implicit impression of a possible cover-up or reluctance to disclose the information. Efforts to stall, hide bad news, or stonewall in the midst of an emerging disaster are at the root of many of the most damaging and disastrous corporate reputation disasters over the past quarter century.

If the crisis has caused harm in some way, then the message should be one of compassion for those who have been negatively affected. It must express concern and empathy for anyone who has suffered as a consequence of the misconduct, without necessarily assuming blame or responsibility. Do not craft a message that may be perceived as insensitive or appearing to lack compassion or concern. Also, the message should be worded to describe the disaster or crisis from the viewpoint of public interest and social norms, not just from that of the company. All public messages must clearly demonstrate understanding of and commitment to the well-being of the community as well as to the interests of all stakeholders.

Many aspects of this message can be prepared in advance. You should develop some phrases, sentences, and vocabulary words that are appropriate (and have the blessing of your senior management) and that can be used as building blocks for emergency message construction. It may help to have preplanned scenarios, detailed response action plans, and premade statements ahead of time. Many find it helpful to begin to script out what and how they would word various messages to specific audiences. Although basic messages can be prepared beforehand, a coordinated comprehensive message strategy appropriate to a specific crisis will only emerge with active teamwork and attentive management.

DIFFERENT TYPES OF NOTIFICATIONS

You may need to send different types of mass notification messages depending on a wide range of factors. Emergency notification communication is an integral component of an organization's emergency and routine communication capabilities. While these systems are most often associated with emergency notification for contacting employees during and after a disaster, mass notification dramatically improves an organization's operational efficiency and bottom line when implemented for day-to-day operations. A mass notification system provides effective communication when you need to quickly deliver information in an emergency. So whereas mass notification is a very useful tool when emergency contact is required, most applications of the technology focus on more mundane, but also critical business processes. These processes realize significant benefit from the use of mass notification, making any organization more efficient and making employees more productive.

ANALYZING AUDIENCES

One of the more important principles is that audiences expect communication during a crisis. It is vital to have a message and get that message out to key audiences. Keep in mind that audience members often exist in multiple categories that span the boundaries of internal and external categories (e.g., a single individual might be an employee, investor, local community member, and buyer of your business product).

The nature of crises suggests certain basic things that are expected to be communicated (e.g., What happened? What is being done about it? Who is affected and how? What should I do next?). However, because many types of emergency incidents can generate anxiety, the tone and implications of your messages is also a significant aspect to consider. It is also a product of human nature that crises raise implicit questions of blame or responsibility, and that "inquiring minds want to know" the answers to such questions. Obviously, one of the biggest communication failures during a crisis is the failure to communicate altogether. However, emergency notification is always more than just "delivering information." Every message conveys an emotional aspect to people who may be anxious or distressed by the situation. Furthermore, whether it is reassurance or an urgent warning of imminent danger, what and how you communicate will affect people in complex ways more than merely "informing" them about an incident. To this extent, message planning requires that you consider the possible implications and how an audience might be reading between the lines of what you say or how you say it. Obviously you must engage in appropriate communication when crises strike, but what is appropriate may be a more complicated question than many would predict.

It is important to understand the expectations of all of the different audiences for your communication during these events. It is also essential to anticipate their agendas and information needs during crises. You must define all objectives when designing messages and selecting the best means of reaching key audiences with the message. The organization must have a consistent message, a commitment to a message strategy, and have the crisis communication team support the effort to "stay on message."

Typical Key Stakeholders

Employees	Local community
Management	Local government
Investors/shareholders	Regulators
Customers	Lenders
Suppliers/vendors	Media watchdogs
Emergency agencies	Special interest groups
Labor unions	

BUILDING A CONTACT DATABASE

Before a crisis begins, it is crucial for your organization to have an already-established contact database for use in any situation. This contact database will come from a variety of different sources. For example, you will need to think about each stage of the crisis and what your company will need to handle at each stage. Do not limit your thinking to just your own organization's members. You may need help from the police or fire departments if the crisis is harmful, you will undoubtedly need the media to inform any and all stakeholders, and you will need your system of emergency notification to be up and functional.

The process of building a contact database is a slow one, much like networking. This process is most effective when it is geared toward emergency notification and management. One way to do this is to meet with outside groups. Meet with government agencies, community organizations, and utilities, and ask about potential emergencies and plans with available resources for responding to them. The following are some common sources of information:

- community emergency management office
- mayor or community administrator's office
- local emergency planning committee
- fire department
- police department
- emergency medical services organizations
- American Red Cross
- National Weather Service
- Public Works Department
- Planning Commission
- telephone companies

- electric utilities
- neighboring businesses

As your organization coordinates with outside organizations regarding the process of emergency communication planning, you should be meeting periodically with local government agencies as well as other community organizations. You may want to inform these businesses about your organization's emergency management plan, both for their approval (if required), and more important, because they will likely have valuable insights and information to offer. At this stage, determine state and local requirements for reporting emergencies and incorporate them into your procedures. You should determine any and all protocols for turning over control of a crisis response to any outside agencies. There are many details that may need to be worked out, including which entrance responding units will use, where and to whom will they report, how they are to be identified, how facility personnel will communicate with these outside responders, and who will be in charge of all response activities.

Other issues to be aware of while maintaining a contact database is to make sure that your organization has taken into account any needs of disabled persons or non-English–speaking personnel. One outside contact that may be helpful in this situation is the government, especially if your emergency notification plan is regulated by the government. While in the process of planning and building a contact database, it is also important to maintain contact with other corporate officers and build credibility. You should communicate with other offices and divisions within your company in order to learn their emergency notification requirements, conditions when mutual assistance may be necessary, how offices will support each other in an emergency, and the names and contact information for all key personnel. This information should be incorporated into your own emergency communication and management procedures.

Building credibility is also an important factor to be taken into account during the planning process. By reaching out to constituents, shareholders, employees, and key community members, you begin to build relationships and lay the groundwork for effective collaboration during emergency situations. A business's reputation can determine how the audience will receive communication from the business during times of crisis. Your reputation and credibility for reliability, trustworthiness, and motives has a direct impact on how the audience will interpret and react to any notification or warning messages they receive from you.

A business prepared for crises will have more credibility with constituents than one that is unprepared. Appropriate handling of a crisis before, during, and after is crucial to retaining good credibility. Thorough preparation, in this sense, also aids your emergency notification success in that your reputation for being on top of these issues will enhance your credibility for any communication you transmit.

Do not overlook proper concern and care for the media in your communication planning. Many typical company heads mandate that the media is not their concern and keeping them (the media) outside the facility gate is perfectly acceptable during a crisis. This view may be shortsighted because the media has the potential to be the louder voice to the public throughout crises. A business should also use its contact database in order to prepare multiple spokespersons and ensure that the message is kept constant and accurate throughout the crisis and through different modes of communication.

INFORMATION POLICY

The information policy of an organization should be one of the foundations for any emergency management plan. Though it is hard to think about such things before a crisis strikes, having a solid and ethical information policy can make the difference in your organization's survival during a crisis. Honesty in the face of an organizational crisis is of the utmost importance if a business wants to emerge from the crisis and still be able to exist as an organization. Deliberate deception in the event of a crisis is self-explanatory in its error. The use of deception often leads to increased uncertainty, lack of trust, and feelings of negativity. This will profoundly alter the culture of a business and may lead to its demise following a crisis (e.g., Enron).

It is important to decide what information will be needed at what times and for which people. An authorized chain of command works in the context of information policy during a crisis situation. In an emergency, it is often good policy to keep people on a "need to know" basis, and this will simplify your organization's emergency communication system as well. It is important to take into account a number of potential challenges and issues (private information, lists of names, contact information, etc.) that inevitably arise during disasters, emergencies, and other crisis situations.

It is critical that information flows freely to and from the communication crisis team and other participants. Unfortunately, this can be hindered by miscommunication that comes in a variety of forms. Communication can be misrouted (sent to the wrong or inappropriate people). Poorly crafted messages can be misunderstood and misinterpreted. Failure to adapt to linguistic, cultural, and foreign language requirements can disrupt communication. Even when you manage to target the right people and adapt to the most appropriate forms of communication, information can still be blocked by a number of events. Communication technology disruptions, people out of pocket and unavailable, unchecked voice messages, poor cell phone service (garbled or dropped calls), situational distractions, and simply confusing messages can block the dissemination of information. These blockages can change the message (distortions and misunderstandings), serve other purposes (e.g., rumors), or misdirect an audience to do something other than the desired behavioral response.

Communication planning should take steps to minimize all these forms of communication challenges. Strategies such as multiple delivery paths, redundant and reinforcing messages, feedback and confirmation techniques, as well as well-crafted messages that are tested and validated for particular audiences. For example, messages can be underloaded, overloaded, or too complex for certain audiences. Messages that are underloaded are those that simply do not tell the audience "enough" information for them to understand and act on the notification. Underloaded messages are often ambiguous and lack the necessary details and specific aspects that constitute an effective message. Such underloaded messages are ineffective in that they frequently do not serve any useful purpose at all and merely add to the confusion and anxiety of the situation. The information flow is so slow or small that it shares little information and leads the other party to frustration, and worse, retaliation.

Overloaded messages on the other hand contain too much information. Overloaded messages tend to overwhelm listeners or readers and are unnecessarily complicated and frequently heavily loaded with jargon. Overloaded messages are too lengthy to be quickly read and understood, and are typically filled with details that might be important to a small target group but only serve to confuse and frustrate most of the people who receive them. Like overloaded messages, the unnecessarily complex messages tend to contain excess verbiage and inconsequential bits in addition to the kernels of vital information. An example might be a weather warning that should merely alert the audience to a dangerous storm, when to expect the storm, what the nature of the threat is, and what steps one should take in order to remain safe. Instead, an overly complex message might try to explain meteorological concepts, probability analysis, numerous variables that could affect the severity or duration of the storm, and/or information about how the forecast warning was prepared or analyzed.

The key to managing the correct loading of messages is to find the most appropriate medium (such as face-to-face interaction or other "rich" media types) for passing those messages along. Messages should be brief and concise, but contain the vital information without unnecessary "baggage." Messages should be front loaded with the most important aspects of the message to occur in the first few words or sentences. A crisis communication plan must have steps in place to avoid blockages or incorrectly loaded messages during a crisis so that the right people get the right information in a timely manner.

Misinformation is another source of difficulty in any information policy during an emergency. Amplified demand for new information as well as impaired judgment and reasoning leads to a susceptibility to rumors and misinformation. This can be disastrous for a company during a crisis.

Businesses can control these difficulties by setting up a plan and have an active communication network. Such communication plans and tools should include the capability for two-way communication with many of the key constituent audiences. Reliable and dependable two-way communication capability gives you the capacity to monitor what your audience knows, thinks, or believes; how they are responding or behaving; the emergence of rumors and misunderstandings; and to confirm behavioral compliance with requests and instructions. In addition, two-way communication capability gives you the capacity to correct rumors and misinformation quickly, obtain current and real-time information from people on the scene, and confirm the quality and reliability of the other field reports you are receiving. This gives you an ability for sustaining quality reconnaissance and surveillance of the situation. Surveillance that can immediately report the first appearance of misperceptions and inaccuracies before they are widely spread.

A crisis creates an information vacuum that needs to be filled as soon as possible. Do not wait too long. If your company does not fill the void, someone else will, and they may not have the best interest of your business in mind. Withholding information can often cast a guilty shadow on a business. In contrast, openness can increase positive perceptions held by the public, the media, and stakeholders in the business. Effective crisis communication includes just the right amount of information. One has to be able to ascertain what constitutes the right amount of information for the right people at the right time. How much information is enough? How much is too much? Your organization's information policy should be unique to your individual needs and risks, as well as to current existing policies on information during routine operations. Everyone in the organization who will participate in the emergency management process must be aware of this information policy in order for it to run effectively within the greater emergency communication response.

To be prepared for the critical decisions about disclosure of information and transparency of data during crises, it is essential to develop and adhere to comprehensive information disclosure guidelines that provide contingencies for different types of situations. Such a policy must ensure compliance with legal and regulatory restrictions as well as meet demands for transparency and fairness. Failure to map out an effective information disclosure plan usually results in an inability to actively meet the needs of stakeholders as well as inviting negative media scrutiny for such failures. Any policy for information disclosure should include specific rules for collecting, processing, retaining, and disposing of appropriate information within the organization to ensure appropriate communication within the organization and proper external information disclosure to the news media. Professional and ethical organizations will strive to ensure total protection of confidential information that respects the privacy of employees as well as that of other stakeholders. Long before preparing to interact with the news media and answer questions, it is imperative to lay down specific policies and appropriate methods for the creation, utilization, storage, conservation, and disposal of company documents and databases. Only with such an information policy in place can an organization proceed to answer questions with the confidence of acting ethically and with integrity.

LEGAL REVIEW

When planning an organizational response to emergency communication, it is necessary to look at legal issues and reviews that may affect and be affected by your organization. During and after a crisis situation, it is commonly necessary to provide damage assessment inventories, notify authorities and family members of any pertinent issues, and answer direct and specific questions from reporters who are trying to get the facts for the news. Potentially there is a large amount of confidential information involved with crisis situations. This includes, but is not limited to, employees' personal information, business and trade secrets, and customer databases and identity, as well as possible questions into the reasons, methods, storage, retrieval, retention, and disposal of all information that is collected. Often as the events of the crisis rapidly progress, decisions about the release of information will have to be made quickly under very stressful and difficult circumstances.

In the instance of a crisis, there will inevitably be many fast-paced, specific questions about the people involved, including those who have been impacted as well as those who are working to respond. The organization must be prepared for these types of legal and privacy questions that seek to probe the background and history of every detail about certain individuals, employees, customers, and business partners. In general you have an obligation to safeguard information that is personal or confidential and to ensure the privacy of all employees. In many cases it is fairly easy to distinguish between private and public information categories. However, during a disaster or emergency situation some of these distinctions become less clear, and in the urgency of the moment it may be difficult to execute good judgment about whether to release or withhold information. This is made more challenging when the reporters are persistent and impassioned in asking questions that appear to be legitimate.

MESSAGE PLANNING

Message planning should be concerned with what you need to say and when you need to say it. This section is focused on the elaborate detail concerned with message planning, but emergency notification communication depends on how well your organization plans out your messages. There are a variety of key best practices for emergency communication planners to keep in mind as they begin to focus on writing messages. For example, communication plans should incorporate flexibility, redundancy, and feedback capability in order to confirm receipt, comprehension, and compliance with the message. Communication plans should be comprehensive, covering anticipated communication with all audiences. This should focus on both the internal and the external audiences during a crisis. Internal audience members are those actually in the organization, your employees. The external audience is comprised of customers, stakeholders, and the broader community in which your organization is located. Emergency communication plans must reinforce messages to these stakeholders. Finally, your emergency communication planning should take multiple channels of communication, two-way communication (feedback options), and resilient communication. In every aspect of this planning, one of the important aspects is the construction of the specific messages that you intend to transmit to targeted audiences to notify them at critical times of an emergency. The construction of an emergency notification message will be covered in a subsequent chapter but it is essential to undertand the place for messages in the overall communication planning.

Creating messages is accomplished by a series of steps taken in a specific order, with your organization determining key target audiences, information needs, and means to sustain communication. You should utilize both push and pull communication options in order to most effectively plan an emergency message. Push communication includes messages that you send to deliver information to targeted audiences in various modalities and channels. For example, push communication may be applying an automated notification system regarding evacuation orders in channels of cell phone, texting, and e-mail. Pull communication is when your audience comes to your message, such as the use of your organization's Web site or 800 numbers to get your information out to any and all stakeholders. Communication is more than just "information" dissemination; it is comprised of framing messages.

Emergency notification is a systematic process that must be detailed enough to handle the crisis situation. Your organization should create notification need matrices, which deal with each of the needs of your organization and all those affected by the crisis in each stage of the emergency situation. All communication must be planned in a multi-channel approach. This plan should include broadcast capabilities to all phones, e-mail addresses, texting devices, instant messaging tools, and more. There should also be an allowance for public address systems and emergency hotlines to get the information out to your audience. Within the business itself, you should make sure there are monitors in the buildings, sirens, campus or public radio broadcasts, and any other options to keep your employees safe. Finally, you should plan for alerts to area news media. It is better that you personally give them information spun the way you would like and release it in your own timing, rather than having the media finding out about a crisis through leaks that paint your organization in a negative light. Each of these steps in the emergency notification process makes up an aspect for all stages of crisis communication.

There are different pre- and postcrisis communication message strategies. This affects what you say, when you say it, to whom you say it, how you say it, and why you are saying it. Your organization should have a specific message plan. This can be accomplished through the use of message maps (see Chapter 8) that are delivered clearly and quickly to keep pace with the time-sensitive nature of a crisis.

COMMUNICATION TOOLS

Communicating with your organization's employees is vital. You must get critical information to those who need it immediately, especially if personnel could potentially be in harm's way. There are a variety of different tools that you can use to do this. Communication networks with the business's community, customers, family, clients, vendors, delivery persons, and those in transit in and around its location should remain open and preferably be preestablished.

The best communication during a crisis is humanitarian communication, the act of informing individuals of the local availability of resources protecting people and property. This type of communication is a necessity in many disasters. Another type of communication that is crucial to emergency management is that stemming from crisis professionals. Law enforcement and emergency responders need full access to the areas that have been affected. At the same time, the business will be trying to evacuate and account for personnel, activate the emergency response team, and control media coverage. An important component of success in this area includes providing identification (such as badges) for key personnel, law enforcement, and emergency responders. The key is to have procedures already in place and ready to be immediately implemented. Local law enforcement and fire and safety personnel should be aware of the identification procedures in order to better assist with compliance and security of the perimeter.

You can improve your emergency response with the use of varying communication routes. Organizations routinely utilize their best information and deploy their most reliable personnel in crisis situations. Yet these same organizations often revert to less-rich communication channels, such as e-mail, fax, or audio, to send and receive complex layered messages about a crisis situation. Although these tools are effective in sending basic data-based information, other less measurable and definable information (such as that used in a crisis situation) cannot be relayed. This communication gap creates tremendous opportunity for failure. However, using rich media, such as face-to-face or phone messages, is the key to successful communication during a crisis. Video conferencing can also provide a richness and immediacy to the crisis communication experience that other communication tools do not. By providing real-time audio, video, and live communication channels in the field connected to regional, state, or national emergency operations centers—or even local hospitals and school systems—your organization's assessment, response, and recovery operations will dramatically improve. Early research has shown that in the absence of personal interaction, video conferencing is essential in the delivery of complicated, multilayered, and descriptive messages. By adding the ability to hold multipoint conferences and stream live crisis information directly from the field, the experience is even further enhanced.

Other alternative communication technologies are emerging. Without electricity and support utilities, many otherwise dependable communication technologies may be down as well. Traditionally, there have been alternative communication technologies able to "fill the connection gap." In major natural disasters, global amateur radio operators have been able to consistently maintain communication connections to entire geographical regions that have otherwise been isolated and cut off from communication.

There are a number of considerations for selecting an emergency alternative communication technology backup plan. The following are some questions that should guide your selection process:

- To whom do you need to communicate in each crisis scenario, and will this alternative communication technology enable you to connect with those key contacts during and after the crisis?
- Does the alternative technology have the capability to communicate (such as through voice and data) the information you need communicated under crisis conditions (e.g., alternative power, range, frequency, and typical interference)?

- Does use of the alternative communication technology require knowledge, skills, or abilities that personnel who are available during crises possess?
- What equipment and costs are required to have complete two-way communication via the alternative communication technology during a crisis?
- Do all personnel have the ability to operate these technologies with no communication privacy during crises?

The key to successful communication is often less dependent on the technology (whether ubiquitous or the emerging alternative), but rather hinges on the processes, procedures, and people involved with the communication. The most common issues involve aspects of duties, responsibilities, interpretation, and checklist reporting. No communication planning can be considered complete until questions about the processes, procedures, and people involved have been asked and answered. Automated notification systems can help with each of these issues, and the use of automated communication tools is emerging as one of the most popular strategies in emergency management.

Automated systems are faster, more accurate, more effective, and often much less expensive than manual communication systems. Automated notification systems, also known as mass notification systems, are designed to deliver a large volume of text, voice, or data messages to a potentially large audience, and in an extremely short amount of time. Normally, they can send messages through multiple communication channels—not just telephone, but also e-mail, pager, fax, instant messenger, personal digital assistant (PDA), and other channels. These systems are capable of accomplishing this feat by utilizing computing, wireless, and telephony technologies that have just matured in the past few years.

The common features of automated notification systems were designed to directly address challenges of crisis communication. Some key ideas in using automated notification systems are the following:

- Make communicating to many as simple and effective as communicating to one.
- Support business processes that require rapid, accurate, and verified communication.
- Address the proliferation of networks and devices that make mass communication more complex and less efficient.
- Communicate quickly, easily, and efficiently with large numbers of people in minutes, not hours.
- Use all contact paths, especially when regional or local communication infrastructure is damaged or not working.
- Ensure two-way communication for better visibility and planning.

- Reduce miscommunication and misunderstandings with accurate, consistent messages.
- Free up key personnel to perform critical tasks by automating manual, time-intensive, error-prone processes.
- Improve overall communication effectiveness by eliminating any single point of failure.

It is important to remember that there are a variety of different challenges, as well as solutions, to using automated notification systems. As each key person is brought into the fold, a hierarchy should be followed so that efforts are not wasted on duplication and, worse yet, contradiction. This hierarchy would typically follow a predetermined organizational chart. Initial notification of key personnel, in particular the crisis communication team, is the primary goal. This first notification should be happening simultaneously as all personnel and the facility are being secured. One example of such an automated emergency notification tool is a system that uses a national notification network to alert key personnel through a system of calls, pages, e-mails, and text messages in a prescribed order. One such business that uses this system has two separate departments for the dissemination of communication: corporate communication and employee communication. Their employee communication department is responsible for communicating emergency information to senior executives, all employees, and, when warranted, also to their parent business. The media is then contacted through the corporate communications department.

COMMON HAZARDS

Though the use of an automated communication tool can help with emergency management, there are still a number of common hazards that must be taken into account when designing your organization's plan. For example, the following list of common communication management challenges are often faced during a crisis:

- anticipating communication needs
- taking the initiative to communicate
- breakdowns of communication systems and technologies
- high levels of stress placed on individuals and teams
- rapidly occurring events and changing information
- aggressive demands for information
- critical analysis from the media and public

These challenges can be overcome by attention to detail during the planning stage of your emergency management strategy. Going through case scenarios of any crisis your organization can fall prey to will help better prepare your organization for surviving potential crises as will education and training of all employees. Core operational considerations of emergency management focus on direction and control of communications, life safety, property protection, community outreach before and after the crisis, recovery and restoration of normal operations, and administration and logistics concerns that can affect each of these considerations.

Another common hazard faced during this stage of your crisis preparation is connecting with your target audiences by choosing the best delivery channels. It is essential to have a media relations strategy as part of your emergency and crisis communication plan. Such a strategy should focus on proactive contact with the news media, speaking up and speaking out on key messages, and of course monitoring and responding to news media reports (both accurate and inaccurate). To successfully accomplish this goal requires having the communication plan together well in advance of any crisis. Even disasters managed in the best possible way can result in coverage that can give your organization a "black eye" in the perceptions of stakeholders. To repair or restore a damaged reputation, it is imperative to craft a message that will address all of the concerns and appropriately position a company for recovery. However, even the best-formed message strategy is worthless if you can't reach the key audiences. The organization cannot rely on the news media alone to get messages out to stakeholders. Choose from a variety of alternative communication technologies that will allow direct contact with critical audiences.

COMMON NEEDS

Along with common hazards faced during emergency management planning, there are also several common needs that factor into any and every organizational crisis plan. The main need for any organization in crisis is to protect its assets—namely, its employees.

It is important for a business to protect its assets. A large part of risk management involves insurance, reinsurance, and reducing potential financial liabilities. However, given the variety of potential disasters and impacts, one asset that deserves substantial consideration for protection plans is the workforce. Obviously, protecting people is a moral and ethical imperative. No other material possession is worth more than the people whose lives are, in part, entrusted to your protection. No cost–benefit analysis could ever replace the fundamental and essential obligation for prudent organizations to always prioritize the protection of the people within and nearby their locales. It is essential to plan to protect your people.

Protecting people is also a legal requirement. There is an implied contractual and due diligence obligation for those in management or ownership positions to protect the health and safety of others in the workplace. Furthermore, various governing agencies and regulatory bodies enforce numerous requirements to ensure that the protection of people remain a priority. However, it is also true that personnel are actually one of your greatest assets. No capital reserve, bond, equipment, or property is worth more to a company than its personnel. If you account for the intellectual capital; institutional creativity and memory; work experience; recovery capacity; knowledge of proprietary information and data; and intrinsic knowledge of processes, procedures, inventories, and systems, not to mention the costs of hiring, training, equipping, and supporting, then the personnel in your organization may be one of your largest single financial investments and asset resources. If you lose all or a significant part of your workforce to displacement from the area, death, physical or emotional injury, or disrupted work lives, the survival of the organization is at risk.

No disaster preparedness planning can be considered thorough unless it specifically includes detailed consideration for the health, safety, and all levels of well-being of the people within an organization. You must take all reasonable steps to ensure the physical safety of people under all contingencies. Furthermore, this plan should address their emotional, mental, economic, and work life continuity needs. Safety is both a short- and long-term goal and should be the fundamental goal of planning. Physical safety and security can only be ensured with a dynamic process that is flexible to changing circumstances and evolving situations. It is a good business investment to help employees prepare for crises. Protecting personnel will require ensuring that payroll is disbursed, benefits are delivered, alternative transportation is arranged, company credit cards are still functional, emergency checks are cashed, and insurance claims are appropriately addressed.

During crises, most personnel simply want to "do something/do anything" in order to feel that their activity is appropriate and useful. This leads us to recognize the importance of including specific behavioral instructions in our emergency notification communication. However, after the adrenaline fades from the body and all other security needs have been met, the typical employee begins to feel a need for a resumption of workplace continuity. This leads us to recognize that it is important to communicate a return to normalcy during the end phases of a crisis or emergency event to address these needs for reassurance and resumption of routine events. You should address concerns about when and where the normal work routine will resume, what the company will do about lost data, if there is going to be a temporary workstation or facility, and what the expectations are about normal events (e.g., meetings and deadlines). All personnel will ultimately need to be assured that work life has returned to normal after these crises or disasters. They will also need to be reassured that you and the company understand their anxiety in dealing with different parameters for the production of work. It is essential to have a road map that gives everyone a consistent plan to follow for protection priorities, recovery targets, and timetables. These priorities should be articulated and well understood by everyone (top to bottom) so that there is a clear sense of "what comes first and what comes next" during and after a major disaster strikes. Obviously, recovery sequence priorities will differ depending on the business, location, or mission. Furthermore, such priorities may not mirror routine business priorities. In general, assets are protected to ensure availability for mission-critical functions and to mitigate hazards and threats to personnel.

EDUCATION AND TRAINING OF PERSONNEL

The establishment of a training program for the education of personnel is a large part of an organization's effective emergency management. When employees and those possibly affected by a crisis are educated and trained concerning their roles in a crisis response, the whole response goes more smoothly. Employee training for the entire organization is essential for several reasons—namely, that it helps employees understand what will be done, and it gives the organization the opportunity to revise what didn't work. To start an education and training program, have one person or department responsible for developing a training schedule for your facility. Distribute the first draft of a potential emergency communication training schedule to group members assigned to this task within the organization and revise as needed. The next step might be to conduct a tabletop exercise or test of the procedures in a "walk-through." A case study group where key individuals describe an emergency scenario and discuss their responsibilities and what communication needs (two way) they would have during each phase of the event can also be helpful. Based on this discussion, you may be able to identify areas of potential confusion, communication needs, and gaps in your communication plans.

The next step in training and education is to conduct the training drills and exercises.

TESTING AND VALIDITY

The testing and validation of emergency messages is of crucial importance to see if they communicate what you think that they should convey. It is not sufficient to write messages that you think mean one thing without verifying that those who receive the messages will interpret and understand the messages to mean the same thing.

Employees, stakeholders, and any other constituents must be assessed in order to determine if they are able to comprehend the message and can understand how they are to respond appropriately during and after the emergency. There are a variety of different ways to test and validate your organization's communication plan. You can use focus groups, test messages, and various empirical techniques for validating the content of your messages. For example, running training scenarios can help immensely. Another example is to ask questions that test how completely the plan has been integrated into the organization's fabric.

The next step involves evaluation and modification of the communication plan. Evaluations can take many forms, among them informal discussions, surveys, formal audits, and feedback from employees or those otherwise in a position to evaluate crisis communication plan effectiveness. After evaluations of the plan, modifications may need to be made in order to design a more effective emergency management plan that includes the most up-to-date communication technologies. Your organization should conduct a formal audit or some other form of evaluation of the entire plan at least once a year.

To engage in a thorough review you will need to systematically ask yourself a large range of self-assessment questions. Although there are many different categories of metrics that can be utilized, the most basic self-assessment should include questions designed to ascertain your level of readiness to communicate during different critical situations and events.

You should endeavor to involve all levels of management in evaluating and updating the communication plan to ensure that it is comprehensive and addresses all of the potential needs and that all aspects of the plan have been agreed on in advance of the emergency. Determine if there are any residual problem areas and shortfalls that should be addressed. It is also helpful to include communication as a specific (and distinct) assessment category for any exercise debriefing or after-action review processes for actual emergencies. Specifically, you must determine if the communication plan going forward reflects lessons learned from simulated training drills and/or actual crisis events.

Ensure that the crisis management group and emergency response team understand their respective communication responsibilities. This includes training for new members (since the last training or exercise). Has the communication plan been updated to reflect changes in personnel, the physical layout of facilities or building, changes in procedures or policies, or changes in regulations governing communication? Another critical area to frequently test is to ensure that the contact list database is accurate and up-to-date.

In addition to a yearly audit, it is also important to evaluate and modify the emergency notification plan at other times, such as after each training drill or exercise, after each emergency, when personnel or their responsibilities change, when the layout or design of the facility changes, or when policies or procedures change. Also, remember always to brief personnel on changes to the plan.

SUMMARY OF KEY POINTS

- It is important to have a communication plan that includes a specific focus on emergency notification.
- Delegation of responsibility and authority for emergency notification communication should be made.
- Update and implement an information management policy and ensure that all emergency notification communication complies with the policy.
- A central aspect of emergency notification communication planning should include a proactive strategy of managing your key messages.
- There are different types of notification. Each of these must be taken into account in the planning process. It is useful to conduct a detailed audience analysis, which is essential for communication planning.
- You should update and keep current your emergency contact databases.
- Be sure to chart the communication relationships that will need to be sustained and honored during an emergency.
- Review and secure approval from senior management, legal, etc., for message templates and messages that will be used in different emergency circumstances.
- Plan messages for various emergency circumstances and include planning for optimal communication tools, target audiences, and common hazards with common responses.
- Implement education and training to ready audiences for emergency notification communication.
- Test and validate emergency notification messages, message delivery systems, audience understanding and comprehension, behavioral compliance, and tracking mechanisms.

CHAPTER 5

SIX PHASES OF EMERGENCIES

This chapter describes the six phases of an emergency crisis: (1) warning, (2) risk assessment, (3) response, (4) management, (5) resolution, and (6) recovery. There are unique needs, challenges, and changes in the target audiences during each of these phases. Thinking about your emergency notification communication needs when planning for these six phases can be helpful and aid the process. It is important to note that your communication needs and your people all change just as the emergency itself changes.

I COULDN'T BELIEVE IT WAS HAPPENING HERE

As commonly defined, an emergency is a crisis situation that poses an immediate risk to health, life, property, or environment. Most emergencies require urgent response to address or prevent a worsening of the situation. While some emergencies are self-evident (such as a major natural disaster that threatens many lives and a large geographical area), many smaller incidents can qualify as true emergencies even though they involve a very confined location or affect few people.

Many emergencies pose an immediate danger to the safety of people involved. These can range from emergencies affecting a single classroom or office to incidents affecting large numbers of people in a community, state, or region (such as natural disasters like hurricanes, floods, or wildfires). Some emergencies may not threaten any people, but can threaten property, production, products, business continuity, or reputations.

Emergency management and security professionals frequently plan for responding both during and after an emergency or disaster. The traditional four stages of emergency management are planning, response, recovery, and mitigation. This model is widely used for training emergency management. Typically these four stages are depicted as a cycle (circle) rather than as a linear arrangement. In this sense, the work at the end of stage 4 (mitigation) is also the beginning of work for stage 1 (planning). This is a helpful reminder that such planning work is not only ongoing, but that there is a vital importance for both lessons learned and the application of those lessons in preparedness.

By trying to focus on the unfolding emergency itself, we quickly begin to see detailed nuances that suggest there may be internal phases within an emergency that would require different categories of emergency notification (as well as the possibility of multiple emergencies occurring simultaneously). I developed these six phases of a crisis which overlap and expand on the traditional four stages of emergency management, focusing in greater detail on the communication processes related to the different circumstances identified in the phases which impact communication planning.

Emergencies and disasters do not "happen all at once." In fact, there are clearly discernible life cycles for crises and emegencies. There may be warnings, warning signs, or no warning whatsover when an emergency incident occurs. Emergency management authorities understand this evolutionary nature. Many models of emergency management break down the sequence of an emergency into distinctive phases or stages. One can find many different models of disasters, emergencies, and crises in the relevant literature, each with different numbers of phases.

For emergency communicaton and notification planning purposes, I advocate the six-phase model. The communication needs, constraints, and exigencies; the specific audiences, status, and receptivity of the targeted audiences; and the challenges for communicating during different periods of a crisis are not static. I will describe these differences in terms of six phases for emergencies (and the appropriate changes in emergency communication).

One final introductory note is necessary. I advocate looking at an emergency situation through the lens of recognizable phases in order to enhance the communication planning process. In reality, however, these phases do not unfold as distinct phases. There is overlap between the circumstances of each of the phases represented. Additionally, in real time there are often no clearly discernible segues or barrier markers to indicate when the circumstances have changed or are changing.

The six phases of a crisis or emergency that can be used to guide emergency notification communication plannig are (1) warning, (2) risk assessment, (3) response, (4) management, (5) resolution, and (6) recovery. There are unique needs, challenges, and changes in the target audiences during each of these phases. Thinking about your emergency notification communication needs under the planning outline of these six phases can be helpful and aid the process.

There may not be a warning phase in every emergency, as many emergencies have no recognizable advance warning to their sudden occurrence. There is no uniformity of time associated with each phase. In practice, some phases may be much longer than other phases. However, planning for emergency communication using the phases as a guideline should provide a sufficient basis to include the possible types of emergency notification required in every emergency situation. The duration of each stage varies and is determined by levels of stress, threat, surprise, and response time. Every stage of the crisis dictates your audience's information requirements and your communication agenda. You should organize your communication plans in a pattern that corresponds with each of the phases.

Every emergency management team should work with partners in their organization to carefully review the major communication needs and to identify target audiences who would need to be notified during each phase of the emergency. For each phase a list should be created that projects who, what, when, and how you should be notifying at these points in an emergency. These lists can be used as checklists and road maps during an emergency and form the backbone for developing specific message templates. These templates form the basis for message maps, which are discussed in chapter 8. For now, a list of audiences and information needs (along with planned delivery channels) for each phase can serve as a general road map for emergency notification communication.

PHASE 1: WARNING

The warning stage is the period when there is a heightened risk of a potential critical event, when there are circumstances making such an event probable, or when a specific threat has been made. Despite the different terminology, the warning phase might be accurately represented by a "watch" issued by the National Weather Service for a storm or other weather event. The conditions are right for an event, and it is time to prepare for the onset of a crisis. For example, receiving a bomb threat (which is different than experiencing an explosion) requires a response that includes notifying key personnel, law enforcement, and risk management constituents. This is an example of a warning stage of a crisis.

Certain types of emergency incidents have very distinct warning phases (e.g., hurricanes and winter storms), whereas other incidents have no warning periods or very subtle warning signs that often go unnoticed (e.g., power outages, workplace violence, and earthquakes).

Communication during the warning stage is often precautionary and is intended to heighten awareness. There may be limited notification and alerts sent to those who are potentially at risk or can be of assistance in assessing the danger or mitigating the threats. The lion's share of communication will focus on interaction among your team and "key constituents" (citizens, students, employees, and other noncrisis team members to whom you are accountable to communicate).

Instructions and notices that either prevent the occurrence of an emergency or mitigate the risk in ways that minimize the adverse impact of an emergency are examples of warning phase communication.

Warnings should be issued to individuals and departments who are assigned emergency responsibilities to alert them of the potential for an emergency. Alerting key staff who direct and control the organization's resources during an emergency would also be an important warning phase notice. This is also the time to start alerting or activating specific actions during emergency situations. Notification could also include informing personnel of the circumstances under which emergency procedures would be activated or become effective and/or under what conditions they would be terminated.

Warning phase notifications should include making status reports, taking stock of preparedness, and alerting personnel of their subsequent notification, recall rosters, and procedures if an incident occurs. The goal is to provide these personnel with the information needed to implement emergency response should such action become necessary. This should include procedures to implement notification of personnel assigned to the Emergency Operations Center (EOC), the response team, and emergency management support functions. The warning phase notices may be the last instructions, reminders, and notices that you communicate before the chaos and confusion of a disaster or emergency springs forth. The warning phase may be "dark clouds on the horizon," but also be the final calm before the storm is unleashed.

Communication during the warning phase includes communication to the EOC, security dispatch, and facilities work order control center. Warning communication should support preparing organizational resources, response field personnel, and readiness to sustain contact during emergencies. Communication in the warning phase may also include providing instructions and reminders for the reporting of damage assessment information to the EOC. In addition, it is not premature to alert all elements associated with your response and recovery to verify their readiness to respond.

Your communication should be consistent with your commitment to take appropriate action to increase readiness as a potential emergency situation looms. Communication undertaken during the warning phase of an emergency situation is designed to increase your ability to respond effectively to the emergency when it occurs. You should consider using any alerts or messages that can increase or confirm the readiness for responding to an emergency, that can mitigate the impacts, or that can position people and resources in order to maximize safety as part of your warning phase communication plans.

Preparing to respond to the warning phase of an emergency situation includes taking the following actions beforehand:

- Developing communication checklists that you follow as standard procedure when the warning phase is activated.
- Providing instructions and directions for inspections of critical infrastructure, reviewing and updating emergency plans and articulating communication protocols, briefing key personnel, contacting and updating key resources, verifying readiness and mobilizing resources (prepositioning), requiring systems checks (possibly, if conditions are right), taking a silent and quick testing of your automated emergency notification warning systems, disseminating accurate, timely, emergency public information, and/or summoning additional staff if needed for a possible emergency

Messages need to demonstrate that the organization recognizes the prospect of a pending emergency or disaster and that its goal is to alert people to take necessary actions that might prevent loss of life and property.

There are also essential alerts that are required to mitigate the impact of an approaching used a lot emergency. Mitigation alert efforts are your last opportunity to make all things ready to prevent, limit the impact of, and quickly respond to an emergency. Warnings should be consistent with your preparedness instruction efforts. If you have time and opportunity during a warning phase, you should distribute brief and urgent preparedness alerts. These may include informing people about how to take the necessary precautions to protect themselves and their property if the emergency were to occur. Many types of emergencies can strike quickly and without warning, requiring instant response. New sentence There are a number of last-minute instructions that could be issued during a warning phase, including actions to take to avoid harm or to prevent an incident from occurring, along with how to be prepared to bounce back after an emergency.

A warning will also affect both you and your audience. Whether it is an approaching storm or a bomb threat, the warning phase will see a rise in concern and anxiety, physiological changes, cognitive effects, and situational and contextual alterations. Recall that stress and distractions during an emergency can impact the ability to focus, be attentive, listen, think, comprehend, and comply with instructions. Messages during the warning phase need to be kept simple and direct. In addition, the alert messages need to be consistent and draw on prior training and expectations.

It is important to determine what types of information and messages might need to be communicated during the warning phase. Some of the basic alert messages should be easy to identify. These could include a list of information content (what are the potential threats/dangers) for possible emergency situations. Also, you should develop language and vocabulary that is both acceptable by legal and senior management strategic review. It is important to consider the meta-message (i.e., tone and urgency) of these messages.

Alert messages during the warning phase should focus on nondramatized, objective descriptions of the threat risks, provide specific behavioral requests, and incorporate a method to confirm compliance (feedback) and status.

Therefore, interactive communication plays key roles during warning periods. Warnings should also trigger assessment and risk analysis communication. Beware of faulty conclusions and too-hasty generalizations. Stick with the facts and be diligent and vigilant in evaluating information before you release it in your alerts. In addition, effective decision making does not happen automatically without training and preparation.

In short, outbound communication during this stage is often precautionary but should accomplish key tasks to alert and advise recipients. Whether intended or unintended, the wording in your notification messages will either motivate your audience to act professionally and appropriately or might frighten them and create undue stress. In addition, disclosures and transparency will build credibility and trust with audiences. You can raise awareness and vigilance with your alerts during the warning phase. In addition, this may help further educate and inform the audience about the potential threats.

PHASE 2: RISK ASSESSMENT

The risk assessment phase is the period when your team (often with the assistance of outside sources) has to assess the risks, potential consequences, and damages before determining the best course of action to avoid or mitigate the (possible) disaster.

During the risk assessment phase, communication is geared toward understanding the nature of the threat and assembling the right people to determine how to handle the situation. The risk assessment phase can overlap with the warning phase as well as the response stage. In many types of emergencies, it is an ongoing aspect of communication that has to be sustained along with the other communication exigencies.

During the warning stage, your key decision makers will need to interact with and assess the situation. This requires sustained communication and information exchange, which in turn requires planning for communication during the stage.

In the moments after an incident occurs and/or is reported, the crisis response team activates the organization's emergency response plan and you begin to notify target audiences. However, communication is primarily focused on your internal decision makers during the risk assessment stage. Most "public" emergency communication occurs during the subsequent response phase.

Communication during the risk stage, although not primarily to public audiences, is just as critical and vital as any other aspect of emergency notification communication. During the risk assessment stage, it is vital to communicate with your team, key personnel, management, and executives. You may also need to notify local law enforcement, health care providers, insurance providers and other relevant agencies. Although your notification may cause them to be on a heightened alert to the danger, the primary purpose of notification during the risk assessment phase is to get and give information essential to ascertain the extent, probability, and severity of the risks related to the emergency.

As with the context of warning alerts, during the risk phase stress levels change decision making, perception of risk, and critical judgment skills. Messages should be clear, objective, specific, and as concrete as possible. The exchange of notification messages should facilitate analytical interaction. There are specific information requirements, in particular the need for rapid and accurate incoming information and information processing (including procedures for gathering, prioritizing, analyzing, storing, retrieving, and discarding information).

PHASE 3: RESPONSE

Once an emergency incident occurs, the emergency response plan is activated. Crisis team members call first responders into action and you begin to notify the public about the incident. Emergency notification would include alerting first responders, those in harm's way, and other key constituents. The response phase begins at the moment when an incident occurs and activation notification is issued to initiate reaction to the emergency. Even with thorough planning, you may still end up improvising some notifications. However, for the most part, you can prepare the messages and alerts you would use during the onset of an emergency incident well in advance in order to speed the issuance and delivery of these notifications.

The response phase requires communication to initiate the activities that are taken during and immediately following a disaster. Effective communication demonstrates your leadership role and professionalism. It also facilitates coordination efforts between local, county, state, and federal agencies. During the response phase, emphasis is placed on quick action, containing the incident, gaining control, protecting people and property, and minimizing the effects of the emergency. All communication that requires the activation of immediate response actions occurs during the response phase.

The response phase requires notifications to activate and coordinate emergency response activities. The level of notification is determined by the scope, size, and type of emergency. In some circumstances one of the most important notices to be disseminated is to actually communicate a "declaration of an emergency" or "activate the emergency response plan."

Specific types of notices in the response stage typically include the following:

- disseminating warnings, emergency information, and action instructions
- requesting information to survey and evaluate the situation
- directing first responders and reactive steps
- positioning personnel and equipment for the response; alerting and activating EOC personnel; reinforcing established guidelines
- issuing instructions for evacuation, sheltering in place, or other behavioral responses

Instructions for actions carried out immediately at the outset of an emergency, need to be disseminated. These alerts may include declaring plans, evacuation, shelter-in-place advisories, and various activation issues.

You may also need to notify incident command posts as well as your own EOC. (If you are following the unified incident command structure, regular and specific notifications will need to be sent and received throughout the emergency.) If an emergency occurs without a warning phase, you will need to activate the response as rapidly as conditions permit. Your instructions will need to reach all of your audience swiftly and be understandable. You will need to conduct evacuation and/or rescue operations as required or issue emergency information and instructions.

Listed here some response phase notifications:

- alerting employees, constituents, or the public to the emergency
- fully activating the EOC and key personnel
- alerting first responders; coordinating emergency operations for maximum survival of people and preservation of property
- keeping everyone informed of changes in the emergency situations as they occur

You will need to communicate with the crisis team; first responders; people at risk; key personnel and executives; local law enforcement and other responding agencies; and citizens, students, and employees. Focus is geared toward making audiences aware of the incident, providing instructions, and seeking confirmation of a response. Basically, it includes emergency notification messages.

Critical factors to consider include (1) context, rapidly changing events, "facts" with low confidence, misinterpretation (receiver orientation) issues, psychological interference (noise), and people and technology breakdowns; (2) the best ways to communicate (decisively; quickly; calmly; directly; exhibiting a richer vs. leaner mentality; avoiding redundancy; exhibiting command, control, and coordination communication; and maintaining directive [informational and instructive] two-way communication with feedback; (3) an emphasis on push communication flow; and (4) what to communicate, such as power-worded messages, in a manner that provides concise, precise, literal, behavioral directions and meta-message factors. Meta-messages (literally, messages about messages) include all of the "implied" levels of meanings or interpretations, sometimes referred to as messages "between the lines." As always, seek confirmation and updated response reports to your messages.

Once the response is underway, there is a subtle transition to the management phase. It is sometimes helpful to think in terms of the first or initial response to an incident in order to focus on the particular needs of the response phase. As first responses transition into ongoing responses, there are changes in the nature of audience members, messages, and notification needs. The emergency notification messages in the response phase are the most critical. It is these "point of the spear" notices that Chapters 7 and 8 in this book expand on in greater detail when considering how to create an effective emergency notification message for the response phase.

After the initial series of messages during the response phase, there is a transition to ongoing management of the emergency rather than immediate responses. No matter how long it takes, the types of information notices, alerts, and messages are all part of the management of the emergency.

PHASE 4: MANAGEMENT

Emergencies either move toward resolution or grow more disastrous with deepening layers of complexity. Managing these processes (with the goal of resolution) requires a lot of notification, alerts, and coordination. Organizations must respond differently according to the progression of the crisis.

Organizations must provide regular status updates to their various audiences, such as alerting audiences of changes or additions to previous instructions, controlling rumors, and conferencing with leadership and responder teams. Typically, the information needs grow more complex with demands for details, causes, and implications. In addition, the circle of people affected by the emergency will have grown.

Course correction may be needed to respond to changes in the situation. The need to keep a wide range of audiences updated is central to notification requirements during the management phase. In addition, in most emergencies, there is a need for communicating with the news media, authorities, and stakeholders.

As the emergency continues, vital information necessary for the response will need to be communicated.

Critical factors to consider when communicating during the management phase include sequential communication breakdowns, information management issues, and effects of fatigue and stress on your personnel. It is best to communicate with your audience as directly as possible, using richer rather than leaner media, principles of redundancy, two-way communication with feedback, sustained multiple channels (modalities), and public communication. It is more effective to utilize both push and pull communication flow during the management phase.

PHASE 5: RESOLUTION

Once the emergency has been resolved and is drawing to conclusion, emergency managers should communicate that resolution to all audiences in the form of all-clear alerts and messages of reassurance. Audiences need to be notified that the dangers have passed and that the status is returning to "normalcy."

Audiences need to be alerted to the closure of emergency and contingency operations. Information about the transition to "recovery" operations needs to be disseminated. Furthermore, recall or demobilize notifications are needed for emergency responders. In most cases, there will also need to be notification of the management protocols and procedures that are back in effect or any changes of command authority or command structure.

Target audiences will include those who have been actively impacted by the management of the crisis: constituents and stakeholders; emergency response personnel; and assigned individuals, agencies, and teams that will take charge of the operational recovery phase. As you develop your notification messages, there are a number of critical factors to consider. These include taking into consideration psychological and cognitive issues along with lingering confusion and misinformation "pockets" such as sequential communication delays, breakdowns, and "information ripples." It is important to get key information to all of those who need it. It is most effective if you utilize both push and pull measures, multiple (direct and indirect) channels, and source credibility (authority).

Notification messages should be simple declarative closure measures. You will need to alert audiences to changes of status, transition and information on anticipated recovery steps, and how to obtain resources or additional information. In all of this, the messages should exude reassurance, confidence, and stability. There are also important meta-message aspects to communicate as the emergency winds down. Notifications during the resolution phase need to communicate resolution in the form of accurate and consistent all-clear alerts.

PHASE 6: RECOVERY

Once the emergency is over and the tasks switch to recovery and clean-up mode, there are still a number of important notification tasks yet to be completed. Typically there are a substantial amount of dispatches, notices, and notification messages involved in recovery following an emergency incident.

Information dissemination is still very useful after the disaster is over. Action reviews and required documentation will be needed, along with measures taken to reduce a reoccurrence, that limit future harm, or that put additional plans in place "for the next time." Recovery communication is both a short-term activity intended to return operation to normal and a long-term activity designed to apply lessons learned from an emergency to the efforts to prepare for the next emergency.

Recovery phase notifications would include those aimed at implementing health and safety measures; protecting, controlling, and allocating vital resources; restoring or activating essential facilities and systems; enforcing police powers in controlling the locations; and establishing access controls, such as erecting traffic barricades. Short-term recovery involves returning vital life support systems to minimum operating standards. Long-term recovery may take years and could involve total redevelopment. Recovery requires a unified commitment and lots of information exchange. Communication is the main component in the success of any recovery effort.

The recovery phase is the period immediately following the emergency resolution phase, when actions will be taken to restore the situation to as normal as possible. The following action requests will need to be sent:

- developing an evaluation of the situation including damage assessment
- reporting damage assessment to the EOC
- planning for restoration, determining priorities, and commencing restoration
- providing assistance and information; providing or arranging transportation
- providing medical and human resources information
- providing information (e.g., schedules, time lines, and work assignments) as needed to get operations "normal" again

Recovery phase communication also includes information exchanges necessary for mitigation efforts. Mitigation refers to measures that prevent an emergency from occurring, reduce the chance of an emergency happening, or reduce the damaging effects of unavoidable emergencies. The after-action review (which occurs during the recovery phase) and the lessons learned from that review are important information resources needed for ongoing mitigation work.

Obviously, many people may be displaced and out of their usual and customary locations in the aftermath of an emergency. They will need many types of information, including changes in schedules, reporting times and locations, where to go for assistance, human resources information, questions about implications and long-term impacts, accountability questions about the emergency, and how the response was enacted.

There will also be objectives that your organization will want to communicate. These will undoubtedly include

- a focus on healing
- getting back to normal.

You must not overlook all of the potential audiences for recovery messages. These would include suppliers, customers, employees, investors, regulators, the community, affected target audiences, and various constituents and stakeholders. Don't overlook assigned individuals, agencies, and teams that have been in charge during the emergency.

This phase is also a major opportunity to manage rumors and misinformation. However, it is primarily devoted to getting things back to business as usual. It is important to get key information to all of those who need it. It is most effective if you utilize both push and pull measures, multiple (direct and indirect) channels, and source credibility (authority). In addition to all of the post emergency information issues, you also need to continue to alert people in the aftermath of an emergency of changed circumstances and people. There is also a need for explanations and analysis to be shared with many audiences. Typically, updates on changes in policies, procedures, and facilities that are being implemented in the aftermath of an emergency event also need to be shared with personnel, employees, and other constituents.

APPLICATION

As demonstrated here there exist several identifiable notification needs for each phase related to who, what, when, and how you should be notifying audiences at certain points during an emergency. Use the six phases to plan notification and alerts that would need to be delivered during an emergency and to form the backbone for developing specific message templates or message maps. For now, this list of audiences and information needs (along with planned delivery channels) for each phase can serve as a general road map for emergency notification communication. The next consideration is to determine what specific purpose or function the notification is intended to serve during each phase for each of the targeted audiences. The following key points of notification functions should help spur your own thinking about what you are trying to accomplish with your emergency notification efforts during each of the phases.

SUMMARY OF KEY POINTS

- There are six phases of an emergency crisis: (1) warning, (2) risk assessment, (3) response, (4) management, (5) resolution, and (6) recovery.
- Each phase of a crisis presents different communication needs, opportunities, and challenges that evolve and change during the life cycle of a crisis.
- Crisis communication plannning should follow these phases, and specific communication preparedness tied to each phase of an emergency should be created. Thinking about your emergency notification communication needs under the planning outline of these six phases can be helpful and aid the process.
- There are unique needs, challenges, and changes in the target audiences during each of these phases. Your emergency notification messages need to be adapted to the changes in your target audiences.

- In some of the phases, there are greater stressors and distractions for your target audiences. Therefore, specific adaptations for emergency notification should be adapted for high-stress phases.
- It is important to note that your communication needs and your people all change, just as the emergency itself changes.

CHAPTER 6

AUTOMATED NOTIFICATION

This chapter presents the new automated notification solutions that can be incorporated as the backbone for an emergency notification plan. The chapter covers the various types of automated systems; compares the effectiveness, functions, and advantages of each; and examines how these systems can greatly increase response time, enhance efficiency, decrease mistakes and failures, and free up personnel to manage other aspects of the emergency, because the automated systems can be operated at maximum efficiency with minimum operators.

TOO MUCH TO DO; TOO LITTLE TIME

The phrase "plan today, survive tomorrow" applies to organizations as much as it does to individuals. Communication failures have historically plagued organizations in their ability to respond to and minimize the human, operational, and financial impact of an emergency. Alerting people during emergency situations continues to be a challenge for organizations of all types and sizes. When disaster strikes and every second counts, organizations need to focus on the mission-critical tasks of ensuring the safety of their people and continuing operations, not on managing the logistics of emergency communication. Nonetheless, traditional approaches to alerting consume extensive resources, time, and the attention of personnel.

Contacting many people quickly is a challenge. There are inherent limitations to how many people can be alerted manually by one person or a small team. Over the years a number of solutions to this challenge have emerged. One of the earliest communication techniques that was created was the telephone calling tree. Even today, the telephone calling tree is used as a common approach for mass notification. However, these manual call trees, when one person calls four people, those four call four more, etc., have been shown to have a number of limitations and challenges unique to such an approach.

Manual telephone calling trees include the following challenges:

- Call trees are slow, time-consuming, and resource-intensive.
- Lack of consistency in messages results in inaccurate information and confusion.
- If someone in your call tree does not perform his or her duties, the message does not reach anyone attached to that branch of your phone tree.
- Lack of an audit trail about who has been contacted, when the message was received and on what device, and the result of the contact (e.g., voice mail or hang up) causes confusion. You have no accurate way of knowing who was called or who received the message.
- Accuracy of data and a central repository that is current and up-to-date is often compromised.
- Sequential communication errors that are inherent to the method (remember the "telephone game") can put people and operations at even greater risk.

A successor to telephone calling trees emerged in the early to mid 1990s in the crossover application of auto-dial technology integrated by sophisticated computer software to manage the task of rapid telephone calling. In quick succession these automated notification systems expanded beyond telephone calls to a wide range of capabilities including "retry until success," multiple contact paths, two-way communication, and rich media applications. This has resulted in more efficient and more accurate emergency notification as well as reducing miscommunication, errors, and rumors.

AUTOMATED EMERGENCY NOTIFICATION SYSTEMS

Automated emergency notification systems can enhance emergency notification communication capability by enabling the ability to reach people faster with the right information. Contacting thousands of people via their many communication devices is as quick and easy as a single phone call or a few clicks of the mouse. These systems eliminate communication interoperability issues by delivering messages across all communication platforms and devices, ensuring successful message delivery.

Automated systems are faster, more accurate, more effective, and often much less expensive than manual communication systems. Automated notification systems, also known as mass notification systems, are designed to deliver a large volume of text, voice, or data messages to a potentially large audience in an extremely short amount of time. Normally, they can send messages through multiple communication channels—not just telephone, but also e-mail, pager, fax, instant messenger, personal digital assistant (PDA), and other channels. These systems are capable of accomplishing this feat by utilizing computing, wireless, and telephony technologies that have just matured in the past few years.

Automated emergency notification systems reduce miscommunication, sequential errors, rumors, and misinformation. They also address many of the problems associated with the telephone game of manual telephone calling trees. Such systems enable you to send accurate, consistent messages to your entire contact base rapidly and efficiently, as well as to establish vital two-way communication linkages with feedback and response capabilities.

The newer next generation systems can perform the following tasks:

1. free up your staff to handle other important tasks
2. save time by automating manual, time-intensive processes and tasks so your team members or employees can focus on their core responsibilities instead of managing communication logistics
3. lower your total cost of crisis and emergency communication

These systems can help you reach more people, more effectively without expanding your staff or overburdening already stretched resources. This chapter will review the basic operational features of these systems, provide some comparisons between different types of systems, and even provide guidance for selecting an automated notification system that is best suited for your emergency communication needs and challenges.

AUTOMATION CAN ENHANCE EFFECTIVENESS AND ACCOUNTABILITY

Automated emergency notification systems offer better visibility and control of message delivery through real-time confirmation and reporting. You know who received your messages, when, and how. Plus, with two-way communication capabilities, you can elicit important information from your message recipients for informed decision making.

Automated systems would seem to be highly useful for crisis and emergency communication with employees, customers, partners, vendors, crisis management, the Emergency Operations Center (EOC), and business continuity team activation and coordination. Such systems can also facilitate on-the-fly conference calling with security personnel, crisis teams, the EOC, or business continuity team members as well with executive management. Such systems play a foundational role in the activation of interim crisis policies and procedures, status update notices during and following a disaster, remote "roll calling," severe weather alerts, office closures and reopenings, and many other applications. Refer to the Additional Benefits for Automated Systems Box for more uses of automated systems.

The common features of automated notification systems were designed to directly address challenges of crisis communication. The following are some key ideas for using automated notification systems:

Additional Benefits for Automated Systems

A mass notification system can also be an integral component of an organization's emergency and routine communications capabilities. Although these systems are most often associated with emergency notification for contacting employees during and after a disaster, mass notification dramatically improves an organization's operational efficiency and bottom line when implemented for day-to-day operations. Just a few common examples include alerting supply chain members about a needed change in delivery schedules; reminding employees about policy changes, deadlines, and other time-sensitive information; and mobilizing information technology staff more quickly after a server goes down. All these benefits make an organization and its employees more efficient and competitive. The benefits of mass notification are already being applied by organizations to increase revenues, cut or avoid costs, and minimize the loss of human life. Organizations have many options when selecting a system vendor.

- make communicating to many people as simple and effective as communicating to one
- support business processes that require rapid, accurate, and verified communication
- address the proliferation of networks and devices that make mass communication more complex and less efficient
- communicate quickly, easily, and efficiently with large numbers of people in minutes, not hours
- use all contact paths, especially when regional or local communication infrastructure is damaged or not working
- ensure two-way communication for better visibility and planning
- reduce miscommunication and misunderstandings with accurate, consistent messages
- free up key personnel to perform critical tasks by automating manual, time-intensive, error-prone processes
- improve overall communication effectiveness by eliminating any single point of failure

There are a variety of different challenges, as well as solutions, to using automated notification systems. The Communication Challenge Box illustrates some of these.

Communication Challenge	
Communication Challenge	Automated System
Heavy demand for information	Able to send hundreds of messages in seconds
Communication systems are unavailable	Utilizes multiple communication networks and paths, built with redundant systems that can survive regional failures
Severe time constraints or little time for investigation or analysis	Leverages speed and delivery reliability to both disseminate information quickly and give decision makers more time
Crisis manager's normal location is unavailable	The notification system and contact data are accessible from anywhere; administrator can delegate authority to an alternate whose location is available
Personnel are scattered	Multiple communication pathways maximize chance of finding and reaching your audience
One-on-one communication takes too long	Thousands of calls can be placed in a few seconds/minutes, and some systems offer conference calling and geographical targeting
Collecting information from the audience is difficult	Automated polling and real-time summaries of polling data can be easily collected
Inconsistent, inaccurate, or incomplete information is issued	Identical recorded or text messages allow accurate and consistent information flow; the speed and volume of automation allows rumors to be quashed quickly

Although nearly all automated notification systems try to address the challenges identified here, they do come in a variety of basic architectures and configurations. Some automated notification systems are operated internally by the businesses that use them, whereas others are operated by vendors. Three popular categories of notification systems available today are "box" solutions, application service providers, and Web-native application service providers. All three will be discussed in more depth later in the chapter.

Some notification solutions send messages to targeted individuals on all contact devices and on all contact paths. The most effective approach uses a sequential, targeted process where each contact path is prioritized sequentially and, once a notification is confirmed, the broadcast stops.

Another key feature allows audiences to control how they prefer to be notified. Contacts can be set up and their preferences defined. When the system is set up initially, contact information for each employee or other individual is created in a directory. For example, an individual may want to be contacted first via landline telephone, with the second choice being via cell phone. A third choice could be through a corporate e-mail, the fourth choice by home phone, and the fifth choice by personal e-mail.

In addition, individuals can be grouped by function or other parameters. For example, an individual can be grouped in a senior management group or e-mail server group. A call initiator can then contact the entire group very easily and quickly.

Automated systems allow both voice and/or text messages to be delivered. When notification is required, an authorized individual in the organization creates a message to be distributed to a group or any selection of contacts in the directory. The communication can be a voice and/or text message and can contain information requesting a response. For example, in an emergency, a message can be sent to all employees to inform them not to come to work that day. The system can also request information, such as the safety and location of employees, and medical assistance needs.

Another key feature is the ability to confirm that the message has successfully been delivered, after which a tracking report can be generated. During the notification, the automated system continues to attempt to contact each individual until a successful resolution is achieved. A real-time report can quickly communicate the overall picture: how many recipients have been reached, what is their status, and so forth. Detailed reports emphasize where individual follow-up is needed.

WHY AUTOMATED MASS NOTIFICATION?

Automated emergency notification can improve the communication process. It facilitates consistent messages to all, resulting in increased coordination and collaboration.

Many of these systems leverage two-way communication and offer survey/feedback capability. Automated notification increases delivery speed of alerts and warnings. This can increase the response time and expand the window for people to seek shelter or safety. Automated systems provide an audit trail for accountability and regulatory compliance requirements.

Automated emergency notification can facilitate decision making. These systems can provide real-time feedback with real-time reporting and data to enable more effective emergency notification communication. In addition, this provides you with the ability to mobilize resources more quickly.

Automated emergency notification also can enhance security and safety. This includes the use of such systems to improve overall emergency preparedness and responsiveness capabilities. Many of these systems enable you to monitor equipment, systems, and facilities during emergencies. Finally, the systems can produce an audit trail for tracking and reporting of incidents and communications during the event to provide the advantage of real-time situational awareness.

Automated emergency notification systems offer a quick, efficient, and effective communication solution for emergencies when critical, urgent, and important informative notifications are essential. Such systems can also increase productivity for emergency management teams as well as better ensure that emergency notification communication will occur even when key personnel are absent or unavailable. These systems allow you to initiate proactive communication as well as to rely on automatic alerts based on your predetermined crisis communication plans. Also, many of these systems can capture inbound communication that will actually decrease in bound calls that you have to handle manually and the need for you to have your personnel visit some field locations and emergency sites.

Perhaps most advantageous is that automated notification systems can reduce costs as well as provide dramatic return on the investment required to put such systems in place. The cost savings are most easily documented in terms of personnel efficiencies and direct reduction in necessary overtime, staffing, and other resources. In addition, in most cases there is also a direct savings in required physical assets—facilities management, systems, and equipment—that are replaced by the automated system.

COMMUNICATION DURING AN EMERGENCY

Mass notification systems are specifically designed to address common communication failures, and many failures could have been mitigated had a mass notification system been part of the disaster response and recovery plan. Mass notification lets disaster coordinators take advantage of whatever communication pathways are open to deliver consistent messages quickly and keep a running tally of the responses to those messages.

Redundancy is one key to the success of notification solutions—not only are messages sent to a given recipient on multiple pathways, but the systems themselves are designed with multiple physical redundancies. For example, a vendor might lease dedicated phone lines from several different national carriers and store identical customer contact information in multiple data centers thousands of miles apart. Although no system should be considered fail-safe, mass notification systems are not only efficient through saving time, but also offer a level of reliability and security that a single system cannot match.

Clearly, not every communication failure can be averted. The scale of a disaster may be great enough to overwhelm any planning efforts. However, in many of the real-life cases cited in this book, mass notification in conjunction with effective planning would have saved lives and property, reassured the public, and gotten businesses and public services up and running much sooner.

Although a mass notification system can never guarantee complete success, certain features can make it as fail-safe as possible. To understand what these are, it is helpful to consider all the steps a coordinator must take in order to communicate successfully during a disaster.

Initiating Messages

The first task facing the emergency coordinator is to initiate the notification messages. This can be a formidable challenge if the command center has been damaged or if communication lines are down. Automated notification simplifies the task by reducing the number of messages that must be initiated. The better systems also provide assistance for message construction, predetermined messages, and the ability to rapidly convey important prepared messages in the system.

A notification system allows the coordinator to issue a single message to an entire list of people—whether that group consists of police SWAT team members, critical vendors, ambulance crew chiefs, parents of schoolchildren, hospital intake liaisons, or reporters. The chances of initiating messages successfully are much greater if the coordinator has to send only five messages instead of 5,000.

The variety of communication media available today often makes people feel they can never really "get away from it all." The benefit is that there is nearly always some way to contact people via the sophisticated notification system.

For the notification system to be truly accessible in an emergency there must be multiple ways to initiate a message. At the very least, disaster coordinators should be able to contact the notification service through the Internet and by telephone. They should not be required to be at a particular computer or a particular telephone to initiate a message. A single dedicated connection is particularly vulnerable to failure.

There must also be multiple ways to record and reformat messages. With a mass notification system, the message is not necessarily delivered in the same format in which it is received. The message initiator should be able to dictate a message to an operator, record a voice message by telephone or Internet, or type a text message using the Internet or a telephone text-messaging device. Live operators or system software should be able to convert text messages to speech and vice versa.

Furthermore, the automated system must be able to accept messages from multiple initiators. Emergency coordinators should be able to delegate authority to several associates so notification won't fail if one person is incapacitated or unavailable.

Finally, the system hardware must have at least two widely separated physical locations, so that it won't become unavailable in the event of a region wide disaster. The system should use redundant electrical power sources, communications carriers, and Internet service providers (ISPs) to minimize the chance that it will be put out of commission.

Delivering Messages

After a message has been initiated, it must be delivered to everyone on the list. There are two important issues involved in this: whether the messages will arrive and when they will arrive. To maximize the likelihood that messages will be delivered, the notification system must be able to send messages to all types of contact devices—landline phone, wireless phone, fax, ISP-based e-mail, BlackBerry (wireless e-mail), pager, PDA—and in as many formats as possible: voice, text, and short message service (SMS).

The system must also permit unlimited contact numbers for each person on the list and allow a different order for each list member. For example, member 1 might designate cell phone first, then e-mail, then fax; member 2 might designate work phone first, then home phone, then pager. In addition, the system must be able to make unlimited attempts to contact each person on the list, until there is confirmation of receipt. Blanket geographical notifications should make use not only of 911 listings but also of any other contact information for the residents of the affected area. In other words, geographical and contact list data should be cross-referenced.

To deliver the messages as quickly as possible, the system must have adequate line capacity. With a sufficient number of lines, it is possible to deliver thousands of messages in just a few minutes. Telephone lines must be dedicated to the system and not shared with other users who will be in competition for them.

SELECTING THE RIGHT TARGET AUDIENCE FOR NOTIFICATION

A well-designed mass notification system must be able to send messages to everyone who needs to be notified. There should be no limit in the system on the number of list members allowed. Messages should be deliverable anywhere, including in foreign countries.

Nearly as important as reaching all the critical participants is sending messages *only* to those who need to receive them. Sending extraneous messages in times of emergency can have serious unintended consequences. These can include chaos and crowding at the disaster site, an influx of unwanted phone calls, and even mass panic.

To filter messages correctly, unlimited lists and sublists must be allowed in the system. For example, the emergency coordinator may need to poll employees from the seventh floor to make sure they were all safely evacuated from the fire on that floor, instruct employees in the network services division to report to the backup site the next morning, or recall some ambulance crews but not others.

Relationships between list members must be tracked. This allows the emergency coordinator to make selections based on the relationships—for example, contacting all parents of only sixth graders in a school. Geographical notification, which is used for evacuating neighborhoods or warning people of potential dangers, must be able to be fine-tuned. For example, the residents of the blocks closest to a fire might be told to leave immediately, whereas those a few blocks farther away might be told to prepare for evacuation.

MAINTAINING ACCURATE CONTACT LISTS

With or without mass notification, one of the primary responsibilities of a disaster coordinator is maintaining accurate contact lists. An automated notification system can help protect data integrity if it is well designed and administered.

There must be a facility to upload existing contact lists. If a list has already been created and vetted by the organization, reentering data would run the risk of introducing errors.

List members should be able to update their own contact information, including their contact path preferences, through a user-friendly Internet interface or by telephone. People are more likely to update their own information correctly, if only because it's easier for them to spot mistakes.

Data must be properly secured. This requires using appropriate security software and developing and implementing adequate security procedures. List members must have confidence that the system administrators will protect their privacy and will not release their contact information to any third parties. Ideally, systems should include an option to conceal personal contact information from administrators.

RECEIVING MESSAGES

Communication flows in two directions. Usually sending out messages isn't enough. The disaster coordinator must find out who has been contacted successfully and sometimes what their responses are. With direct, one-on-one communication, getting an answer is not usually an issue, although it may be if the caller has to leave a message. An automated notification system, on the other hand, needs a mechanism to receive and report responses. To facilitate two-way communication, the system must be able to receive a response such as a touch-tone signal to confirm that a message has been delivered successfully.

The automated system must be able to receive multiple responses such as touch-tone signals to answer questions posed by the original message. For example, if first responders are being notified, the coordinator's message might ask them to "press 1" if they are already at the disaster site, "press 2" if they are on their way there, and "press 3" if they are unavailable to respond to the emergency. Real-time reports of all message delivery attempts, confirmations, and polling results must be easily available by Internet and fax. Both summary and detail reports are necessary. Summary reports can quickly communicate the overall picture such as how many recipients have been reached, how many are on their way, and so forth. Detailed reports can show where individual follow-up is needed. For example, in a neighborhood evacuation, rescue personnel can focus their efforts on the houses where residents indicated that they needed help.

PERFORMING OTHER CRITICAL TASKS

Emergency coordinators have other tasks besides sending and receiving messages. However, as we have seen, one-on-one communications are so time-consuming under the best of circumstances that they can delay recovery and even lead to loss of life. When other communications failures are added to the equation, coordinators may end up being preoccupied almost exclusively with communications.

Any functioning automated notification system will greatly reduce personnel time spent on communication and will free emergency personnel to deal with rescue and recovery work. Being able to initiate a few messages and receive hundreds or thousands of responses formatted in a readable report a few minutes later is an enormous time-saver.

In addition, a well-designed notification system will have several features that are specifically geared toward making emergency personnel more effective. Also, conference bridging capability included in the elite systems allows real-time communication among some or all members of a list. In essence, these are spontaneous conference calls. Conference bridging can be used when the return message is more complicated than "I am on my way." It can enable coordinators to start planning even before they reach the emergency command center, and under some circumstances, it could supplement radio communications at a disaster site.

COMMUNICATION TECHNOLOGY AND TOOLS

Automated notification also supports advance message planning efforts. The ability to create and store messages in a library before a disaster occurs means that coordinators can begin the rescue and recovery process simply by clicking on a button. The ability to store messages for scheduled release allows disaster coordinators to create a series of messages in a single sitting. This not only saves time in creation but also reduces their risk of being unavailable to initiate follow-up messages. Finally, the system should be easy to use and should not require extensive training. Just as coordinators should not be spending hours making phone calls, they should not be trying to remember complicated command sequences or searching for user manuals.

There are a number of different types of automated mass communication products currently available. Some of these offer unique advantages over other somewhat similar systems. The following section describes the basic categories of such systems and some of the important features and functions of each.

On-Premise "Box" Solutions

This type of system is operated by a business itself. With a common box solution, businesses license some form of automated communication software, purchase the hardware to run it on, and then operate it in their own data centers using their own information technology (IT) staff. Vendors or third parties may serve as consultants during the implementation, particularly if the software needs to be customized. The system may also require the leasing and testing of additional phone lines, installation of backup generators, redundant copies of software and data, and regular installation of hardware and software upgrades. For most businesses, especially those that do not operate large data centers, maintaining this entire infrastructure internally can pose a challenge. Other concerns with a box solution include a long implementation period and the difficulty of scaling capacity on demand.

Application Service Provider

This type of system is hosted by a vendor. An application service provider (ASP) solution describes a notification system that is deployed, hosted, and managed from a site other than the business's own facilities. Many such solutions are Web enabled after previously existing as a box solution. Implementation is typically shorter than a box solution, but depending on the true nature of the ASP, there may still be issues with customization costs and scalability. Regardless, an ASP solution is considered a step up from a box solution, if for no other reason than the fact that the communication system is accessible through any Internet connection. If an emergency manager is out of the office when an emergency strikes, he or she can still access the automated notification system and communicate effectively. Also, because an ASP is housed off-site, it is much less susceptible to becoming damaged or affected by a localized crisis.

Web-Native ASP

A Web-native solution resembles the basic ASP but is specifically designed and built for multiple users to access over the Internet. Organizations pay a reasonable usage fee for full access to the system. Many businesses select this type of specialized service for the same reasons they buy electricity from the utility company. First, it's rarely cost-effective to generate your own electricity because power companies operate at a much more efficient scale. Second, specialization breeds expertise in the field, making it easier to deliver to customers the latest advancements in features and technology. The same characteristics hold true for most companies selling Web-native notification services. The systems are larger in scale, have redundant infrastructures, operate efficiently, and can easily adjust their capacity up or down.

Emergencies create demands that must be actively managed in order to mitigate or prevent catastrophic physical, financial, or reputational harm. As always, an automated communication system should be evaluated for its inherent ability to help a crisis team perform their management tasks.

CHOOSING AN AUTOMATED EMERGENCY NOTIFICATION SYSTEM

On the surface, many automated emergency notification systems closely resemble each other. Peel back the outermost layers and you will find that they are quite different. A side-by-side comparison of competing mass notification solutions demonstrates clear differences in speed, performance, reliability, and effectiveness. The better notification systems on the market today provide access to a robust telecommunications and data infrastructure with performance and capacity that typically exceeds in-house systems without a large investment in equipment, software, or support costs. There are several useful guides available to help you in comparing and selecting an automated emergency notification system that is right for your needs and situation.

In short, there are four basic types of systems with which you should be familiar. For each of these you should understand their basic features and capabilities. It may be helpful to provide a short comparison list for these basic categories of systems.

FOUR BASIC TYPES OF AUTOMATED NOTIFICATION SYSTEMS

1. On-premise model systems, in which a vendor sells you the hardware and/ or software for the communication system that you then host on your own company server and integrate into your existing communication pathways. Most first-generation systems were on-premise systems.

2. Hosted model systems where the company or organization subscribes to an external service and the provider hosts all of the hardware and software within the vendor's facilities. Typically the business activates the external vendor to disseminate the communication.

3. Hybrid systems, which are a combination between on-premise and hosted systems. Hybrids are an interesting phenomenon because they are a combination of having some of the infrastructure at your location and some of the infrastructure at the vendor. A common example is running the primary server out of your data center but then having the vendor host the telephony capacity for you so that they actually place the calls.

4. The Software-as-a-Service (SaaS) model systems that are typically on a subscription basis hosted by a vendor. An SaaS delivery model comes with multiple data centers in an active—active configuration. ACT-SaaS service provides customers with extraordinary scalability and unparalleled availability and security, lower implementation and maintenance costs, free upgrades, vendor-delivered maintenance, and fast implementation. ACT-SaaS enables customers to access powerful software over the Internet at maximum performance levels without purchasing or maintaining hardware, software, or telecommunications equipment.

VIRTUAL HARDWARE VERSUS PHYSICAL HARDWARE

Historically, whenever a new application was brought into an IT environment, they had to put in a new server, such as a new print server, e-mail server, or human resources server. This caused the amount of servers within a data center to grow to an unmanageable number. So within the past five years, instead of having one physical server for each application, IT departments embracing a virtual technology may have one server that actually runs five or six virtualized servers.

As far as the infrastructure still goes, there are two basic types of environments: (1) dedicated hardware environments, including a premise-based system and a hosted system where every customer has its own unique server platform, and (2) a shared environment, such as the SaaS solution, where there's one monolithic infrastructure that all of the customers share or are a part of. The dedicated hardware environments often have higher up-front costs because when you come onboard, they're not just creating an account for you on the system, but they have to actually go out and buy and install hardware to operate your environment.

SOME POINTS TO CONSIDER WHEN CHOOSING AN AUTOMATED NOTIFICATION SYSTEM

The institutionalization of the business continuity and emergency management functions has led to an increased awareness at the executive level of the importance of proper emergency planning. It has also clearly demonstrated that having the necessary tools to communicate during times of crisis is essential. There are more than 50 different vendors and solutions, and although the adage that "one size does not fit all" is true, there are several factors that should be evaluated when making a vendor selection.

Much like the development of business continuity planning tools, in the recent history of mass notification systems, there have been three phases of technological innovation. The first-generation systems were on-premise (computer server-based) systems that you would buy from a provider and maintain and utilize on your own. The second generation of notification technology, the ASP, and the third generation of notification technology is based on the SaaS model. The SaaS delivery model allows notification vendors to dynamically share capacity and resources across all data center resources, providing a much higher level of capacity and scalability than is available using first-generation on-premise or second-generation ASP delivery models.

The delivery model is the single most important factor in determining the quality of notifications that each vendor will be able to provide. In the third-generation delivery model, certain vendors are able to provide enhanced redundancy.

Ease of Use

When choosing mass notification systems, check for the ease of use for nontechnical users. Do not merely watch while a mass notification vendor walks you through the system's processes. Insist on an experiment to see if you could do it yourself. Just see if you can walk through the process and quickly and intuitively figure it out or at least begin the process without any coaching. If you can do so, you're probably going to have a product that anybody can use during an emergency.

Site Redundancy and IT Architecture

Look for site redundancy or no single point of failure in the system. What that means is that every aspect of the architecture is replicated into another facility. Therefore, if it has a Web server at one site, it should have a Web server on another site. That way if the Web server fails, you're not going to get blocked from being able to access the system. Vendors will take a lot of shortcuts in this way. They may not fully replicate the entire infrastructure across the entire span of operations to ensure continuity and continuous operations. They may have a primary site that's fully powered and then a secondary site that has maybe half of the available capacity. So if they have to transition to their fail-safe site, they may not have as much capacity available to meet their customers at that point in time.

Another key aspect to look at from an architectural technology standpoint is whether the vendors actually own their own infrastructure. Many vendors currently in the market are resellers of automated notification systems, and the relationships between sellers, providers, and users can often get a little tangled and confusing when it comes to service and support. Most of these vendors will not advertise the fact that they are resellers (because then a lot of customers will just go to that other company and buy from them directly instead of through them). So because they don't willingly admit to it, it's something that you have to ask them about and maybe press them on a little bit to really make sure that they do not have such an arrangement set up.

It is also important that automated notification system vendors do their own development work. A lot of vendors outsource entirely all development and quality assurance efforts with their products. If they're not building anything, it's actually more of a virtual product. If these outsource development efforts are also through an agreement with the original equipment manufacturer, it creates almost a virtual company that doesn't really have anything, except a sales team to build and deliver it.

Real Versus Virtual Hardware

One key difference between different products on the market centers on whether the system is running real hardware or virtual hardware.

A lot of systems, to reduce those higher up-front costs, will install virtual servers for their customers. So even though you have a virtual server that's unique to you as a customer, you may still be running on a shared hardware platform with a lot of other customers. It's not truly a dedicated system at that point because when you're in a shared hardware environment, if one of those customers is doing something very actively, they may consume more server resources, which then affects your ability to send out communication.

If the system is sharing some type of hardware using a virtual server, you should find out exactly what aspects are being shared. Does the system depend upon sharing telephony aspects, and are they sharing actual servers or hard drives across the board? This also may have security impacts for you or affect other types of decisions that you should know about or information that you want to know about before you actually commit to a specific system. In addition, it is important to know how server and site redundancy is accomplished. If the vendor is buying a piece of hardware for you, they have to make it truly redundant. They may have to buy two or three of those pieces of hardware, which increases the cost.

A shared hardware environment, such as the SaaS solution, tends to have lower up-front costs because the hardware has already been acquired, installed, and maintained. Not having to do any of this hardware infrastructure work to get you set up and running saves time and costs. It also tends to have a standardized configuration. The security infrastructure is the same for all customers, making it very simple to apply that security template across the entire customer base instead of an individual base, as you would find in a dedicated environment. So even though it's a shared infrastructure and it may be perceived to be less secure, overall this hardware tends to actually have much higher security than the dedicated ones.

Capacity

It is also important for you to know how the vendor and system build capacity. There are only two real capacity models available: dedicated and shared. Dedicated capacity means that you buy a port and have that port or telephone port dedicated to you. This comes with a very high relative cost, and the capacity is often limited by your budget. The benefit there is that you get the certainty of your communication speeds. The other type is a shared environment. This is actually the most common capacity model on the market today. Instead of dedicating specific ports to specific customers, the vendor creates a shared-capacity pool that all the customers share. This provides much lower initial costs, as well as ongoing costs, allowing the vendor to provide much larger pools of capacity than individual customers can buy themselves through a dedicated system. So instead of buying yourself 10 ports, you may have access to a pool of 10,000 ports that are shared with a lot of different customers.

The next part of the capacity equation is whether the vendors actually own their own capacity or rent it. Some vendors will actually not acquire their own capacity pools but will rent that capacity from third-party telephony aggregators such as telemarketing firms or collection calling companies. They do this because it allows them to build a large theoretical pool that makes for a very low cost. Unfortunately, it also makes the delivery of messages difficult to guarantee. Even though they may have access to 500 telephone lines from a specific telemarketing aggregator, those lines may be in use when you go to use them. They theoretically have access to those lines, but because they don't really own them, they can't guarantee the availability when you want to use the system.

One really important question to ask is how the vendor delivers capacity. A key point that notification system customers get tied up in is that vendors will promise access to huge pools of capacity—being able to deliver hundreds of thousands and millions of calls per hour. The problem with this is that access to a capacity pool does not mean that they can actually deliver on that capacity. If the vendor is oversubscribed or if the system is being heavily utilized, you may find that the only available capacity for you is less than what you could have afforded if you would have bought a dedicated port solution.

Compatibility

When comparing automated notification systems, it is helpful to determine whether the system is compatible with your existing systems and how data and system updates are processed. For example, do the updates allow you to be automated? Do you have to send a spreadsheet in an e-mail to the vendors for them to process for you? Do you have to do it all manually, or is there some type of automated way so that you can set the system up, let it run, and keep that data fresh for you?

AUTOMATED EMERGENCY NOTIFICATION SYSTEMS

Many automated emergency notification systems are currently on the market. It is important to select a comprehensive automated emergency notification solution that streamlines voice and text communication to tens, hundreds, or thousands of recipients through virtually any delivery method for daily operations and emergencies. The better systems provide a secure, reliable, scalable, and easy-to-use method for organizations of all types and sizes to communicate flexibly, and in a variety of situations with constituents, customers, employees, vendors, partners, emergency response teams, students, and others.

Implementation and Initiating

Implementing a comprehensive, fully integrated automated emergency notification system along with a complete set of message maps is a major step toward your readiness to meet the communication needs and challenges for emergency situations. There are many considerations about the interconnection between messages and systems technology that you'll need to know before implementation.

It is oversimplistic to focus merely on technical capacity for bandwidth or callout thresholds per minute. Although it is important to know how many calls or text messages a system can produce in a specific amount of time (many of the available systems on the market have sustained callout rates of 100,000 per hour for voice messages and 200,000 per hour for SMS and text messages), the real questions on which to focus concern how many of those messages will actually be received, read, understood, and appropriately acted on. There will always be a number of variable contingencies (e.g., target audience mobility and external infrastructure limits) that must be overcome by such a system. Therefore, it is important to ask deeper questions about whether the system utilizes multiple contact paths, redundancy, and continuous contact attempts until receipt is confirmed; recipient response options; and the net effective rate that such a system can produce in given circumstances with specific audiences.

With some systems, it may be theoretically possible to deliver 30,000 30-second messages for more than an hour with multiple attempts. However, external factors (e.g., customers overwhelming the cellular phone capacities in the emergency situation) may affect your communication attempts. Thus, it may be to your advantage to simultaneously transmit SMS messages of the same warning (which can be received in short-burst packets even when it is impossible to make or receive a cell phone call). Therefore, the system should have the capability for redundancy, overlapping message modalities, and continuous sending functions to compensate for these external variables. On the other hand, there are also inherent limitations for SMS modalities, not the least of which is that current systems are capacity-limited to less than 200 characters per message. This reinforces the need for redundancy and overlapping message modalities when alerting target audiences with emergency notification messages.

In some major emergencies, the entire cellular system for carriers has been rendered inoperable (most infamously in lower Manhattan on 9/11). Therefore, the principal of backup modalities and redundancies for message delivery must extend beyond the boundaries of individual cell phones. Even if the cellular system itself is not destroyed, the dramatic increase in usage rates might itself overload the capacity of the system. It is not uncommon that during routine rush-hour commutes cellular customers may encounter the "No Signal Available" message, indicating that they are cut off from that communication modality.

Even if the text or telephone message is successfully transmitted, it may prove inadequate to effectively "communicate" the information or nature of the warning if recipients can't get the gist of it straight away. Messages must be kept brief (the percentage of listeners who are attentive to a message begins to fall after as few as 27 seconds, and the percentage of readers of messages drops significantly after as few as 30 words). Therefore, it is imperative that key information and instructions be placed in the first part of an emergency notification message.

It is important to remember that recipients of emergency notification messages will produce an exigent need for additional information. Because you are limited in how much you can include in an alert message, it is important also to quickly (and automatically, if possible) update sources of more information (e.g., specialized Web pages, call-in hotlines, and directions to turn to for broadcast news media outlets, Twitter, Facebook, MySpace, and blogs).

A comprehensive crisis communication plan will include both messages that you push (actively broadcast or target to your audiences) and messages that pull your audiences to sources for them to retrieve. For example, pulling audiences to your Web site where you have frequently updated notification messages posted can complement "broadcast" messages that you are pushing to your audience. A well-balanced emergency notification plan would utilize this push–pull method to quickly alert and warn as well as to satisfy all of the deeper needs for information on a wide variety of issues. It is important to not only provide timely warnings to constituents, but also to ensure that you have plans and methods in place to address the information needs of your stakeholders. This also includes how you handle the emergency communication as an aspect of your strategic communication, which can affect perceptions of your reputation and image. Finally, although it may not be a prime consideration for emergency notification, your plans must also include how you will communicate with the news media both during the short term and in the longer term of the emergency. Media relations are a serious factor to consider as you develop your emergency notification plans.

AUTOMATED EMERGENCY NOTIFICATION

Communication failures have historically plagued organizations in their ability to respond to and minimize the human, operational, and financial impacts of a disaster. When disaster strikes and every second counts, organizations need to focus on the mission-critical tasks of ensuring the safety of their people and continuing operations, not on managing the logistics of communications.

Although some systems use the term "mass notification," that name may regrettably limit the conceptual and planning processes for establishing an emergency notification system. In some respects, mass notification conjures up images of the old public warning sirens or broadcast media alerts to mass audiences with nonspecific, generalized warnings. It also may imply a one-way "blast" of messages and a central software system purely focused on launching messages rather than on an integrated communication system. It is important to note that many contemporary solutions are designed as comprehensive "event and/or emergency management" solutions that include notification capabilities as well as reporting and tracking data customized for the user. The goal is to give administrators a view of all situational requirements, audiences by group, messages sent, responses received, and awareness of the problem areas that need to be addressed. As a result, the system provides much more than just mass notification broadcasts and becomes a powerful tool for emergency management communication.

Modern comprehensive integrated automated emergency notification empowers organizations to plan, manage, sustain, and (after action) report on the communication during the emergency. With such notification systems, one person can communicate with tens, hundreds, or thousands of people anywhere, anytime, via any communication method, including phone (landline, mobile, and satellite), e-mail, instant messaging, text messaging (native SMS), fax, BlackBerry, PDA, pager, and more.

Most automated notification systems allow the user to (1) select a group of individuals or organizations to which to send a message, (2) create the message, and (3) launch a notification broadcast across the various channels of communications to these individuals.

There are two components to any automated emergency notification system. First, there is the front end, which is the user interface that one uses to operate the system. This is where a lot of the features and functionalities exist, and because this is the primary interface to the overall system, it's what a lot of people tend to focus on. The front-end application for most mass notification systems provides a wealth of different features enabling an organization to communicate with its employees, its customers, or any of its other constituents. However, every notification system has a back-end infrastructure as well, and this is really the engine that operates the overall system. The back-end infrastructure is what makes the calls go out or the e-mails get sent in a timely manner. A notification system must have both of these components working quickly, effectively, and consistently.

Notification messages are constructed in a way similar to creating e-mail. First, you determine what kind of message will be sent: an emergency notification, a time-sensitive notification, or a standard message if the information is important or informative. An emergency message has priority and will move through the network faster (e.g., an ambulance on a busy street always has the right of way). Second, the user chooses recipients either individually or by an unlimited number of groups (e.g., the fire department, police, EOC team, or a city). Third, the user creates a message that can be saved and reused. It can be created using any kind of phone, microphone attached to a computer, text to speech, or by using a live operator. Fourth, the user designates what contact paths will be used (e.g., cell, e-mail, text). The contact paths you choose should also take into account whether you'll want a confirmation, along with the escalation, number of transmissions, length of the transmissions, and other variables.

Once the notification is sent, a real-time dashboard is displayed on the screen that tracks the number of notifications that have been sent and confirmed. A real-time report is also generated that provides the details for each notification such as the time, date, confirmation, and status of the call (e.g., voice mail, hang-up, and the ability to click on the contact path in red and get the detailed information).

The system needs to support multiple languages that reflect your demographics. From a user interface, it needs to be intuitive and menu driven. Some notification solutions blast messages to all contact devices and on all contact paths. The most effective approach uses a sequential, targeted process where each contact path is prioritized sequentially. Once a notification is confirmed, the broadcast stops.

There are a series of steps that you should take to ensure that you are ready to deliver your emergency notification messages within moments of the onset of an emergency situation. This would include setting up your contact list and various contact preferences. You would also want to create your message templates. Once you are ready, these systems allow you to distribute your messages in no more than a handful of simple steps.

1. Contacts set up and preferences defined. When the system is set up initially, contact information for each employee or other individual is created in a directory. This information includes the order in which the employee would prefer to be contacted. For example, an individual may want to be contacted

first via landline telephone. The second choice is to be contacted via cell phone. A third choice is to be contacted through a corporate e-mail, the fourth by home phone, and the fifth by personal e-mail. In addition, individuals can be grouped by function or other parameters. For example, an individual can be grouped in a senior management group or an e-mail server group. A call initiator can then contact an entire group very easily and quickly.

2. Voice and/or text messages created. When notification is required, an authorized individual creates a message to be distributed to a group or any selection of contacts in the directory. The communication can be a voice and/or text message and can contain information requesting a response. For example, in an emergency, a message can be sent to all employees to inform them not to come to work that day. The system can also request information, such as the safety and location of employees, along with medical assistance needs.

3. Message delivered and report generated. During the notification, the system continues to attempt to contact each individual until a successful resolution is achieved. A real-time report can quickly communicate the overall picture—how many recipients have been reached, their status, and so forth. Detailed reports emphasize where individual follow-up is needed.

ACT-SAAS

One of the more important features of some of these systems is the capability for ACT-SaaS. ACT-SaaS service provides customers with extraordinary scalability, unparalleled availability and security, lower implementation and maintenance costs, free upgrades, vendor-delivered maintenance, and fast implementation. ACT-SaaS enables customers to access powerful software over the Internet at maximum performance levels without purchasing or maintaining hardware, software, or telecommunications equipment.

Unlike some ASP-based mass notification systems, ACT-SaaS notification solutions focus more on what the customer wants rather than what the solution provider can deliver. With superior performance, scalability, and lower total cost of ownership, the ACT-SaaS notification system is the number-one choice of large organizations over ASP, on-premise,

---

Application Box: Everbridge

One vendor, Everbridge, provides an automated notification system via a proprietary ACT-SaaS service, an advanced SaaS delivery model with multiple data centers in an active–active configuration—the only mass notification provider to offer this level of security, performance, and availability.

and simple SaaS solutions, which is a direct reflection of the change in business requirements and demands by organizations.

The ACT-SaaS mass notification system gives customers dedicated availability plus access to additional communication resources across multiple data centers, ensuring the highest level of message throughput—several times faster than on-premise or ASP solutions, which are limited by port capacity or server access in a single data center. The vendor maintains all aspects of the system infrastructure, avoiding problems caused by notification solutions that depend on third-party technology to deliver messages.

ACT-SaaS enables everyone—employees, customers, and more—to log in to the system from anywhere, 24/7/365. A notification provider should employ multiple data centers in the United States, Canada, and the United Kingdom using a proprietary ACT-SaaS active–active configuration and security—so the system is always available when you need it. What happens to your contact data in a natural disaster, terrorist attack, or power outage? With ACT-SaaS, data reside on advanced infrastructures, not on third-party leased equipment. Built-in redundancy ensures continual access regardless of the situation.

On-premise software requires an expensive up-front purchase of perpetual licenses and annual maintenance fees in addition to the internal resources necessary to manage the equipment, telecommunication lines, backup power, data backup, redundant networks, and more. ASPs require restrictive "ports of capacity" purchases, resulting in a dramatically higher total cost of ownership than ACT-SaaS at a much lower capacity. All ACT-SaaS costs are included in one annual subscription agreement, requiring less capital up-front and delivering considerable cost savings over time. Large companies choose ACT-SaaS for its security, cost savings, and ability to scale as needs increase; smaller companies find ACT-SaaS to be the logical choice because of the flexibility of its pay-as-you-grow structure. ACT-SaaS is scalable and extensible. As an organization grows, so can its notification solution. ACT-SaaS offers dramatically faster implementation times. Rolling out an ACT-SaaS solution to all or part of your organization is easy; there is no additional hardware or software to buy and no time spent installing applications or training staff. Implementations are measured in days and weeks versus other solutions that require several months or more to deploy.

Therefore, you should use an automated notification system to reach people faster with the right information. Contacting thousands of people via their many communication devices is as quick and easy as a single phone call or a few clicks of the mouse. With the automated notification system, you also eliminate communication interoperability issues by delivering messages across all communication platforms and devices, ensuring successful message delivery. Use an automated notification system to reduce miscommunication. As messages travel from person to person, information often gets lost or altered from its original intent. The automated notification system enables you to easily send accurate, consistent messages to your entire contact base.

In addition, the system can lower your total cost of emergency notification communication. The automated notification system provides access to a robust telecommunications and data infrastructure with performance and capacity that typically exceeds in-house systems without a large investment in equipment, software, or support costs. You reach more people more effectively without expanding your staff or overburdening already stretched resources. In addition, the system can lower your total cost of emergency notification communication.

The system can better ensure effectiveness and accountability compared with manual or "on-the-fly" emergency notification efforts. With better visibility into message delivery through real-time confirmation and reporting, you know who received your messages, when, and how. Also, with certain automated systems' unique two-way communication capabilities, you can elicit important information from your message recipients for informed decision making.

INITIATING COMMUNICATION WITH AN AUTOMATED NOTIFICATION SYSTEM

The first task facing the emergency coordinator is to initiate or accelerate the information flow. This can be a formidable challenge if the communication center or EOC has been damaged or if communication lines are down. Automated notification simplifies the task by reducing the number of messages that must be initiated. An automated system allows the coordinator to issue a single message to an entire list of people—whether that group consists of employees, customers, parents of schoolchildren, first responders, or reporters.

The chances of initiating and delivering messages successfully are much greater if the initiator has to send only a few messages instead of thousands. There should be multiple ways to initiate a message. At the very least, emergency coordinators should be able to access and use their notification system through the Internet and by telephone. The crisis communication team should not be required to be at a particular computer or a particular telephone to initiate a message. The system should also be able to deliver messages from multiple initiators. Managers should be able to delegate authority to several associates so notification efforts won't fail if one person is unavailable.

After a message has been initiated, it must be delivered to everyone on the delivery list. There are five important issues: (1) whether the messages will arrive; (2) when the messages will arrive; (3) whether the recipient actually reads, sees, or hears the message; (4) what the recipient will understand the message to mean; and (5) what the audience will do in response to the message.

To maximize the likelihood that messages will be delivered, the notification system should be able to send messages to all types of contact devices—phone, cell, fax, computer (e-mail and instant messaging)—and PDAs of all types in as many formats as possible (such as voice, text, SMS). The system should permit multiple contact paths for each person on the list and allow a different order for each list member. The system must be able to make unlimited attempts to contact each person on the list until there is confirmation of message receipt.

Communicating with the Right People

Nearly as important as reaching all the critical audiences is sending messages only to those who need to receive them. Sending extraneous messages in times of emergency can have serious unintended consequences, including chaos and crowding at the disaster site, an influx of unwanted phone calls, and even mass panic. To filter messages correctly, unlimited groups and subgroups should be allowed.

Delivering and Receiving Communication

Communication should flow constantly in two different directions during a crisis. Just sending out messages isn't enough; the crisis manager must find out who has been contacted successfully and, sometimes, what are their responses. An automated notification system can be a great mechanism for receiving and reporting such responses. To facilitate two-way communication, the system should be able to receive an active response to confirm that a message has been delivered successfully. The system should be able to survey or poll recipients.

Communication Efficiency and Ease of Use

The many automated notification services on the market today vary widely in terms of capacity, data security, and cost. With those major considerations always in mind, the greatest communications utility for an organization will obviously come from an automated system having features and functionality that best match how the organization will need to communicate in a crisis. Advanced features such as conference calling and geographical targeting are important to consider because they maximize communication options for a crisis manager. Feature-rich systems are more likely to overcome common communication obstacles like phone line jams or loss of Internet connectivity. Many automated systems offer message libraries, where created messages can be stored, as well as the functionality to create crisis scenarios connecting specific prepared messages with the exact groups they will be sent to when an incident occurs.

An automated notification system should be easy to use and should not require extensive training. Just as crisis communicators should not be spending hours making phone calls, they should not be trying to remember complicated command sequences or searching for user manuals. Stress and anxiety during a crisis will make communication difficult, and an automated notification system should reduce this stress. Emergency management teams have other critical tasks besides sending and receiving messages. However, as we have seen, one-on-one communications can be stressful and time-consuming under the best of circumstances and can delay a coordinated response or even lead to loss of property or life. A quality automated notification system will greatly reduce time spent on communications and will free emergency personnel to deal with crisis mitigation, response, and recovery work. An automated notification system is an ideal way to fill the information void quickly, while carefully delivering the right message to the right audience. This speed of information leads to the next section, dealing with and understanding the news media.

FUNCTIONS OF NOTIFICATION

One of the most critical functions for emergency notification is connecting with and alerting your own people, including your emergency responders. The next most important audiences for notification communication are those constituents to whom you are accountable for their safety and well-being and for whom you have information about threats and risks that need to be rapidly disseminated, properly understood, and appropriately acted on. Previously described were the types of disruptions and communication challenges that an emergency will create. How do you assemble your emergency response team? How do you activate your EOC and set your emergency plans in motion? Do you have a process and system for keeping control of all of your people, including those in the field? What are your communication redundancies and backups when systems fail and when you are prevented from using your routine communication forms?

There is a difference between successful notification and effective communication. Notification is a key part of effective communication, but there are many other variables and factors that go into whether the overall communication and response process was ultimately effective.

One aspect of the emergency context is that you need to have the capacity to provide warnings and alerts at the same time that you need to ensure the continuity of your business operations. These automated notification systems can also solve the business communication challenges of coordinating with your vendors, suppliers, delivery partners, and customers during a major emergency or disruptive crisis.

Dealing with Business Interruptions

E-mail and network interruptions caused by server crashes, power outages, application errors, upgrades that do not work properly, or other problems can have a devastating impact on any organization. Organizations that rely on e-mail or the Web to conduct business, such as selling products via a Web site or receiving orders via e-mail, can suffer significant revenue loss during such a downtime incident. An emergency notification system can provide substantial cost savings and revenue benefits by helping IT staff to resolve problems more quickly.

In addition to network- and e-mail-related business interruptions, there are a variety of other types of interruptions that a mass notification system can help to resolve. For example, a utility company that must issue a "boil water" order to customers because of a contamination problem can do so rapidly using a mass notification system. Because such a system can also collect feedback from message recipients, the utility company can understand in real time who has received the message and who has not. A utility company can also employ a mass notification system for nonemergency issues such as collections and making the payment collection process faster, more effective, and less labor intensive. Schools can also employ mass notification to inform parents and students about a wide variety of events, such as school closures due to a storm or power outage, or simply to send out a reminder to return a signed form by the planned deadline.

Supply Chain Notification

One of the most important benefits of mass notification is the ability to maintain an efficient and effective supply chain. Because many organizations have chosen to minimize inventories to keep costs down, they have become much more vulnerable to supply chain disruptions such as storms, labor disruptions, and other problems. However, a mass notification system can mitigate much of this risk by allowing companies and their partners to respond to potential disruptions much more quickly.

Customer Service Management and Outreach

An automated notification system also provides organizations with the ability to notify customers proactively and efficiently about a variety of time-sensitive offers, such as upcoming sales, promotions, and special deals. For example, a notification system can be used to notify customers about a 48-hour sale on a certain item and allow the customer to place an order simply by responding to the notice. Companies can also use a mass notification system to remind customers of service or warranty expirations and allow them to renew the service for another year.

There are three fundamental benefits of automated notification in the context of customer service management:

- Notification can increase revenue for an organization by proactively notifying customers.
- Costs are reduced by enabling a single individual to send out and manage the responses to a notification campaign.
- Notification can build "stickiness" for a company or brand by allowing frequent, low-impact interactions with customers.

Routine Employee Notification

Automated notification offers many benefits in the context of informing employees about routine events, such as meetings, annual sign-up periods for health benefit plans, and notifications about new corporate policies. The use of a notification system can significantly increase the response rate for these events, inform management about who needs more detailed information about an issue, improve overall employee productivity by making sure that employees stay on schedule, and reduce the overall costs associated with informing employees about important events.

There are many other aspects of having command of your communication capabilities during an emergency event in addition to issuing warnings. This would include having control of communication for the response to the emergency, coordinating your operations, and meeting other business needs. The following checklist provides some examples.

EMERGENCY/CRISIS/DISASTER RECOVERY COMMUNICATION

- coordinating the efforts of first responders (e.g., security, IT, the human resources department, and Student Affairs)
- directing employees, students, tenants, and citizens to take specific actions (e.g., evacuate, work from home, refrain from drinking contaminated water)
- sending status updates to employees, students, and citizens
- Notifying employees, students, and faculty about school or office weather-related closures, fires, floods, and air quality issues

OPERATIONS

- escalating IT incidents; e-mail or systems related
- reducing inbound calls by keeping stakeholders informed of the situation
- communicating any type of information that requires a confirmation of receipt
- announcing staffing, training, Golden Guardian, programs, or meetings
- managing facilities for incidents (e.g., leaks or noxious odors)

A series of Application Boxes are provided to illustrate the use of mass notification systems for use by a city, a utility, and first responders. In each of these examples, the capabilities of the emergency notification system deployed solved a unique business problem for the organization, as well as extended their command of the communication processes in all circumstances.

Application Box: City of Inglewood, California

The city of Inglewood needed a fast, easy, and effective way to communicate with citizens, businesses, officials, and internal departments.

Challenge

- Slow, costly, and labor-intensive process for contacting residents (using calling trees)
- Demanding interdepartmental communication and coordination during crises

Solution

- Reliable and effective mass notification solution to send consistent information to a large, geographically targeted audience quickly
- Easy to use for average computer users

Results & Return on Investment

- Increased productivity, inter- and intradepartment coordination, and collaboration
- Decreased time and costs for mailings, flyers, door knob hangers, overtime, and resources
- Improved safety and security of constituents
- Seamless communication among departments

Application Box: Park Water Company

Park Water Company (PWC) needed a high-capacity notification system to notify thousands of customers in minutes during emergencies and for routine operations.

Challenge

- Did not have an automated system for sending out geographically tar-geted messages
- Labor-intensive and costly customer service notifications; PWC had to send letters, post street signs, and place door hangers to schedule main-tenance or planned service interruptions

Solution

- A notification solution to integrate with its customers, service operations and deliver quick, reliable communications targeted to customers in a specific geographical area

Results & Return on Investment

- Substantial time and cost savings, and elimination of costly community outreach efforts
- PWC was able to improve its customer service and satisfaction levels by proac-tively pushing information to residents, reinforcing their right to be informed.
- Improved emergency preparedness and response capabilities

**Application Box: City of Camarillo, California,
Disaster Assistance Response Team (DART)**

The city of Camarillo used an inefficient and unreliable pager-centric notifica-tion system to engage DART volunteers (first-responder support organization for the Ventura County Fire Department and Sheriff's Department) to respond to emergencies and other needs.

Challenge

- Reliance on pagers as the only contact path represented a single point of failure.
- Roughly 50 percent of all messages sent through this pager-centric sys-tem never reached the intended recipients.
- The system was not able to track and identify who had received the mes-sage or when they received it.

Solution

- Citizen alerts using multiple contact paths as a way to ensure a higher message completion rate and the system's delivery confirmation func-tionality were key differentiators for DART.

Results & Return on Investment

- Using a Web-based, fully hosted mass notification system, message con-firmations and responses soared by an average of 90 percent.

- The message delivery-tracking capabilities dramatically increased the system's value, effectiveness, and performance in meeting DART's needs.
- Dramatic improvement of DART's operational processes by sending routine team meeting instructions and other daily communication and promoting city of Camarillo events

---

Application Box: Salesforce.com

Salesforce.com needed a reliable system for communicating internally with employees at a moment's notice in an emergency.

Challenge

- Large, diverse group of employees using different contact devices
- A crisis management team that had been depending on e-mail blasts
- A manual phone tree used for emergency communication and to assemble the team

Solution

- An SaaS system with multiple data centers in an active–active configuration
- A system that mimics the company's organizational structure, enabling the team to handle emergencies by department, office location, geographical territory, or across the entire enterprise

Results & Return on Investment

- Quicker crisis management team response to emergencies
- Faster messaging in a crisis
- Better visibility into and ability to respond to employee safety concerns

---

Application Box: AirTran Airways

AirTran Airways needed a high-capacity notification system to coordinate messages pertinent to the state of the airline's performance metrics and other messages related to critical events driven by irregular operations, passenger or crew matters, and emergency situations.

Challenge

- Difficulty communicating across a diverse team
- Inefficient, complicated emergency communication process that used paper communication
- Lack of flexibility with paper notifications meant that there were no confirmations, polling, or large-scale communication

Solution

- A powerful notification solution able to reach thousands of people to dispatch information about on-time performance, weather, delays, crew scheduling, and maintenance with just a few simple steps

Results & Return on Investment

- Elevated awareness of on-time performance
- Faster response times and decision making
- Productivity gains while keeping operating costs low

Application Box: Greater Baltimore Medical Center

Greater Baltimore Medical Center (GBMC) relied on outdated call trees and lists to coordinate both routine and emergency communications. With short-notice or no-notice Joint Commission visits, the possibility of pandemic flu outbreaks, and the Center's proximity to two recognized terrorist targets, administrators realized the pressing need for a quicker, more efficient communication system.

Challenge

- Reliance on department-centric call trees for both emergency and routine communications
- Challenges complying with Joint Commission requirements
- Proximity to recognized terrorist targets—Washington DC, and Aberdeen Proving Ground
- Difficulty handling staff shortages in an efficient manner

Solution

- An easy-to-use emergency notification system versatile enough for routine and emergency communication uses
- A system backed up by unparalleled customer service

Results & Return on Investment

- Using a Web-based, fully hosted mass notification system, GBMC has streamlined their response to emergency drills and satisfied Joint Commission emergency management compliance requirements.
- GBMC is able to schedule extra personnel on short notice.
- GBMC uses the Everbridge system on a daily basis for routine communications between a variety of groups: maintenance, executives, incident command, and decon teams.
- GBMC has no hardware or software to manage on-site.

Automated notification solutions play a central role for emergency notification, as well as a number of business communication problems. The more advanced systems overcome most of the challenges for emergency notification communication including time constraints, personnel limitations, high-mobility target audiences, stale databases, avoiding single points of failure, lost channels, need for redundancy of channels, two-way interaction demands, integration with premeditated messages, and documentation.

SUMMARY OF KEY POINTS

- Contacting the right people at the right time with the right message is the basic challenge for effective emergency notification.
- This challenge can be addressed by use of new automated emergency communication solutions.
- The benefits of automated notification solutions include increased efficiency and cost savings; higher accountability; ease of use; fewer personnel needed to initiate, deliver, and confirm notification; more precise audience targeting; response confirmation; and providing documentation to satisfy new regulatory requirements.
- Automated notification systems can address many of the common communication challenges for emergency notification, including maintain updated contact databases and lists, elimination of sequential communication breakdowns, higher levels of accuracy, means for collaboration and teamwork, and coordinating inbound information processing.
- Some automated notification systems can be preloaded with message templates and premeditated emergency notification messages.
- There are different types of automated notification systems, each with different functions and features, and some that provide significant advantages over others.
- There are a number of basic questions to ask when you are selecting an automated notification system.
- Automated notification systems offer functionality and other uses beyond emergency notification.

CHAPTER 7

EMERGENCY MESSAGES

This chapter focuses on emergency notification messages. The chapter reviews the functions of an emergency notification message, the implications (intended and unintended) of emergency messages, and the anatomy of an emergency notification message. The key points covered include describing the basic structure of an emergency notification message and key principles of emergency notification messages.

WHAT YOU SAY AND HOW YOU SAY IT

After a notification message has been initiated, it must be delivered to everyone on the delivery list. There are five important issues: (1) whether the messages will arrive; (2) when the messages will arrive; (3) whether the recipient will actually read, see, or hear the message; (4) what the recipient will understand the message to mean; and (5) what the audience will do in response to the message. Although the delivery issues may be covered by use of an automated notification solution, the core of an alert's effectiveness remains the content of the message that has been delivered to the recipient. Far too often, the importance of a carefully constructed message is neglected while attention is placed on the technology that enables the alert warnings to be delivered. A complex notification system is worthless if the message that is delivered fails to inform and motivate the recipient to take action.

You should draft sample notification messages for common hazards and possible emergencies. Consider which people will be affected by the threat or danger. Walk through every possible emergency scenario and be ready to demonstrate your readiness for notification. Make choices about types of messages, delivery channels, timing, and redundancies. Determine a priority of channels for communication. Ask yourselves these questions: Do you know how these messages will be delivered, how the message will be received, (3) whether there is a confirmation process, and (4) if the automated system that is in place that can be initiated rapidly and effectively? Are the messages that you are drafting tied in with preemergency education and training efforts? What are your deep background education information resources, and how will your audience know them? Are you prepared to issue alerts and notifications the consequences of which might be life or death?

BASIC PRINCIPLES FOR CREATING EMERGENCY NOTIFICATION MESSAGES

Emergency notification messages may need to be issued at any time during an emergency. However, the most critical alerts are frequently those that are issued during the response and management phases and occasionally during the warning phase. These alerts are often life-and-death notifications that are essential. They have to work to inform and motivate audiences to take action to get them out of harm's way. However, even for notification messages in other phases, there are basic functions that any notification message should accomplish.

FOUR FUNCTIONS

A typical emergency notification message has at least four basic functions that it needs to accomplish. These functions are (1) information, (2) meta-message, (3) behavioral request and instructions, and (4) feedback request. These four functions have been referred to as the primary building blocks for a notification message.

Information

Perhaps most obviously, an emergency notification message needs to provide the vital information that the message seeks to warn recipients about. At the most fundamental level, the message must contain the key elements of the nature of the threat, the risks or threats involved, and the timing aspects of the emergency. The importance of getting the right amount of information in a message (avoiding the extremes of information over- or underloading the message) and the use of vocabulary and terms that will be meaningful to the recipients are always important.

In some cases, specific code words can be utilized (e.g., "code adam," "active shooter," "code blue," and "flash flood warning") and can be used for informational content (if the recipients have been trained to decipher or interpret the code).

Information content for emergency notification messages needs to be precise, objective, and as literal as possible. Information content can be obfuscated by the use of unnecessary jargon, ambiguous language, or imprecise descriptions. Information should be presented in descriptive, objective, and nondramatic terms. Better messages use more concrete, literal, and precise wording.

Meta-Message

There is no such thing as a purely objective or neutral message. All messages contain some degree of spin or implication. Most listeners or readers of an emergency notification message pick up on the "subtext" of a message, often described as reading between the lines. Typically, recipients make interpretative decisions about a message's urgency or seriousness. Critical life-and-death choices are quickly made by recipients of emergency notification messages merely based on the judgments about the saliency of the message. Researchers have discovered that during the South Asian tsunami, many of those who ultimately perished had in fact received warnings but found them so incredible or failed to understand the real urgency of their immediate need to flee to higher ground that they lost their lives anyway.

On the other hand, warning messages that consistently overdramatize the risks, which customarily turn out to be false alarms, can inversely create a Chicken Little effect that results in warning messages being ignored.

Assessing the implicit or inferential tone of an emergency notification message is an important component for understanding the quality of a message. Audiences will also "read into" messages in an attempt to discern the tone or seriousness of the message. If you fail to take this aspect into account when constructing messages, chances are that you will then leave the door wide open for a wide variety of possible interpretations. On the other hand, if you take these aspects into consideration when you are constructing a message, you will exercise control and provide some parameters for the range of possible (mis)interpretations that your target audiences might read into the tone of your message. They will take it as seriously (or not) as you provide the meta-message content "between the lines" of the words you choose (or don't choose), the arrangement, the inflection, or the "spin" of what your message says.

Behavioral Request and Instructions

Merely alerting or informing about a period of potential danger and giving the audience an appropriate sense of urgency is not enough to constitute a complete emergency notification message. Every effective emergency notification message should provide a specific behavioral request for the recipients or direct their attention to instructions provided during their training or education during the precrisis period. Without providing instructions about "what to do," an emergency notification message is inadequate.

Feedback Request

In addition to providing specific instructions, a thorough emergency notification message should also incorporate information and the means for recipients to respond. Many automated notification systems provide the capacity for receivers to answer a poll (e.g., confirm their relocation to the evacuation rally point), obtain additional information (e.g., Web page link), or even report their safety or danger status. In other systems, the messages might provide invitations for feedback.

Beyond the polling functions, the most important things that you will need to learn from recipients of your emergency notification messages are to confirm that they have received, appropriately understood, and appropriately responded (behaved in response) to the warning message that they have received.

DANGER–ACTION STRUCTURE

A template of warnings should be prepared in advance of an emergency that you can drawn on for use in hazardous situations. The basic formula is danger–action.

Key words and phrases describing dangers—such as "active shooter," "tornado warning," and "HAZMAT warning,"—can be vetted in advance of the emergency. Key words and phrases for actions, such as "lockdown," "Take shelter now," or "Evacuate now," can be conjoined with a list of informational messages to form the building blocks of emergency notification messages. These key word lists are the first step in creating more effective emergency notification messages.

The model suggests that you should write narrow-purpose notification messages to inform what the danger is and what action the recipient should take. Do not give convoluted instructions. Convey complex information and instructions using simple, brief, and concrete language. Avoid using technical, industry-specific jargon that may confuse and intimidate an audience already under stress. Identify things for people to do in response to the threat.

Consistent with this model, the tone of the message should indicate a willingness to cooperate and share authority and responsibility. You will also need to provide important roles and responsibilities. Tell people how to recognize problems or symptoms. Tell people how and where to go to get further information. Continue to help the audience understand the risks. Empower and enable appropriate risk–benefit decision making by your audience. Gain understanding and support for emergency response plans. Listen to your audience, and correct any misinformation or misunderstandings as quickly as possible.

3 & 30 PRINCIPLE

As discussed in a previous chapter, individuals' perceptions and attention are impacted during an emergency. Their abilities to grasp multiple key points in a given message are limited, and their attention capability is also restricted. If there were ever a time when messages need to be brief and concise, this is it. It is necessary to organize complex information and make it easier to be understood by the reader or hearer. This is similar to the expectations for lead or front-page media and broadcast stories. They usually convey only three key messages in less than nine seconds for broadcast media or 27 words for print. It has been suggested that optimal messages are those that convey key information in three short sentences and that convey no more than three key messages in 27 words.

The general rule of thumb is that the greatest number of recipients who perceive and attend to a message will listen or read the first few seconds or words of the message. Gradually, individuals in the audience stop reading or listening because of fatigue, distractions, diminished cognitive capacity, or failure to recognize the relevance or importance of the message or because they are making predictive assumptions—based on past experiences or projections of what they think it should say—(frequently incorrect) about what the remainder of the message will be. All of these tendencies for audience erosion of understanding and comprehension are accelerated by time pressures, other distractions, cognitive impairments, and other stressors.

Statistically, the first significant drop in reading or listening to a message occurs somewhere around the 27th to 30th second or word. After that time period, the total audience that is still attuned to the message and engaged with reading or listening continues to diminish. In cases when there is a clear perception of the personal relevance of the message, the time frame is extended. The number of audience members still attending to the message after different periods of time is based on a number of factors.

This suggests, consistent with common folk wisdom about messages, that it is most strategic to put the most important information and instructions as early in the first part of the message as feasible.

Conversely, sending a multiple-paragraph warning alert where the most important factors are left until the end of the message may miss many in the audience, even among those who received and attended to the message but who faded out in terms of attention and perception before reaching the vital facts.

To adapt to this reality, it is helpful to attempt to construct emergency notification messages that can fit into this message footprint to ensure that the widest possible attentive audience will read the key parts of the alert. Such messages must be carefully premediated to have the maximum effect on the intended audience. It may be necessary to provide a longer alert notification, but the test is to determine if the most important essentials are communicated in the first three sentences and 30 words.

One useful technique for writing notification messages is to attempt to write an emergency alert message in no more three sentences and in no more than 30 words. These compact 3 & 30 messages are what can be used for actual alerts. I suppose that one could use a 3 & 27 or 3 & 33 principle just as well, but I have found that 3 & 30 is a practical target for those who are writing messages. It is easy to remember (and my students demonstrate great recall of the concepts behind the 3 & 30 principle as well as the label), and it is a nice alliteration that comfortably rolls off the tongue. Thus, I suggest that one think in terms of a 3 & 30 message for a response phase emergency alert message.

The 3 & 30 messages have the widest possible applications and are compatible with almost every communication device, including those that are character- and byte-capacity restricted. It may be difficult to create such brief, concise messages. However, having done so, you will have far superior notification messages compared with longer and more rambling alert texts. It may be that you only need to alert and produce recall from your audience so that they can supply much of the "what is happening and what should I do" parts of the message. The alert message may be far more of activation than an "education" message. Either way, the 3 & 30 message can be used for both these purposes.

I think that this is a key element to aid in the construction of such messages. Remember that if you have done your job correctly, this is not the first time that you have communicated with your people about, for example, an evacuation. You don't inherently have to fully educate them to all evacuation routes, procedures, and assembly points in a 3 & 30 message. Rather, you should be able to create a notification message that resonates with the audience based on prior communication and training. Nonetheless, it usually takes several drafts to get a message compressed down to the essentials in three sentences and 30 words. The payoff for this effort is that such messages work much more effectively when used for emergency alerts.

60 & 6 PRINCIPLE

As discussed previously, the average individual suffers from diminished cognitive functions during peak stress periods of an emergency. We know that the ability to comprehend and understand messages decreases during these periods, and we also know that the typical person has a loss of about four grade levels in verbal or reading ability.

To adapt to these tendencies, it is important that you simplify the grammar, syntax, vocabulary, and reading level of your emergency messages for general-population audiences. Based on norms in North America, your messages should be written at a sixth-grade (or lower) reading level.

There are a number of different measurements for text readability. It may surprise you, but some of these measures are controversial and subject to fierce debate among academics. Despite the controversy, for practical reasons, the readability formula that I most often use when instructing notification message writers is the Flesch–Kincaid readability formulas for both grade level and reading ease.

The Flesch Reading Ease scale measures comprehension difficulty of text on a 100-point scale. The Flesch–Kincaid Grade Level scale computes a grade-level score for a written message. Consider the following statement:

My field experience has demonstrated that in addition to writing notifications at a sixth-grade or lower reading level, it is best if the notifications have a reading ease score of at least 60 or greater (on the 100-point scale).

The preceding sentence, for example, taken as a reading passage unto itself, has a grade reading level of about 19.9. The sentence also has a readability score of about 31.

If we rewrite the sentence as follows, the two sentences have a grade reading level of about 8.1 and a readability score of about 59:

Notifications should be written at a sixth-grade reading level or lower. Notifications should have a reading ease score of at least 60 or greater.

In a third draft of the same basic statement, the grade reading level drops to 5.4, and the reading ease score rises to 74:

Notifications should be at a sixth-grade reading level. They should have a reading ease score of at least 60.

Although no approach is perfect in this regard, my experience in field applications suggests that these are good guidelines for the writing of simpler, more concise, and easier to read notification messages. There are other formulas available (and some less controversial), but Flesch–Kincaid offers the most widespread availability of these equations in software and other electronic services.

THE COMBINATION FOR EFFECTIVE NOTIFICATION MESSAGES: 4/DA, 3 & 30, AND 60 & 6

To summarize, the recognition that a notification message must address the four primary functions, and alert messages should follow the danger–action arrangement (4/DA) form are crucial for optimizing the effectiveness of notification messages during emergencies. The message needs to be written in three sentences and no more than 30 words to ensure the largest attending audience. The content of the messages should have a reading ease score of 60 or higher and a sixth-grade reading level or lower. My students typically memorize a single equation to help them remember my approach to writing notification messages as the 4/DA—3 & 30—60 & 6 principle or rule. I like to think of the equation as a "combination" for unlocking the secrets of more effective notification messages. This just may be the proper combination to saving lives during the coming disaster or emergency.

ANATOMY OF AN EMERGENCY NOTIFICATION WARNING

The following is a dissection of a basic emergency notification message. While there can be wide variation in the types of notices that are created and disseminated, we can analyze some of the basic things that all emergency notification messages should contain. Using the 4/DA—3 & 30—60 & 6 formulas for response phase notifications, we can begin to see the outline of what types of elements need to be included and arranged in our notices. The Sample Message Box provides a detailed example of the method in action.

Sample Message Box

Framework

RE: ALERT

From: [Credible Known Source]

Danger: There is a *serious* emergency [describe incident including time and location in the building]. Provide essential information and consider tone (meta-message).

Action: [Instructions]. State behavioral request/instructions.

[Feedback request]

You can arrange the message in various formats to match different communication modalities (e.g., e-mail, SMS, or as a script to be read for an audio message). Therefore, there is no one standardized format regarding spacing, line breaks, or other typographical features. Furthermore, risk communication research has not found any empirical evidence supporting the trend for font choices that significantly affect attention, perception, or behavioral response in a positive way. This means that although widely used in many different emergency alert messages, font manipulation techniques (e.g., ALL CAP MESSAGES, different colors, **bold text,** or exclamation marks!!!!!) have not been shown to have any significantly better results than the same message without the font manipulations. In addition, this same body of research also suggests that danger symbols (e.g., skull and crossbones or bright-red X marks) also have little effect on attention, perception, and/or behavioral response in target audiences.

Sample Message 1

From:	Earl Hutchinson, Chief of Public Safety
Subject:	Danger Warning—Immediate Lockdown!

An armed intruder has been reported in the Central Administrative Building (CAB). If you are in the CAB seek shelter, lock the doors, stay put, and keep quiet. Stay away from windows. Law enforcement is responding. Do not leave a secure place until you receive an official all clear.***

You should draw on your stock word choices (e.g., intruder, shooter, and crazy person) and your stock message templates to create notification messages. You can vary these formats and use successive messages to alert your target audiences.

This initial message accomplishes three of four functions (information, meta-message, and behavioral instructions) following the danger–action structure. The text of the message scores a 73 on the reading ease scale and is at the fifth-grade reading level (thus, this message exceeds the minimum threshold for understandability as set by the 60 & 6 principle). This text is five sentences and 49 words (which is longer than the optimal alert message according to the 3 & 30 principle). Message writers might want to determine if a series of shorter messages might be better suited for the needs of this emergency situation. On the other hand, the critical information needs may require that a slightly longer version of this alert be used. The 3 & 30 and 60 & 6 principles are merely guidelines for recognizing that your audience has limits to what they can process and understand in a brief alert message. This message might be followed by another notice. Here is an example of a secondary urgent notice.

Sample Message 2

From:	Earl Hutchinson, Chief of Public Safety
Subject:	Danger Warning—CAB Lockdown!

Law enforcement has arrived and the CAB lockdown is still active. Continue to remained sheltered, stay put, and keep quiet. Do not move until you receive an official all clear.

[Optional]

To confirm that you are inside CAB, please press *1.

To confirm that you are not currently inside of CAB, please press *2.

This (main text) secondary message accomplishes three of four functions (information, meta-message, and behavioral instructions), and the optional additional two sentences would fulfill the fourth and final function. The second message still follows the danger–action structure. The text of the message scores a 73 on the reading ease scale and is at the fifth-grade reading level (thus, this message exceeds the minimum threshold for understandability as set by the 60 & 6 principle). The main body of this message is three sentences and 30 words (which is the optimal alert message length according to the 3 & 30 principle).

As more information becomes known, additional information could be supplied about what is happening, the specific threat, the actions people should take to further protect themselves and others, and where to go for more information. At some point an "all clear" message should be sent in the resolution phase to indicate that there is no longer a threat. The "all clear" message can be longer and more complex than initial response emergency notification messages. In addition, the "all clear" notification might contain lists of additional resources, various status-polling functions, and more background details of what happened.

Because these messages will need to be adapted to the specific event for a specific situation in a specific organization, it is impossible to simply borrow a list of notifications to use. You will need to create basic templates for various types of notifications that you may need to disseminate at each phase of the emergency. You will want to revise these as you assess, validate, and train for emergency operations.

MANAGING MESSAGING BEFORE, DURING, AND AFTER THE RESPONSE PHASE

Messages should acknowledge the facts and the risks with empathy. It is important to explain and inform about risk. On the basis of nearly 75 years of research, social scientists know that "panic" is a rarity in emergency alerts. The preponderance of evidence suggests that honesty and frank presentations of the dangers and threats is almost always received without starting an uncontrollable panic. There is little empirical justification for deception or shielding risks from people. Such actions are misguided and can create far more intractable problems in the long run than they avoid. I think that transparency and disclosure should be a prime goal in crafting messages. This means that you should describe what you know, don't know, and what you are doing about it in factual and objective terms. It is also important to commit to continued communication throughout the emergency and to your pledge to keep communication channels open.

As already noted, crisis situations include high levels of stress, time pressures, and limited and changing information, as well as the burden of making important life-and-death decisions quickly, accurately, and under intense scrutiny. These affect both your audience and your own team. Messages should be carefully crafted to work under these difficult conditions.

Driven by the dramatic changes in public information caused by the "information age" and the Internet, communicators today must meet three imperatives that define audience expectations: the demand for speed, for direct communication, and for honesty and transparency. Emergency notification messages simply must provide the essential information to have an informed and aware audience; they must also provide specific directions of what to do, address concerns, and reassure the receivers. However, some simplistic emergency notification models simply insert "information." Well-crafted messages are fraught with the potential for misunderstandings, failures, backlashes, and terrible consequences. "Raw" information (which is constantly changing as the "facts" of the situation change), of course, is not ready for distribution to all of your constituents. Because the communication team has access to the situation reports being provided by those involved in the incident and the response, they can immediately begin drafting emergency notification messages, media releases, fact sheets, employee messages, and executive leadership updates. Approvals are critically important because they provide accountability for the distribution of critical information. However, far too often these critical messages are written in haste during the developing crisis.

The guidelines suggested here are certainly not absolute. You have to weigh the choices and consequences in determining how much to include or how long an alert notice should be. Message writers might want to determine if a series of shorter messages might be better suited for the needs of this emergency situation. On the other hand, the critical information needs may require that a slightly longer version of the alert be used. The 3 & 30 and 60 & 6 principles are merely guidelines for recognizing that your audience has limits to what they can process and understand in a brief alert message.

Adopting an audience perspective, identify which information the audience members may need to have clarified, interpreted, or amplified and if any are likely to have specific unaddressed concerns. Then compile the information needed to provide at appropriate times. Finally, determine the most reliable, redundant, and understandable methods for getting that information to the audiences at the right time.

How a business manages or fails to manage emergency communication may make the difference in their ability to manage an emergency.

INFORMATION DISCLOSURE

A crisis creates an information vacuum that needs to be filled as soon as possible. Do not wait too long. If your company does not fill the void, someone else will, and they may not have the best interest of your business in mind.

The following is an example of poor message management: After the *Challenger* explosion in 1986, NASA delayed contact with the media for hours in search of details. When they finally made their presentation on air, all they did was repeat what millions of viewers had already seen. This was the first of many of NASA's public relations blunders in the ensuing crisis.[1]

An example of better message management is as follows: After the Tylenol poisoning scare in 1986, Johnson & Johnson sent out "half a million warning mailgrams to distributors, doctors, and health care practitioners by mid-afternoon of the day on which the first deaths were announced. Its domestic employees received two letters to keep them updated and to thank them for their support. The business established a toll-free consumer hotline that received more than 30,000 calls."[2]

Withholding information can often cast a guilty shadow on a business. In contrast, openness can increase positive perceptions held by the public, the media, and stakeholders in the business. After the Tylenol poisoning scare, Johnson & Johnson's "public disclosure and media relations efforts demonstrated that the business placed social responsibility before all other considerations." Effective crisis communication includes just the right amount of information. But what constitutes the right amount of information? How much information is enough? How much is too much?

Stress affects comprehension in an emergency. Overloaded messages may be too complex for an individual in a crisis to understand or interpret, whereas underloaded messages may not give clear instructions or present clear rationales for action. As previously noted, overloaded and underloaded messages lead to high rates of communication failure in a crisis.

A crisis plan can determine what constitutes the right amount of information by assessing how people understand, interpret, and act on messages. There are many factors that affect understanding, interpretation, and decision making during a crisis, such as

- cognitive processing capabilities
- perceived risk
- Information loading
- attitude–behavioral consistency
- balance
- uncertainty reduction drive
- situation awareness
- selective attention
- reaction time
- semantic memory

Cognitive processing involves thinking, reasoning, remembering, imagining, or learning. These abilities typically decrease as stress increases. To start with, everyone possesses different cognitive abilities and limitations, which in turn affects decision-making capabilities in a crisis. People perceive risks differently. Unknown risks are perceived to be greater than risks that are well understood. Selective attention limits what people may notice and remember during a crisis. Reaction time may also be affected during times of crisis. Factors that can affect reaction time include recognition, choices, number of stimuli, fatigue levels, reasoning, remembering, imagining, or learning. All of these concepts must be kept in mind in order to effectively communicate during a crisis.

NEGATIVE MESSAGES

Negative dominance also occurs. During times of stress it takes four positive statements to balance one negative statement. Stress negatively affects the cognitive process. Thinking of what to say and how to say it in the middle of a crisis leads to the possibility of mixed or erroneous messages. Messages may be too long, too short, or may not address relevant issues. The wrong message can contribute to already existing panic and confusion. Business reputations may suffer, and poorly worded answers to questions can affect an organization's survival after the disaster. The perception that an organization behaved in a competent manner during a disaster is key to successful recovery.

COMMUNICATION CHALLENGES RESOLVED: LINK TO MESSAGE MAPS

In the 21st century, effective emergency communication plans, whether with the media or through the media to targeted constituents, are an obvious must-have. Without an effective communication plan, chaos can flourish in an already catastrophic situation. As evidenced by 9/11 and Hurricane Katrina, the most problematic issues are often more centered on communicating effectively. These challenges directly affect an organization's ability to stay in business. Sending the wrong message can be just as harmful as—or even more than—not planning for the problem at all.

Successfully managing major crises requires creating a comprehensive communication plan and developing a number of specific, concrete messages that can be used in a variety of different delivery mechanisms.

One final aspect for emergency notification communication is sustaining communication consistency despite constant change. The nature of threats, audiences, contexts, premessaging education, circumstances, legal and regulatory conditions, and the sophistication, of the tools available are always evolving and are never static for very long.

TESTING AND VALIDITY WORK

The testing and validation of emergency messages is of crucial importance and, if not done on a frequent basis, can undermine your organization's entire response to the crisis itself. Employees, stakeholders, and any other constituents must be reached, be able to comprehend the message, and be empowered to respond appropriately during and after a crisis. There are a variety of different ways in which to test and validate your organization's communication plan. For example, running training scenarios can help immensely. Another example is to ask questions that test how completely the plan has been integrated into the organization's fabric. Even with well-mapped emergency notification messages the task of testing and revising your communication plans is never really ever "complete and finished." This is an ongoing process of refinement and specialization of your communication plans.

SUMMARY OF KEY POINTS

- After a notification message has been initiated, it must be delivered to everyone on the delivery list. There are five important issues: (1) whether the messages will arrive; (2) when the messages will arrive; (3) whether the recipient will actually read, see, or hear the message; (4) what the recipient will under-stand the message to mean; and (5) what the audience will do in response to the message.

- Basic principles for creating more effective emergency notification messages.

- A typical emergency notification message has at least four basic functions that it needs to accomplish: (1) information, (2) meta-message, (3) behavioral request/instructions, and (4) feedback request.

- The basic emergency notification message should follow a danger–action structure format. This is called the 4/DA structure.

- An emergency notification message should be written in no more than three sentences and 30 words. This is called the 3 & 30 principle.

- An emergency notification message for general population audiences should be written at a readability scale rating of at least 60 and no higher than the sixth-grade reading level. This is called the 60 & 6 principle.

CHAPTER 8

MESSAGE MAPS

This chapter presents the Chandler Method for mapping messages for emergency notification. It includes an explanation of the benefits of message maps, the technique for creating message maps, examples of basic and advanced message maps, and the role of stock message templates.

The Chandler Method for Message Mapping calls for messages to be drafted in advance of a crisis, for templates for all categories of messages to be approved in advance of an event, and for developing a comprehensive series of messages that complement the emergency notification message and target specific audiences or specific objectives. Once information has been approved for release, it needs to be distributed. Message mapping offers a road map to utilizing the optimal channels for message distribution. The expectations of doing the right things and communicating well go far beyond the initial notification. The initial emergency notification message is only a part of a larger communication strategy. Emergency notification messages must be accompanied by a continual stream of updated information available in all the ways that today's audiences choose to receive that information. The real challenge that today's leaders face is not just how they can quickly notify a large group of individuals, but how they can then continue to keep them well informed with timely, accurate information and how can they respond to the expectations that today's audiences have for direct interaction.

PREMEDIATE EMERGENCY NOTIFICATION MESSAGES

Message maps convey information specific to an organization, such as work resumption, post disaster insurance availability, and bereavement policies. Your business can use examples of other company's message maps, but you must design your own for the unique aspects of your organization. For example, a message map detailing what a southwestern organization will do in the event of an earthquake will not be useful for a northeastern company. Designing a message map that is unique to the organization also serves the needs of different demographic groups within a company, with multiple messages for various demographic groups. A message map must be sensitive to the functions of each aspect within an organization.

The message map is a critical part of crisis communication management and must use all of the crisis communication tools covered thus far. Most important, the message map must be written at or below a sixth-grade reading level, because of the effects of stress. I have used message-mapping approaches in my training, consulting, and university curriculum for about 30 years.

During my academic and professional roles I noticed the importance of having "talking points" for a variety of communication situations. As my work moved further into the crisis communication field, I tended to draw on my previous experiences, and the idea for mapping out messages in advance of an emergency, which one could draw on as needed to guide communications seemed a natural fit. I realize that there have been others who have also seen the advantage of such mapping of messages, and there have emerged other mapping approaches from other sources over the years. I am pleased, however, that some of the specific techniques and principles that I advocate have been associated with me though my teaching, consulting, speaking, writing, and training roles, and that a few years ago these approaches began to earn the nickname of the "Chandler Method" for message mapping. I use the descriptive term in this book to stay consistent with the usage among practitioners.

There is a need to have a navigational chart for your emergency messaging. To ad lib or try to spontaneously generate messages in the midst of an emergency is to risk problems and failures. What follows is a method for mapping out emergency messages that you can follow (and adapt) as a checklist for emergency messaging during each of the unfolding phases of the emergency.

MESSAGE MAPS: BLUEPRINTS AND ROADMAPS FOR EMERGENCY NOTIFICATION COMMUNICATION

The message map serves as a way to organize complex information into simple actions and commands that will facilitate successful handling of a crisis. In order to fulfill this basic function of crisis communication, the message map is written using the 4/DA, 3 & 30, and 60 & 6 rules of the Chandler Method. Remember, the best chance of getting an audience's attention occurs within the first nine seconds of a broadcast or during the first 30 words of written material. For example, the classic response to fire: stop, drop, and roll, conforms to the ideal message map system. It is easy, catchy, and short, containing only the pertinent information for a specific crisis. In this manner, complicated messages should be distilled into easy-to-remember actions that are useful for all members of an organization.

Message maps should never be created during a crisis; in order to be effective they must be proved useful *in advance*. Creating message maps ahead of time allows organizations to take into account knowledge, attitudes, and beliefs that suggest how target audiences will react to messages. They should not be hard for everyone to understand or written with technical jargon or high-reading-level words specific to a certain department within the general organization. Message maps should not be long, convoluted dissertations on what to do in a crisis. Short and simple is the key.

BENEFITS OF MESSAGE MAPPING

Creating message maps prior to a crisis ensures messages will be specific and appropriate, which is essential to disaster preparedness. Planned message maps deliver clear, consistent communication throughout a crisis, as well as allowing consideration of how the message will affect and motivate all constituencies. Planned message maps do the following:

- provide a road map and checklist for emergency communication
- eliminate the potential for dissemination of incorrect information
- reduce communication breakdowns
- respond to rumors more effectively
- meet elevated communication demands
- are adaptive (can be written in multiple languages or versions)
- ensure the right message reaches the right people at the right time

EASY ACCESSIBLE EXAMPLES OF MESSAGE MAPS

The federal government, including the Department of Health and Human Services (DHHS) and the Centers for Disease Control and Prevention (CDC), has developed and gathered resources that they have made available in the public domain to aid health officials as they communicate with the public in the first hours of an emergency. If relevant, you should use these materials for your own emergency communication planning. These publically available resources are also helpful for those outside of the health provider segment as models, examples, and learning tools. There are a wide range of materials relevant to risk and crisis communication prepared by the CDC and DHHS presented on the PandemicFlu.gov Web site, which is federal government information and is in the public domain. That means this information may be freely copied and distributed. Many checklists and other materials are available in PDF format for ease of duplication. They request that you use appropriate attribution to PandemicFlu.gov.

The CDC has also developed and made available a number of emergency notification message briefs and message maps. For example, the CDC and DHHS have a number of very helpful message maps for the public health sector regarding influenza pandemic, although these message maps are for precrisis (prepandemic) messaging (the kind of information and education that would need to communicate in advance of an emergency). You may use them freely, including copying or redistributing. You can download a PDF file containing all of these at http://www.pandemicflu.gov/news/pre_event_maps.pdf.

In consultation with the CDC, the study teams also examined public communication needs related to four different potential health threats and related general hazards. Each team researched all four threats; however, each study team concentrated on one threat in terms of analysis, report writing, message development, and verification analysis. These reports and materials are available in both English and Spanish at the Web page "Communicating in the First Hours" found at http://www.bt. cdc.gov/firsthours/resources/index.asp/.

CREATING EFFECTIVE MESSAGE MAPS

The chapter will explore the process for creating message maps for your organization. However, there is a connection between the creation of notification messages and the more expansive message maps that will guide their use.

If message maps are essential to disaster preparedness, why don't more organizations have them in place? Creating a message mapping strategy takes time, energy, and resources. The process involves input from many members of an organization. Although time-intensive, crisis communication planning can save lives, company assets, and organizational reputations. In the long run, it is economically more effective to take the time and resources to ensure excellent preparation. To create a message mapping strategy,

- determine core constituent audiences. Who is involved in or affected by the company? List all possible stakeholders (including employees, customers, vendors, suppliers, government regulators, investors, and media). Employees can also be divided into subcategories such as managers, fieldworkers, and clerical staff.

- walk through every possible outbreak or disaster scenario. What do you want to communicate to employees? Ask all "what if" questions any stakeholder may have. Paychecks, alternative work sites, telecommuting, health information, and more need to be considered.

- make choices about the types of messages. Consider legal, public relations, and financial and business implications and operations.

- determine channels of communication. How will these messages be communicated? How will the company know the message was sent? Is there a confirmation process? Is there an automated system in place or will the organization need to set up a phone bank to contact others?

- hone and refine actual message maps. Traditional message maps reduce important, emergency-relevant concepts to no more than three short sentences that convey three key messages in 30 words or less. Each primary message should have no more than three message points. The Application Box illustrates the basic message map process.

STOCK MESSAGE TEMPLATES

A stock message template is a predefined outline that is used as a foundation for a message map. The template can be adapted to create a message map for a particular crisis in a particular organization. The crisis planning team modifies the stock template to create message maps for crisis communications within the organization. Stock templates for message maps are created by using a hypothetical situation to generate a message map before a disaster occurs. Each stock template covers a particular type of crisis. A stock template provides an outline from which to start planning how the organization will respond to a particular crisis. For example, one section in a stock template provides for the contact information of specific individuals within the organization who have particular skills or information that can be useful in that particular crisis. The crisis planning team adds this information to create the message map from the template.

You should organize and categorize the message maps in both a database as well as in hard-copy binders for rapid referral. You could use a 100- or 1,000-base numbering system that gives you room for expansion and development but keeps the entire set of messages in a general sequence and relationship to one another.

For example, the CDC suggests that message maps should be developed for emergency communication during a pandemic. Here is a (partial) list of some the CDC-recommended message maps for the pandemic emergency:

101. What is pandemic influenza?
102. How is pandemic influenza different from seasonal flu?

Application Box: Example of a Basic Message Map from the CDC

Traditional basic message maps reduce important, emergency-relevant concepts to no more than three sentences that convey three key messages in 30 words or less. For example, the DHSS released a message map in January and February of 2006 regarding contagion control during a pandemic.

Message 1: People should stay informed about prevention and control actions.

1. Public health officials will share information about prevention and control actions.
2. Information about prevention and control actions will be shared in a variety of ways including through the CDC hotline and Web site.
3. Informed public participation and cooperation will be needed for public health efforts.

Message 2: People should use information about prevention and control actions to care for themselves and their loved ones.

1. Public health officials will provide information on the science and symptoms of the specific disease.
2. People should practice good health habits including eating a balanced diet and getting sufficient rest.
3. People should discuss individual health concerns with their health care provider, health department, or other trusted source.

Message 3: People should take actions to keep from spreading germs.

1. People should cover coughs or sneezes and wash their hands frequently.
2. People should stay away from sick people as much as possible.
3. If you are sick, stay away from others as much as possible.

When constructing message maps, planners have a number of key tools at their disposal. Three basic message map tools are stock templates, word choices, and creating goals and strategies.

---

103. Have there been influenza pandemics before?
105. What are the chances there will be pandemic influenza again?
108. How much warning will we have in the United States if a pandemic starts?
109. How fast would pandemic influenza spread?
110. How many people are likely to get sick in a pandemic? How many will die?

You can organize your message maps in a typology where 100-level maps are basic (background messages). These might be building blocks for other messages that are put in sequence, such as 200-level messages containing evacuation messages and 300-level messages about first aid. You can even go further and use subsequent numbering to indicate follow-up messages. For example, a 150-level message offers a basic message, and the 250-, 350-, 450-level maps offer either connected or subsequent messages as follow-up.

For each message you should develop three or four main points that are the keys to that message. The most important part of a message map is the detailed answers. The questions are designed to be used by the crisis communication team as a template for what information might need to be disseminated before, during, and after an emergency.

For each of the questions, provide three to four succinct answers. For example, the answers to question map 101, "What is pandemic influenza?" are as follows:

- Pandemic influenza is a global outbreak caused by a new influenza virus.
- Pandemic influenza is different from seasonal influenza (or "the flu").
- Timing and consequences of pandemic influenza are difficult to predict.
- Preparing now can limit the effects of pandemic influenza.

For each bulleted point, add three to four subpoints that explain the answer in more detail. The content of these itemized points inform and educate message recipients about the risks involved and how the crisis may affect them. The following are the detailed points for each item in response to the previous question:

- Pandemic influenza is a global outbreak caused by a new influenza virus.
  - The virus may spread easily, possibly causing serious illness and death.
  - Because so many people are at risk, serious consequences are possible.
  - Historically, pandemic influenza has caused widespread harm and death
- Pandemic influenza is different from seasonal influenza (or "the flu").
  - Seasonal outbreaks of the flu are caused by viruses that are already among people.
  - Pandemic influenza is caused by an influenza virus that is new to people.
  - Pandemic influenza is likely to affect many more people than seasonal influenza.
- Timing and consequences of pandemic influenza are difficult to predict.
  - Pandemic influenza has occurred three times in the last century.
  - Flu viruses are constantly changing.
  - The most serious was the 1918 pandemic that killed tens of millions of people worldwide.

- Preparing now can limit the effects of pandemic influenza.
  - The World Health Organization, the U.S. Department of Health and Human Services, and countries throughout the world have developed emergency plans for a pandemic influenza.
  - Informed public participation and cooperation will be needed for effective public health efforts.
  - Individuals should stay informed about pandemic influenza and prepare as they would for any emergency.

The four points are short phrases that serve as a general answer to the main question. The three to four subpoints provide more detail and give you a road map to where you are trying to go with this message. This organizes the answers clearly and makes the outline easy to read by breaking up the answers into separate parts.

It is helpful to provide additional information such as a Web site or a phone number that relates to the question you are addressing. For example, when a storm is approaching, it is helpful to know how to find the weather radio station in your area so that you can get current information. In addition, refer the reader to other questions in the message map that provide related information.

For example, for question 100 from the pandemic flu example, this is what the informational section at the bottom of the message looks like:

For more information

- see related maps
  - 105. What are the chances that there will be pandemic influenza again?
  - 202. What is being done to prepare for pandemic influenza?
  - 215. What can individuals do to prepare?
- call the CDC hotline at 1-800-CDC-INFO (1-800-232-4636). Go to http://www.pandemicflu.gov for more information.

MESSAGE MAPPING MODEL

The Message Mapping Model (Chandler Method) is essentially a more sophisticated version of traditional message mapping combined with some rules and principles derived from communication theory and research regarding message construction for audiences during crisis contexts. This model of emergency communication also makes use of three different levels of messages, capitalizing on the idea that preemergency information needs are quite different from actual mid-disaster needs. In the preemergency phase, audiences may not find messages relevant or compelling. Preemergency audiences are unlikely to remember even distilled messages, while mid-disaster audiences need more specific information. Messages created using this system are intended to develop and hold audience attention over time.

Message maps are risk communication tools used to help organize complex information and make it easier to express current knowledge. Crises often come without warning and can have a major impact on a company, particularly if the organization does not have a crisis plan in place. Action must be taken immediately, and response time becomes extremely limited. During a crisis, personnel within the organization may suffer from sleep deprivation, sensory overstimulation, physical discomfort, fear, isolation, and incessant pressure. When people experience these feelings, it is impossible to expect them to perform and react as they normally would. It is crucial to have a crisis communication plan that outlines in detail what responses your company will release when faced with an emergency situation. A prepared message map is a guide to lead individuals through a crisis when their thought processes may be impaired by stress.

Effective communication, coordination, and control during and after disasters are achievable to the extent that you have a workable plan for communicating. It is imperative that a complete crisis communication plan be created prior to a disaster. The crisis communication plan describes what to do before, during, and after a disaster. The plan should explain how your organization plans to communicate with people who could be potentially affected by the crisis.

Message maps address questions that people would ask of your organization if a particular crisis were to occur. Message maps start out very broad. For example, a company experiencing a product recall should first define what a product recall is. Do not assume that all of the organization's constituents are familiar with their vocabulary. Messages must include the context of the situation in order for a message to be acted on reliably, consistently, and appropriately. The following is the first question addressed in a product recall message map:

101. What is a product recall?

- A product recall is an official request to return a product to the maker.
  - Recalls are usually issued because of the discovery of a safety issue with a given product.
  - In simple cases, products can be brought back to the maker to be fixed.
  - In extreme cases, a product can be permanently removed from the market.
- A specific batch of the product, or the entire population, can be recalled.
  - If a certain batch of a product is faulty, only that batch must be recalled.
  - In such cases, it is the choice of the company whether to recall the entire population.

- Recall stipulations are decided by the government and consumer protection laws.
- Major product recalls occur in a variety of businesses.
  - Children's toys and other electronics are constantly recalled for malfunctioning electrical parts.
  - Car parts are often recalled because of their potential to seriously harm the consumer in the event of a malfunction.
  - Food products are often recalled because of long-term health risks.
  - Prescription medications and over-the-counter medications are often recalled after research demonstrates negative long-term effects.

When developing a stock message template, begin with broad questions and progress toward more specific messages to cover the whole gamut of questions that might be asked. By doing this, no question will go unanswered, and the company with a premade stock template will benefit by being sufficiently prepared to answer even the most basic questions that would otherwise be easy to overlook. Although the answer to the question posed above may seem simple now, it would be more difficult and time-consuming to conjure up that answer in the midst of a disaster.

If crisis planning must occur during a disaster, the process of creating crisis communication adds to the distress that individuals in the organization are already experiencing. It is much better to have message maps beforehand.

To create a stock template for your company, envision a crisis that could occur. For example, if your company is located in the southeast, your company may be at risk for experiencing a hurricane. If your company is located in the north and blizzards are likely, create a scenario to fit that storm.

Many types of natural disasters, such as blizzards or hurricanes, show signs of warning. If your company is faced with this type of disaster, the message map for the precrisis phase will be longer than the maps for the crisis and postcrisis stages. This is because there are many steps that can be taken to lessen the repercussions a storm can create, and the organization needs to notify people of these. An example of a message in the preemergency stage of a hurricane is as follows:

103. At what point should the office close if there is an approaching hurricane?

- Be informed of the location of the storm and the intensity.
  - Watch local news stations and listen to their instructions.
  - News station will keep you updated on when the storm will hit and the amount of damage it will likely cause.

- Typically, employees should be sent home after a hurricane warning is issued.
- Make sure the office building is securely prepared before leaving.
- Everyone helps each other out during a hurricane.
- Maintenance will most likely handle the preparation.
- Employees need to secure their own homes, so make sure the office is secured days before the hurricane hits.
- Inform employees what they should do with important documents before they leave (if there is time).
  - Documents should be stored in a safe during the storm.
  - Data should also be backed up and kept at an off-site location.
  - A designated person should have a master copy of all important, backed-up storage devices so that business can resume.

During an emergency, time is crucial. Crisis communications must be clear and targeted, and keep this in mind as you create message maps. The most important information must be relayed in a simple and specific message that all receivers will comprehend even if operating under high stress. The message map includes prepared messages for the different stage of a crisis. During a crisis, these messages can be quickly refined so that clear, accurate messages can be released quickly.

When a company responds to a crisis, messages that communicate risk are crucial. Risk communication messages are designed to communicate warnings, threats, consequences, dangers, and specific behavioral requests or guidelines to target audiences. Receivers are intended to understand these messages and react in some way.

Messages must be tailored to each specific audience, depending on what is expected of them. Different target audiences may receive different messages. For example, the crisis communication team may receive a different message than what the accounting department receives. Target audiences might be stakeholders, upper management, the crisis communication team, or the maintenance organization. When creating a stock template, identify all target audiences specific to the crisis you are planning for. Detailed information about the communication needs of each target audience is part of preparing the stock template. Then the needs of each individual target audience can be addressed when preparing crisis communication messages in the message map.

When determining what specific information to include in a message map, think of what is essential to convey to your target audience. Remember that transparency and honesty build credibility and increase the likelihood that your messages will be received and considered by the audience. They can also prevent any accusations that the organization did not confront the crisis properly.

Stock templates must be tested and rehearsed. Create your sample messages with a specific point, terminology, best delivery channel, and intended response in mind. By testing and rehearsing the crisis communication plan, individuals will be familiar with their role, how to adapt the message plan to the exigencies of a particular crisis, and when to release which messages.

WORD CHOICE

Word choice can affect the outcome of a crisis. How people respond to a crisis communication message, such as a warning, is affected by the word choice used in the message. While developing crisis communication messages, you must consider word choice. Your whole strategy may prove futile if a message is not understood as intended.

First, word choice is vital to ensure that the message is presented clearly and does not invoke overreaction. When creating your stock template, remember that messages will be dispersed to different audiences. Have a list of synonyms readily available to tailor wording in messages to different target audiences if necessary. Different wording might be appropriate when you are relaying information to a group of distressed employees rather than to the crisis communication team. The wrong message can contribute to chaos and confusion. Certain words are more calming than others.

An example of good word choice helped to avoid panic when worried family members telephoned USAir after Flight 427 crashed near Pittsburg in 1994. Trained phone operators responded with "Yes, sir. his/her name is on the list" instead of "Yes, sir. he/she was on the plane." Each answer elicits a different response. Saying "he/she is on the list" is less harsh than "yes, he/she was on the plane." The word *plane* may evoke images of the crashed plane, and the particular family member on the flight, further heightening emotional anxiety.

Word choice and readability are intimately related. Many types of disasters can strike an organization. Part of managing a crisis is making sure that all communications are clear, effective, and motivate the recipients to take the intended action. Crisis communications, particularly in the early stages of a crisis, must be understood immediately, even in a time of shock and confusion. These messages convey what is happening, what recipients of the message should do to protect themselves, and what steps the organization will take to resolve the crisis.

It is important to remember that there are six different phases of a crisis or emergency. Word choice can differ depending on which stage of a crisis the communication will be released. The stock template includes sections for each of these phases as well as the pre- and the postemergency periods. Within each phase, the informational needs and target audiences differ.

During the warning phase, words such as *warning* and *caution* alert employees and potentially others that some kind of crisis may occur. This captures their attention, ensuring their compliance as the crisis progresses. Messages developed for the warning phase tend to be more informative as opposed to the response or management stages, which aim to invoke behavioral actions from recipients.

During the response and management phases, it is especially important to keep words simple and messages clear. The crisis phase usually requires action from the recipients of the message. Messages that require behavioral compliance should be very straightforward and not ambiguous. For example, the following message demonstrates a clear message that requires action from the recipient:

Make a list of retailers who bought the product. Tell all customers about the recall. Plan to alert individuals within 150 miles of the recall. Inform call centers.

This message describes what the recipient should do in the event of a product recall. These messages should be easy to read and comprehend. There should be no ambiguity message should. The readability of this message is at a fifth-grade reading level. All audiences could understand and react to this message, even in a state of panic.

Resolution and recovery phase message maps deal with the end game for an emergency. The wording of messages for these phases should be clear and easily read, although this is not as imperative as it is for response or management phase's messages when lives may hang in the balance. The recovery phase messages should focus on how to get a company back on track.

During the recovery phase, there also should be an evaluation of the actions taken during the crisis phase. A stock template should include a section on how to evaluate the success of crisis communications. Evaluating crisis actions are crucial to analyzing how an organization can make its crisis communication plans more effective. For example, the following list describes measures for evaluating the success of a product recall.

301. How should a company measure a recall to see if it was successful?

- The company should set a high recall benchmark.
  - There should be a benchmark established for a successful recall rate.
  - A high benchmark recall rate could be considered anything over a 50 percent return.
  - The key factors in a high return are comprehensive customer recall rates and high risk perception by the consumer.

- The company should set a medium recall benchmark.
  - A middle benchmark is considered anything between a 30 percent and 50 percent recall return.
  - Recalls can also be judged as successful if no injuries or deaths occur and if there is a lack of complaints after the recall.
  - A medium benchmark could be considered successful if there is no loss of reputation or adverse effects on image.
- The company should identify a low recall benchmark.
  - A low recall benchmark is the lowest possible recall return, typically less than 30 percent.
  - Very-low-value items with low perceived risk warrant a lower benchmark.
  - At a low benchmark, success could be defined as no alarm to consumers or any injuries or deaths.

The wording in this section of the message map is more complex than the precrisis and crisis messages, but it is still very straightforward.

During a crisis, demands for information occur when stress is high, time is short, and informational resources are limited. During this time, employees might face aggressive questioning from media reporters. When the company is in the spotlight and exposed to criticism and interrogation, word choice is especially crucial.

The crisis communication team should analyze each part of a response and look at how it may be perceived by the public. Look at the response as an isolated comment and not as part of a longer answer. Each phrase of a sentence can carry many interpretations. Be sure that information is clear and informative.

Messages should not include too much information nor should they include too little. You don't want to overload people with information, but not including enough information could be equally as damaging. If you do not tell employees and other stakeholders exactly what is going on, their safety could be put at risk. For example, in the product recall, consumers must know *exactly* what safety hazards the product presents. Consumer safety is more important than covering up a mistake.

RESPONSE TIME

How long it takes an organization to respond to a crisis can affect the outcome of the crisis. When a crisis occurs, people want information and they want it immediately. If an organization fails to address the issue right away, someone else will, and this usually leads to negative attention because that person may not have the organization's best interest in mind. They may not have accurate facts or up-to-date information or may have a reason to deliberately portray the situation in a bad light at the expense of the company. The following is an example of the importance of a company's immediate response.

After the Tylenol poisoning scare in 1986, Johnson & Johnson sent out half a million warning mailgrams to distributors, doctors, and health care practitioners by mid-afternoon of the day on which the first deaths were announced. Its domestic employees received two letters to keep them updated and to thank them for their support. The business established a toll-free consumer hotline that received more than 30,000 calls."

The company immediately took accountability for the crisis events and worked quickly to remedy the wrongs caused. The public responded favorably because the company took responsibility and proceeded with appropriate measures to deal with the situation, and they did it in a timely manner.

The method also integrates with longer term strategic communication efforts (including training and educational communication as well as prepositioned vital information and providing access instructions that can be used during an emergency) that work together for precrisis issues: crisis alert communication, acute crisis, and postcrisis applications.

Some information is complex and requires extensive text in order to be sufficiently informative. The concepts in this book are hopefully sophisticated so that they would not be able to be reduced to a three sentence, 30-word message. So too, an evacuation plan that incorporates a buddy system; assembly and rally point locations; and instructions for equipment, doors, lights, and other standard evacuation procedures that is far too complex to try and accomplish in an emergency notification message. There is a place for books, handbooks, procedure manuals, online resources, and longer memoranda in order to educate or communicate vital information. In fact, the knowledge obtained from these information efforts should be instantly "recallable" by people when they are notified in an emergency. It is too late to stop and start reading a 200-page evacuation procedure manual when the call for evacuation arrives. However, if properly trained in advance, having received quick reference guides to aid recall, and training that was systematically reinforced, an individual can truly be empowered to react appropriately when the emergency alert is received.

Part of the Chandler Method for this type of alerting includes creating a three-tier message reinforcement of these deep knowledge resources in the targeted audiences. Once you have provided sufficient (and ongoing) education and training, it is appropriate to plan out a systematic process of reinforcing those instructions and knowledge by creating a three-tier message system that can work as a bridge between the background education and the specific alert message, which should enable the individual to recall and follow the instructions as he or she has been trained and reinforced.

THREE TIERS FOR AN ALERTING MESSAGE

These three types of message formats are best represented as three tiers:

- Tier 1: Long-term basic core messages. Core messages intended for long-term use should be reduced to phrases of no more than three or four words, such as "Click It or Ticket." Core messages can be used in all phases of a crisis and as such must be extremely simple and redundant.
- Tier 2: Three easy-to-remember phrases. Second-tier messages are only moderately repetitive and are used to convey information during alert phases. Rhythm is important in tier-two messages. A tier-two message would be "Stay Alert, Stay Awake, Stay Alive."
- Tier 3: Three sentences with limited word counts. Third-tier messaging is appropriate for the response and management phases of an emergency. These should be carefully crafted messages that can be used directly for notification purposes. Third-tier messaging uses three sentences with limited word counts to provide detailed, specific information. Third-tier messages are more personally relevant to specific audiences, specifically those in danger. These messages have the lowest amount of redundancy and contain the greatest amount of specific information.

Tier 3 messages include the categories of emergency notification messages that can be mapped in advance of the crisis. The creation of Chandler Message Maps is very similar to that of traditional maps. However, the reductive nature of Chandler Message Maps means that messages are created from most complicated to least complicated:

- Begin with the overall goal in mind.
- Determine the three subpoints that relate to the goal.
- Create three sentences for each message goal (tier 3).
- Reduce sentences to three short phrases (tier 2).
- Reduce phrases to three or four words (tier 1).

You should have a comprehensive communication plan that includes how you are going to educate and train, as well as consistently reinforce strike* and alert your people so that they are best prepared to react appropriately during an emergency.

THE ROLE OF MESSAGE MAPS FOR RAPID DISSEMINATION OF ALERTS

Message mapping is an essential communication tool in crisis preparedness and recovery. Message maps allow organizations to successfully manage major business interruptions, thus limiting damage to personnel, property, and business viability. The maps are both road maps and checklists that can expedite the process of alerting all of the relevant people and to provide a status report on how much of your communication plan that you have accomplished at any point in the emergency. Automated notification systems are particularly appropriate for using message maps when there is a need to get the information out quickly. An automated notification system can deliver voice and text messages to one, ten, or thousands of people within minutes. There are proven vendors of automated notification services that enable corporations, government agencies, and schools to achieve considerable savings through rapid and efficient communication in routine, urgent, and emergency situations.

PREPARATION FOR USING A MESSAGE MAP

There should be one voice emanating from the organization presenting the facts as accurately, quickly, and convincingly as possible to ensure a heart of integrity and proficiency radiating from the organization. Everyone in the company should know who to refer questions to in order to ensure the confidence of a congruent message. From there, the message needs to be divided to meet the interests of the audiences and stakeholders unique to a business. This will require preplanning before the crisis strikes to lessen the load when time is scarce.

Success requires careful preparations in order to ensure the effectiveness of corporate communications. First, the crisis communication team must have a list of all audiences and stakeholders. Second, they must list all communication options available and then decide which channels are most appropriate for which audiences. Although a crisis will always entail numerous complications unaccounted for, getting the crisis team thinking about this process will prepare them. Even if they cannot follow the original plan, they can build on brainstorming. Third, decide the message for each audience and send it out as quickly as possible.

Step 1: Recognize Your Audiences

All effective communication is strategically designed and adapted appropriately for specific "target" audiences. Every audience has unique attributes and perspectives. Each member of various audience groups has (shared) information needs, priorities, and concerns. Different audiences perceive information, situations, risks, rewards, salience, and valence differently. Communication is most effective when it is prepared with the nature and characteristics of the intended audience in mind. Communication is least effective when it is created without consideration of the targeted audience or only a general and vague notion of who will be hearing or reading the messages. Communication that is written from the perspective of the sender or creator of messages is typically the most obfuscated, confusing, and indecipherable. One of the important rules for effective communication is to know your audience before you decide what, how, when, and where to attempt to communicate with them.

"Particular audiences should be served by particular messages if the communication is to do a specific job of work. Vague content in communication brings about vague results. Carefully researched, sharply refined and aimed messages with achievable desired effects are what is required."[1]

Your company is affected by and affects a broad range of people. When an emergency strikes they will want to know what is going on. To make sure all stakeholders get the correct message and remain congenial to the organization, the crisis communication team needs to be committed to getting them the correct information quickly and conveniently. Employees are top priority—without them a business cannot survive. They will also be an immediate information source to people outside the organization. After employees, a list of other stakeholders will follow. Although some audiences are more important, communication travels rapidly in our fast-paced world. The following list possible audiences and stakeholders, but these will be unique to every company. The crisis communication team should keep a detailed notebook of the stakeholders unique to your business with all contact information. This list should be updated regularly.

Stakeholders in your business may include the following:

- employees
- suppliers
- Wholesalers
- retailers
- community members
- community leaders
- family members of employees
- customers
- news agencies

- investors
- board of directors
- insurance representatives
- business partners
- government and law enforcement officials
- Industry activist groups
- unions

Step 2: Choose Your Methods of Communication

After recognizing all audiences, set about strategizing *how* to communicate and in what order. The method of communication will vary depending on your company, audience, and the type of crisis. Look at what methods of communication are available and best for the situation. Examine modes of communication already in place, plan how to use those channels in different types of crises, and then look for alternative channels. It may help to create a worksheet.

Be Creative

Because of the unanticipated effects of a crisis you may need to be creative with modes of communication. After 9/11, some business executives used rather surprising resources to communicate to their employees. The CEO of Oppenheimer appeared on CNBC to announce that it would be operational as soon as the market reopened and published a full-page letter in several large New York newspapers. After 9/11, American Airlines used a means of communication unique to their business. They were able to use the monitors for printing itineraries and tickets, which were located throughout the airport, to instead communicate to employees. Tim Doke, vice president of corporate communications, explained, "Voice mails were transcribed and sent to the machines that print itineraries and tickets—as well as posted on the Internet and e-mailed to employees. . . . This meant that even maintenance people on tarmacs who might not have Internet access at work could be kept informed." Lastly, at the *New York Times* headquarters, the CEO, Russell Lewis, immediately began informing and reassuring employees over the emergency loudspeaker system throughout the building.[2]

It is vital to communicate information within the premises when crisis strikes. For example, it is important for people to know who the crisis management team is, where emergency rations and water are, or if a room has been inspected for bombs or poison. These are just a sample of situations that may occur. Part of the preplanning should include a detailed list of potential hazards. From this list decide what types of communication may be necessary and create premade signage or other communication strategies. One university uses green windbreaker jackets that the crisis management team keeps in their offices to wear in the event of a crisis so they can be identified. Also consider how to get information from the field to the crisis communication center. Also keep detailed records of the situation.

Immediate Actions

Immediately after a crisis hits, the crisis communication team should launch and update key information channels. If power, phone lines, and the Internet are working, immediately record updated voice mail and revise the Web site with situation updates and contact information. The more open and upfront you are the more likely you are to be greeted with respect rather than discontentment in ensuing days.

Contacting the press is the next priority after informing employees. When a story breaks, the media will be in a mad rush for information. The sooner a business can get the message out correctly and help the reporters do their job, the better. As soon as possible, start sending press releases to the media. Although it is not always necessary, you may want to also hold a press conference. Press conferences allow a single message to be communicated to a broad audience, allowing for an even message across multiple news sources. As mentioned in previous examples, the press may also be a vital tool to inform stakeholders.

Step 3: Craft Your Message

Each audience is going to have different concerns in mind. Families of employees will want to know if their loved ones are okay and how to contact them. Stockholders will want to know how this situation affects them financially and what's going to happen to their stocks. Again, this is where a graph is helpful in analyzing what messages need to go to what audiences. In general, answer the basic questions: who, what, when, where, and why. In addition, keep the following things in mind:

- First and foremost, be honest. Most people are more offended by a business lying about a crisis than they are about the crisis itself.[3] John Budd, the former vice president of Emhart Corporation, learned this the hard way after neglecting to communicate that $8 million was missing from one of their divisions. The media discovered the fault and ran damaging stories for the next 10 days. Budd's advice, "Just tell it."[4] According to one executive, "Stonewalling and otherwise holding back on information about a crisis is the most common mistake made by executives."[5]
- Your message should be oriented toward action.[6] It should be showing what the company is *doing*.
- Positively define the business's identity.
- If it is a crisis that involves harm, compassion should also coat the message. What you communicate will be heard by many people who do not have the same knowledge and experience as you. You do not want to come off as insensitive by lacking compassion or concern.
- Talk from the viewpoint of the public's interest, not your company.[7]
- Speak in personal terms whenever possible.
- State the most important facts at the beginning.
- Do not exaggerate the facts and do not give unconfirmed information out, ever.[8]
- If you don't want a statement quoted, then don't say it.

It will help to have preplanned messages for all possible scenarios, detailed response action plans, and mapped messages reviewed ahead of time. The crisis communication team may want to create a booklet of possible crisis scenarios that can affect the organization and make press releases, signs, statements, possible questions and answers, pertinent background information sheets, videos, or sound bites ahead of time that can be sent out immediately. Within a week after the Food and Drug Administration reported multiple accounts of syringes found in Pepsi cans in 1993, PepsiCo "released" a video that had been prepared well in advance (it was already on file with television networks and stations) that documented Pepsi's safety precautions used during canning.[9] Although the PepsiCo video did not discuss any specific contaminant (e.g., syringes), it clearly showed the thorough safety precautions that were used in the canning/bottling process that would make it highly unlikely that any foreign contaminate could ever accidently or maliciously be inserted into cans of the product. They saved weeks of time required to produce such a video by having it done in advance, and they placed their information response on the air almost instantaneously after the first reports were made public. This example provides an apt object lesson on the time advantage and quality advantage that having your messages prepared in advance affords compared with ad hoc, post facto message construction.

Strategic Executive Crisis Communication Keys	
Effective Executive Communication Characteristics	**Ineffective Executive Communication Characteristics**
Honest	Exaggerating
Concise	Overdramatizing
Clear	Saying "No comment"
Accurate	Insensitive remarks
Precise and literal	Trivializing concerns
Correcting inaccuracies	Arguing
Organized	Attempting humor
Respectful	Sarcasm
Compassionate	Irony
Sympathetic	Jargon
Pleasant	Being too technical
Poised	Speculating
Articulate	Lying
Following through	Alienating
Concerned	Evading

Word Choice

Word choice is also vital when communicating during a crisis to make sure the message is presented clearly and does not cause overreaction. After a storm, one university had to make sure their outgoing messages said, "classes canceled and offices closed" not "campus closed." If all audiences hear that the campus is closed, vital workers may not come to work, which could only escalate problems. When criticism forced Intel to recall its Pentium processor, carefully chosen words that would not cause alarm to customers and shareholders suggested that they could exchange their version for a newer model.[10]

Some spokespeople may be tempted to respond with "no comment" by default in response to media inquiries. Nothing is more damaging to a business's image. This answer is known to produce distrust in the organization, implying guilt.[11] In an article in the *Journal of Corporate Public Relations*, Bernard Charland states, "When a business responds to media inquiries with 'no comment,' it usually reflects disregard for the media and the public interest. Not commenting is a mistake that damages [press] relations and negatively impacts a business's reputation. It usually indicates a lack of strategic management information and flies against the premise of corporate responsibility."[12] The contact information of the inquirer (most likely a reporter) should be recorded, followed by a quick response. If someone makes a promise that he or she will find out information, then he or she must follow through.

Although "no comment" should never be an option, sometimes "no" is a legitimate answer. It is okay to say no when the reporter has a bias and will report the issue with a negative slant or when asked to interview about a scandal or when confronted with loaded questions. If you cannot confirm that the reporter is from the agency they say they are from, your company should refuse to answer with anything other than "no." A similar answer is also acceptable if the information requested by a reporter will take an unreasonable amount of time or if the information releases important information that will reveal too much to competitors.[13]

Be Available

Immediately after a story breaks or your business issues a press release, you will likely encounter people looking for more information. Someone from the crisis communication team needs to be available at every hour of the day to accommodate audiences who are on time schedules, office hours, or time zones different from the rest of the business. In addition, this person should have detailed information and all the contact information for the personnel of the rest of the office so others can be summoned immediately.

Handling Misinformation in the Media

"Corporate management must be factual, honest, and forthright, make certain they keep the media informed. . . . I believe the media assumes the same responsibilities when they enter into the dialogue."[14] The media may try to get the story correct; however, sometimes they will give inaccurate information. Not all misinformation calls for immediate alarm or correction.

If the misinformation is not vital information, sometimes it is best to simply let it go. It may be sufficient to call the station and have them correct the information for their files so that it is not reported incorrectly again.

Remember that when you ask for a correction, it may make audiences remember the error more. When contacting the station, remember that the reporter and/or editor may get defensive because it is a direct slap to their journalism abilities. Sometimes it is appropriate to write a letter to the editor to get the facts straight. On rare occasions you will want to insist on having a correction printed. This may be in the case of specific numbers that have an effect on stocks. However, it is sometimes possible to advertise the correct information in discreet manners.[15]

During a crisis event, common sources of misunderstanding arise from a variety of different sources too numerous to list. The goal will be to recognize the source of misunderstood messages and learn to navigate around those sources.

CONCLUSION

Although your organization may have an excellent crisis management plan, if there is not lucid communication within the company that flows out, then its integrity will not be seen, and it may easily become the villain. Thus, it is vital to fill the information void after a crisis with the correct information without delay. Attempting to ignore the crisis may only exacerbate the problem. Careful preparations are required before a crisis strikes and time is scarce. First, recognize the audiences. Second, choose the methods of communication. Third, decide what messages to tell to which audiences. After a crisis it is vital for the crisis communication team to be available around the clock and know how to appropriately handle misinformation.

Establish a commitment to emergency notification. Have a plan. Develop communication systems capable of meeting the needs for effective emergency notification. This would include warning and alert systems capable of providing timely, accurate, and comprehendible information as well as consistently providing appropriate authorities with complete information regarding an emergency.

The importance of effective emergency notification communication is indisputable. During an unfolding emergency it is essential to notify and alert individuals, contact the crisis management team, and manage the command, control, and coordination communication functions essential to respond, mitigate, and save lives. Notification of impacted or vulnerable individuals is essential whether the emergency is the result of a natural disaster, industrial accident, workplace violence, active shooter, or major terrorist incident. Effective emergency notification can also distribute timely information about ongoing risks, medical and psychological resources, human resources, and personnel information; communicate with families and the surrounding community; and keep all key processes functioning even when people are displaced from their desks, phones, and usual locations. The time to prepare to successfully notify people during your next disaster or emergency is now.

One major component of effective emergency communication is message mapping, the process of creating prepared messages that can be used in a wide variety of urgent situations. There is definitely a role for message mapping, such as the Chandler Message Mapping Model for emergency communication preparedness.

SUMMARY OF KEY POINTS

- Emergency notification messages should be premeditated and prepared in advance of an emergency incident.
- Message maps are blueprints and road maps for emergency notification communication.
- There are a number of benefits for message maps, including high-quality messages, review, faster send time for messages, strategic planning, compatibility with automated notification systems, and forming checklists for notification due diligence.
- The process for creating message maps includes determining message goals by hazard and phase of the emergency, identifying target audiences, developing stock message templates, and organizing the messages into matrixes and message points.
- The Chandler Message Mapping model is a more complicated approach for mapping out messages.
- Message maps rely on strategic elements such as word choice, tiers of message types, source or spokesperson characteristics, and constructing better messages.

NOTES

INTRODUCTION

1. WKMG. http://www.koinlocal6.com/news/local/story/Boil-Boring-Water/40xNrUFxQUqXLRQA-cIDug.cspx/ (accessed August 21, 2009).

2. Ibid.

3. Ibid.

4. Ted Brown, Selecting an Emergency Communications Solution, Disaster Resource Guide. Cited in Disaster-Resource Guide.com. http://www.continuity eguide.com/articles/07p_144.shtml/ (accessed January 15, 2010).

5. PS Docket No. 07-287. FIRST REPORT AND ORDER. Adopted: April 9, 2008. Released: April 9, 2008. FCC 08-99A1, http://hraunfoss.fcc.gov/edocs_public/attachmatch/FCC-08-99A1.txt/ (accessed January 15, 2010).

6. Ibid.

7. Ibid.

8. Ibid.

9. P. Davidson, "Nationwide Cellphone Alert System in the Works," *USA Today*, April 8, 2008 http://www.usatoday.com/money/industries/telecom/2008-04-08-fcc-emergency_N.htm/ (accessed January 15, 2010).

10. Ibid.

11. Ibid.

12. Ibid.

CHAPTER 1

1. D. O. Reihart and R. D. Baier, (2009) "Communication: The Indispensible Part of Emergency Medical Services," *Journal of Lancaster General Hospital* 4, no. 2 (Summer 2009), http://jlgh.org/content/Report4_v4i2.htm/ (accessed May 1, 2010).

2. The Federal Response to Hurricane Katrina: Lessons Learned, February 2006, ed. Frances Fragos Townsend, Assistant to the President for Homeland Security and Counterterrorism. http://georgewbush-whitehouse.archives.gov/reports/katrina-lessons-learned/ (accessed May 1, 2010).

3. Ibid.

4. Ibid.

5. M. Chertoff, National Emergency Communications Plan, July 2008; revised August 7, 2008, http://www.dhs.gov/xlibrary/assets/national_emergency_communications_plan.pdf/ (accessed May 1, 2010).

6. Ibid.

7. Ibid.

8. Ibid.

9. Ibid.

10. L. K. Moore and Shaun Reese, (2008) Emergency Communications: The Emergency Alert (EAS) and All-Hazard Warnings. Congressional Research Service, The Library of Congress. September 2, 2005. Updated August 25, 2008. CRS Report for Congress: Received through the CRS Web, http://www.au.af. mil/au/awc/awcgate/crs/rl32527.pdf/ (accessed May 1, 2010).

11. Ibid.

12. Ibid.

13. Ibid.

14. Ibid.

15. Ibid.

16. Implementing Recommendations of the 9/11 Commission Act of 2007, Public Law 110-53, August 3, 2007, http://www.nctc.gov/docs/ir-of-the-9-11-comm-act-of-2007.pdf/ (accessed May 1, 2010).

17. Ibid.

18. Ibid.

19. U.S. House of Representatives, Implementing Recommendations of the 9/11 Commission Act of 2007, Conference Report to Accompany HR 1, July 25, 2007, http://surfacetransportationisac.org/SupDocs/9-11CommAct.pdf/ (accessed May 1, 2010).

20. Ibid.

CHAPTER 2

1. Intergovernmental Oceanographic Report 2006. Annual Report Series, 13. Intergovernmental Oceanographic Commission, UNESCO, http://unesdoc.unesco. org/images/0015/001531/153144e.pdf/ (accessed May 1, 2010).

2. Indian Ocean Tsunami Warning System, http://marketing.reachinformation. com/Indian_Ocean_Tsunami_Warning_System.aspx/ (accessed May 1, 2010).

3. Integrated Tsunami Watcher Service, http://www.iibc.in/itws/ (accessed May 1, 2010).

4. Grand Traverse County Michigan, Emergency Management, http:// www.co.grand-traverse.mi.us/departments/health/Emergency_Management/ Emergency_Management_Homeland_Security/ICE_In_Case_of_Emergency.htm (accessed May 1, 2010).

5. Ibid.

6. Ibid.

7. Ibid.

8. Kilkenney County Council Online, http://www.kilkennycoco.ie/eng/ RSSLatestNewsAndAnnouncements/In%20Case%20Of%20Emergency%20-%20 ICE.shortcut.html/ (accessed May 1, 2010).

9. Ibid.

10. Ibid.

11. Ibid.

12. National Oceanic and Atmospheric Administration's National Weather Service, http://www.weather.gov/chat/er.php/ (accessed May 1, 2010).

13. L. K. Moore and Shaun Reese, Emergency Communications: The Emergency Alert (EAS) and All-Hazard Warnings. Congressional Research Service, The Library of Congress. September 2, 2005. Updated August 25, 2008. CRS Report for Congress: Received through the CRS Web, http://www.au.af.mil/au/awc/awcgate/crs/rl32527.pdf/ (accessed May 1, 2010).

14. Ibid.

15. Ibid.

16. Ibid.

17. Ibid.

18. Ibid.

19. Ibid.

20. Ibid.

21. Ibid.

22. Ibid.

23. Ibid.

24. Ibid.

25. Ibid.

26. Ibid.

27. National Commission on Terrorist Attacks upon the United States, The 9/11 Commission Report, 2004. Washington, DC: Government Printing Office. The Commission closed on August 21, 2004. This site is archived at http://govinfo.library.unt.edu/911/report/index.htm/ (accessed May 1, 2010).

28. Ibid.

29. Ibid.

30. Moore and Reese, Emergency Communications.

31. Ibid.

32. Ibid.

33. Ibid.

34. Ibid.

35. Ibid.

36. Ibid.

37. Ibid.

38. Ibid.

39. Ibid.

40. Ibid.

41. Ibid.

42. Ibid.

43. Ibid.

44. L. K. Moore, Emergency Communications: The Emergency Alert (EAS) and All-Hazard Warnings. Congressional Research Service, The Library of Congress. September 2, 2005. Updated January 26, 2009. CRS Report for Congress: Received through the CRS Web, http://assets.opencrs.com/rpts/RL32527_20090126.pdf/ (accessed May 1, 2010).

45. Moore and Reese, Emergency Communications, p. 11.

46. Moore, Emergency Communications.

47. Moore, Emergency Communications.

48. Health Alert Network, Centers for Disease Control, 2010, http://www2a.cdc.gov/han/Index.asp/ (accessed May 1, 2010).

49. Ibid.

50. Ibid.

51. Japan Starts Disaster-Alert System Using Satellites, February 9, 2007, http://www.reuters.com/article/idUST35898/ (accessed May 1, 2010).

52. IEICE Technical Committee Submission System, July 9, 2009, http://www.ieice.org/ken/paper/20090709HaNW/eng/ (accessed May 1, 2010).

53. Ibid.

54. Japan Starts Using Satellite Disaster-Alert System, http://www.newscientist.com/article/dn11169-japan-starts-using-satellite-disasteralert-system.html/ (accessed May 1, 2010).

55. For example, see Chapter 7 of Sheriff's Office Policy and Procedure Manual, Colorado Springs, CO: El Paso County Sheriff's Office. January 1, 2004, http://shr2.elpasoco.com/PDF/policy/chapter_07/731_policy.pdf/ (accessed May 1, 2010).

56. Ibid.

57. Amber Alert: America's Missing: Broadcast Emergency Response, Office of Justine Programs: U.S. Department of Justice, January 13, 2010, http://www.amberalert.gov/ (accessed May 1, 2010). See also, How CodeAmber Began, Code Amber News Service (CANS), Amber Alert About Us, http://codeamber.org/about.php/ (accessed May 1, 2010).

58. Ibid.

59. Georgia's Public Alert System, Georgia Bureau of Investigation, http://alerts.gbi.georgia.gov/02/gbi/alerts/0,2614,67865199,00.html/ (accessed May 1, 2010).

60. MAILE Amber Alert, Department of the Attorney General, State of Hawaii, http://hawaii.gov/ag/mcch/main/maile_amber/ (accessed May 1, 2010).

61. Morgan Nick Amber Alert, Arkansas State Police, https://www.ark.org/asp/alerts/mnaa/index.php/ (accessed May 1, 2010).

62. Amber Alert: America's Missing: Broadcast Emergency Response, January 13, 2010.

63. Ibid.

64. Florida Launches Sliver Alert, October 8, 2008, http://www.wctv.tv/home/headlines/30654919.html/ (accessed May 1, 2010).

65. Florida's Silver Alert Plan, Frequently Asked Questions, http://www.fdle.state.fl.us/MCICSearch/Documents/SilverAlertFAQ.pdf/ (accessed May 1, 2010).

66. Ibid. See also Amber/Silver/Blue Alert Programs, Texas Department of Public Safety, http://www.txdps.state.tx.us/dem/pages/amberalertprogram.htm/ (accessed May 1, 2010).

67. Ibid.

68. Ibid.

69. Ibid.

70. Ibid.

71. Ibid.

72. P. Davidson, (2008) "Nationwide Cellphone Alert System in the Works," *USA Today*, April 8, 2008, http://www.usatoday.com/money/industries/telecom/2008-04-08-fcc-emergency_N.htm/ (accessed May 1, 2010).

73. Daily Open Source Infrastructure Report for 10 April 2008, Department of Homeland Security, http://www.globalsecurity.org/security/library/news/2008/04/dhs_daily_report_2008-04-10.pdf/ (accessed May 1, 2010).

74. P. Davidson, "Nationwide Cellphone Alert System in the Works,"

75. P. Davidson, "Nationwide Cellphone Alert System in the Works,"

76. P. Davidson, "Nationwide Cellphone Alert System in the Works"; see also Daily Open Source Infrastructure Report for 10 April 2008.

77. Ibid.

78. Welcome to Manhattan, Illinois! http://www.villageofmanhattan.org/index.asp?Type=DYNAFORM&SEC={4C485771-9A7A-4B01-A3BB-AACFFA3A5C1C}&DE=/ (accessed May 1, 2010).

79. Emergency Numbers, City of Lubbock, Emergency Management and Homeland Safety, http://eoc.ci.lubbock.tx.us/emNumbers.aspx/ (accessed May 1, 2010).

80. Ibid.

81. Ibid.

82. Community Emergency Alert Network, Faifax County, Virginia, https://www.fairfaxcounty.gov/CEAN/; see also Frequently Asked Questions, http://www.fairfaxcounty.gov/cean/faqs.htm/ (accessed May 1, 2010).

83. Ibid.

84. Ibid.

85. Welcome to Alert DC, District of Columbia, https://textalert.ema.dc.gov/index.php?CCheck=1/. Note that this site requires cookies to be enabled. See also Alert DC, http://alert.dc.gov/eic/cwp/view.asp?A=3&Q=563034/ (accessed May 1, 2010).

86. Ibid.

87. Ibid.

88. Ibid.

CHAPTER 3

1. A. Skraba, M. Kljajic, and M. K. Borstnar, "The Role of Information Feedback in the Management Group Decision-Making Process Applying Systems Dynamic Models," *Group Decision and Negotiation* 16, no. 1 (2007):77–95. See also R. Y. Hirokawa and M. S. Poole, *Communication and Group Decision Making* (Newbury Park, CA: Sage, 1996).

2. I. Bonn and S. Rundle-Thiele, (2007) "Do or Die: Strategic Decision-Making following a Shock Event," *Tourism Management* 28, no. 2 (2007):615–20.

3. K. Cameron and D. Whetton, *Organizational Effectiveness: A Comparison of Multiple Models* (New York, NY: Academic Press, 1983), 60.

4. R. C. Chandler, J. D. Wallace, and S. Feinberg, *Six Points for Improving Crisis Communication Plans: The Application of Visual Communication for Effective Crisis Response* (Minneapolis, MN: Tandberg, 2007).

5. G. King, III, "Crisis Management and Team Effectiveness: A Closer Examination," *Journal of Business Ethics* 41, no. 3 (2002):235–49.

6. Ibid.

7. Ibid.

8. R. C. Chandler and J. D. Wallace, "The Role of Videoconferencing in Crisis and Emergency Management," *Journal of Business Continuity and Emergency Planning* 3, no. 2 (2009):161–78.

9. Ibid.

10. Ibid.

11. Ibid.

12. Ibid.

13. R. C. Chandler, J. D. Wallace, and S. Feinberg, *Six Points for Improving Crisis Communication Plans: The Application of Visual Communication for Effective Crisis Response.*

14. R. C. Chandler and J. D. Wallace, "The Role of Videoconferencing in Crisis and Emergency Management."

15. R. Fleischauer, R. Vergudo, and J. Newberry, (2000). *Crisis Communications Guide and Toolkit* (Washington, DC: National Education Association, 2000), 13–5.

16. Ibid.

17. Ibid.

18. Ibid.

19. Ibid.

20. Ibid.

21. Ibid.

22. Ibid.

23. Ibid.

24. Ibid.

25. Ibid.

26. Ibid.

27. Ibid.

28. Ibid.

29. Ibid.

30. Ibid.

31. P. Argenti, "Crisis Communication: Lessons from 9/11," *Harvard Business Review* 80, no. 2 (2002):108.

32. B. Reynolds, Crisis and Emergency Risk Communication. Presentation to the 8th National Biosafety Symposium (CDC), Atlanta, GA, 2004; see also "Introduction," The Public Official's Guide to Disasters, http://www.mapleton.org/ULCT%20Information/Public%20Officials%20Guide%20to%20Disasters.doc/ (accessed May 1, 2010).

33. Ibid.

34. Ibid.

35. Ibid.

36. Ibid.

37. Ibid.

38. Ibid.

39. "Introduction," The Public Official's Guide to Disasters; see also Be Ready Utah, http://bereadyutah.gov/DownloadPreparednessGuides.html (accessed May 1, 2010).

CHAPTER 7

1. O. Lerbinger, *The Crisis Manager: Facing Risk and Responsibility* (Hillsdale, NJ: Laurence Erlbaum Associates, 1997), 42.

2. Ibid., 47.

CHAPTER 8

1. A. Gregory, (2000). *Planning and Managing Public Relations Campaigns* (London: Kogan, 2000), 116.

2. P. Argenti, "Crisis Communication: Lessons from 9/11," *Harvard Business Review* 80, no. 2 (2002):108.

3. O. Lerbinger, *The Crisis Manager: Facing Risk and Responsibility* (Hillsdale, NJ: Laurence Erlbaum Associates, 1997), 30.

4. Ibid., 45.

5. Ibid., 32.

6. B. T. Blythe, *Blindsided: A Manager's Guide to Catastrophic Incidents in the Workplace* (New York, NY: Penguin Putnam, 2002).

7. O. Lerbinger, *The Crisis Manager: Facing Risk and Responsibility*, 32.

8. Ibid., 32.

9. Ibid., 29.

10. Ibid., 38.

11. Ibid., 31.

12. M. K. Pinsdorf, *Communicating When Your Business Is under Siege* (New York: Fordham University Press, 1999), 45.

13. See C. M. Howard and W. K. Mathews, *On Deadline: Managing Media Relations* (Prospect Heights, IL: Waveland Press, 2002), 95–8.

14. Ibid., 55.

15. Ibid., 93–5.

GLOSSARY

ACT-SaaS: Active Software-as-a-Service (SaaS) delivery model for automated emergency notification with multiple data centers in an active–active configuration. The ACT-SaaS service provides scalability, availability and security, lower implementation and maintenance costs, free upgrades, delivered maintenance, and fast implementation. ACT-SaaS enables customers to access powerful software over the Internet at maximum performance levels without purchasing or maintaining hardware, software, or telecommunications equipment. See also SaaS. (ACT-SaaS is a registered mark of Everbridge, Inc.)

Alert: Notification that a potential disaster or emergency situation is imminent, exists, or has occurred; usually includes pertinent information and a behavior directive request.

Assembly Point: The designated area at which personnel (i.e., customers, students, employees, visitors, and contractors) assemble if evacuated from their building or site.

Asynchronous Communication: When message and reply do not occur in real-time exchanges (synchronous communication) and there is an unpredictable delay in receiving or responding to a message.

Automated Notification System: A hardware or software (computer or Web-based) technology that allows for automatic mass notification message distribution on multiple communication channels (e.g., SMS, e-mail, and cellular phones) requiring minimal personnel and time.

Business Continuity: The ability of an organization to continuously operate so as to sustain operations and production, to provide service and support for its customers, and to maintain its viability before, during, and after a business disruption.

Business Continuity Plan: Documentation of plans and the planning process of developing (and documenting) contingency arrangements, communication, and response procedures that enable an organization to respond to a disruption or emergency event and effectively resume critical functions after an interruption.

Business Impact Analysis: A process designed to prioritize business functions by assessing the potential quantitative (financial) and qualitative (nonfinancial) impact that might result if an organization were to experience a particular business disruption, emergency, or disaster.

Call Tree: A documented procedure that describes the telephone calling responsibilities and the calling order used to disseminate messages using sequential telephone calls as prescribed by the calling tree. A manual process of successive telephone calls to disseminate alerts and emergency notifications.

Common Alerting Protocol (CAP): Standard for new, digitized alert networks using multiple technologies.

Communication Center: Area of crisis command or emergency operations or separate facility where the communication technology for inbound and outbound exchanges are centered. Typically includes a wide range of communication technology and various communication modalities.

Crisis: A critical event that if not handled in an appropriate manner, may dramatically impact an organization's profitability, reputation, or ability to operate or an occurrence and/or perception that threatens the operations, staff, shareholder value, stakeholders, brand, reputation, trust, and/or strategic or business goals of an organization.

Crisis Management Team (CMT): A team consisting of key managers and executives and other key role players (i.e., media representative, legal counsel, facilities manager, and disaster recovery coordinator) and the appropriate business owners of critical functions who are responsible for recovery operations during a crisis.

Danger–Action Structure: Basic formula for constructing an emergency notification message informing what the danger is and what action the recipient should take.

Disaster: A sudden, unplanned catastrophic event causing unacceptable damage or loss: (1) an event that compromises an organization's ability to provide critical functions, processes, or services for some unacceptable period of time or (2) an event where an organization's management invokes their recovery plans.

Emergency: A sudden event that creates a potential threat to safety, property, and routine processes, which demands an immediate and appropriate response.

Emergency Alert System (EAS): A national warning system in the United States put into place in 1997, superseding the Emergency Broadcast System and now jointly coordinated by the Federal Communications Commission (FCC), the Federal Emergency Management Agency (FEMA), and the National Weather Service (NWS).

Emergency Operations Center (EOC): A site from which response teams or officials (municipal, county, state, and federal) provide direction and exercise control in an emergency or disaster. It may include a command center used by the crisis management team during the early phases of an emergency or crisis. An organization should have both primary and secondary locations for an EOC in case one of them becomes unavailable or inaccessible. It may also serve as a reporting point for deliveries, services, the press, and all external contacts.

In Case of Emergency (ICE): Campaign to encourage mobile phone users to store the word "ICE" in the address book of mobile phones with the name and phone number of the person who should be contacted in the event that the cell phone owner is injured and unable to communicate this information.

Information Management Policy: A documented policy that specifies information or materials that can and cannot be released during emergencies, including the securing or safeguarding of all sensitive information, electronic or otherwise.

Message Map Matrixes: Message maps organized into specific checklists (sequences) of actionable emergency notifications to disseminate at predetermined points of an emergency, as well as subsequent follow-up messages until predetermined confirmation and acknowledgments have been received. Frequently includes emergency notification messages (written in advance) ready to ready to be launched in an emergency notification system.

Message Maps: Written documentation containing key message templates (basic message talking points) organized by phases of an emergency situation, categorized by message goals, target audiences, optimal delivery (communication modalities) paths, and message sources, as well as additional (cross-referenced) information.

National Emergency Communications Plan (NECP): Addresses gaps and determines solutions so that emergency response personnel at all levels of government and across all disciplines can communicate as needed, on demand, and as authorized. The NECP is the first national strategic plan aimed to improve emergency response communication and complements overarching homeland security and emergency communications legislation, strategies, and initiatives.

Notification: Communication message that provides current information (e.g., warning or alert) about a risk, threat, or situation along with a request for response or behavioral compliance. Typically, notification messages during emergencies are considered as urgent dispatches that are essential to inform, warn, disclose, or persuade.

Public Law (PL) 110-53 [Title IX]: Specifically addresses private-sector preparedness and defines important business continuity provisions to be carried out by the Department of Homeland Security. The combined results of these various requirements will be to eventually establish an "Accreditation and Certification Program" for private-sector preparedness that provides businesses and organizations with a clear road map for strengthening preparedness, response, recovery, and the ability to continue operations.

Rich and Lean Media: The relative depth, range, and quality of a communication medium to convey communication characteristics including tone; and nonverbal, contextual, and complex aspects of an interchange. Video communication is a richer medium than a (leaner) telephone call because of the additional nonverbal and context factors that can be observed and taken into account while seeking to understand and be understood.

SaaS: Software-as-a-Service (SaaS) delivery model for automated mass communication solutions with multiple data centers in an active–active configuration.

Short Message Service (SMS): A communication service standardized in the Global System for Mobile Communication (GSM), using standardized communication protocols allowing the interchange of short text messages between mobile telephone devices.

Stock Message Templates: Predefined outline of approved key words or phrases that can be used as a foundation for a message map.

The Warning, Alert, and Response Network Act (WARN Act): As signed into law as Title VI of Public Law 109-347, required the establishment of a Commercial Mobile Service Alert Advisory Committee by the FCC to make recommendations on technical requirements, standards, regulation, and other matters needed to support the transmittal of emergency alerts by commercial mobile service providers to their subscribers.

Web-Native Application Service Provider: Automated notification system designed and built for multiple users to access over the Internet. Organizations pay a reasonable usage fee for full access to the system.

4/DA—3 & 30—60 & 6: Combination of (Chandler Method©) emergency notification message construction rules.

3 & 30 Principle: Optimal emergency notification message length that conveys key information in no more than three sentences (with no more than three key message points or one per sentence) and in 30 or fewer words (also referred to as the 3-3-30 rule).

60 & 6 Principle: Optimal emergency notification message complexity and grammar reading ease rule that calls for messages that score at least 60 on the Flesch Reading Ease scale and no more than the sixth-grade reading level using the Flesch–Kincaid Grade Level scale.

INDEX

9/11, 11, 19, 42, 77, 139, 167, 187
1998 Florida wildfires, 73
2003 California wildfires, 72
2006 White House Report, 10
2007 Southern California Wildfire, 36–37
3 & 30 Principle, 158–159, 162–163, 168
4/DA-3 & 30–60 & 6, 161
60 & 6 Principle, 160–164
911 Commission Report, 9

Accreditation and Certification Program, 13
Active Shooter, 35, 45, 66, 155, 157, 192
ACT-Saas, 52–54, 133, 142–143
Alarms, 22–23
Alert DC, 50
AMBER Alerts, 46; Levi's Call, 46; Maile AMBER Alert, 46; Morgan Nick AMBER Alert, 46
American Red Cross, 37, 90
Analyzing audiences, 89
Assembly Point, 159
Australian Country Fire Authority, 38
Automated emergency notification systems, 32, 45, 51, 121–122, 126, 132, 137–138
Automated Notification, 120–154; w/ACT-SaaS Service, 142

Basic principles, 155
Behavioral request, 155–157
Bernard Charland, 190
Blueprints and roadmaps, 170–171

Business Continuity, 8, 13, 51, 106, 122, 134
Business Continuity Plan (BCP), 134

C-3 Inefficiencies, 60
Call (Phone) Tree, 121, 152
CAP, 38
CDC, 44, 73, 81, 171–172, 174
Challenger Disaster, 165
Chandler Messages, 184
Chandler Message Mapping Model, 192
Chandler Message Maps, 184
Chandler Method, 169–170, 176, 183
Crisis Management Team (CMT),
CNBC, 187
Cognitive impact of emergencies, 66–68
Collaboration Issues, 60
Command Center, 127, 131
Commercial Mobile Service Alert Advisory Committee, 12
Common Alerting Potocol (CAP), 38
Common Challenges, 56, 81
Common Emergency Communication Challenges, 56–57
Common hazards, 33, 100, 101, 105, 154
Common needs, 101–103
Communication breakdowns, 51, 62, 70, 85, 115, 117; People, 63–66; Inattentional blindness, 65; selective attention, 65, 67, 166; misunderstandings, 63; situational risk, 64; selective perception, 65–66; situational awareness, 64

Communication Center, 14, 16, 70, 114, 187
Communication Challenges, 55–83, 93, 146–147, 167
Communication Challenges, 74; Rumor Control, 74; Phone Line Jams, 74; Loss of Internet Access, 74; Media Intrusion, 74; Scattering of Personnel, 74; Media Mistakes, 74–75; Credibility, 75; Panic and Alienation, 75–76; Media, 76
Communication Challenges Resolved, 167
Communication failures, 120, 126, 140
Communication Planning, 6, 9, 19, 82, 84–105, 107, 171, 172
Communication Processes, 69–70
Communication tools, 16, 56–57, 62, 71, 73, 97–99, 105, 170, 177
Community Emergency Alert Network (CEAN), 49
Congressional Research Service, 38, 40, 42–43
Contact database, 89–92
Core Messages, 84, 184
Creating effective message maps, 172–173
Crisis Communication Plan, 55, 81, 84, 81, 93, 101, 104, 118, 126, 139, 159, 172, 177, 180–181
Crisis Communication Priorities, 76–77; Preparation, 77; Planning, 77–78; CCT, 79; Organizational Personnel, 79; External Relations, 79–80; Media, 80; Stakeholders, 80
Crisis Communication Roles, 55
Crisis management, 51, 55, 59, 62, 77–79, 82, 104, 122, 187, 191–192
Crisis management plan, 77, 191
Crisis Management Team (CMT), 78, 187
Crisis preparation, 101

Danger-Action Structure, 157, 162–163
Delivery Status Notifications, 32

Department of Health and Human Services (DHHS), 171–172
Department of Homeland Security (DHS), 11, 12, 26, 40, 42
Digital Emergency Alert System (DEAS), 42
Digital Signage, 29
Disaster, 166, 171–173, 176–178, 180, 192

EAS (Emergency Alert System), 39–42, 45, 47
EBS (Emergency Broadcast System), 21, 39–40
Education and training of personnel, 103
Effective Notification Messages, 161
Emergency Broadcast System (EBS), 21, 39
Emergency Alert System (EAS), 39
Emergency Contact Database, 84, 105
Emergency Interoperability Consortium (EIC), 38
Emergency Message, 141, 154–168
Emergency Notification Basics, 20–54
Emergency Notification Plan, 48, 74–76, 80, 84–86, 91, 105, 120, 139
Emergency Notification Planning, 84
Emergency Notification Processes, 7
Emergency Notification Systems, 32, 45, 47, 50, 121–122, 126, 132, 137
Emergency Operations Center (EOC), 16, 109, 122
Emergency Warning sirens and alarms, 23–24
Emhart Corp., 188
Enron, 92
EOC, 122, 141, 146

Facebook, 33, 36, 139
Fairfax County Virginia, 49
Fax, 51, 98–99, 122, 128, 130, 140, 145
FCC, 12, 30, 40–41, 47–48
Federal Emergency Management Agency (FEMA), 40–41, 43
FEMA's National Continuity Programs Directorate, 42

First messages in an emergency, 58–59

Five Communication Steps for Success, 81; Solid Plan, 81; First with Information, 81; Express Empathy, 81; Be Honest and Open, 82

Flesch Reading Ease Scale, 160

Flesch-Kincaid Grade Level Scale, 160

Fort Collins, CO, 49

Four functions for emergency notification messages, 155

Global System for Mobile Communication (GSM), 204

Handling Misinformation in the Media, 191

Health Alert Network (HAN), 44

Homeland Security Advisory System (HSAS), 43

Hurricane Katrina, 9, 167

ICE (In case of emergency), 27–29

Immediate Actions, 187–188

Improving Emergency Communications Act of 2007, 11

Indian Ocean Tsunami Warning System (IOTWS), 24

Information Disclosure, 16, 61, 94–95, 165

Information Management, 84, 87, 105, 115

Information Management Policy, 87, 105

Information policy, 14, 86, 92, 94, 95

Information Quality, 60

Instant Messaging (IM), 32–33

instant messenger, 32, 99, 122

Integrated Emergency Notification in the Public Sector, 47–48

Integrated Public Alert and Warning System (IPAWS), 40

Integrated Tsunami Watcher Service (ITWS), 24

Interoperable Emergency Communications Grant Program, 11

J-Alert, 44

John Budd, 188

Legal review, 95–96

LEPC, 90

Lubbock, Texas, 49

Managing the message, 87–88

Manhattan, Illinois, 48

Mass Notification Systems, 38; History, 38; EBS, 39; EAS, 39–40

Meebo, 33–34

Message Maps, 48, 97, 108, 118, 138, 167, 169–192

Message Maps for rapid dissemination of alerts, 184–185

Message planning, 18, 84, 89, 96–97, 131

Message Planning Tools, 84

meta-message, 64, 111, 114, 155–156, 162–163

Methods of Communication, 31, 187, 191

Mobile Instant Messaging (MIM), 33

Mobile Phones, 25–27, 30, 49, 52

NASA, 165

National Emergency Alert System, 21

National Emergency Communications Plan (NECP), 21

National Incident Management System, 11

National Oceanic and Atmospheric Administration (NOAA), 40

National Preparedness Guidelines, 11

National Response Framework, 11, 40

National Science and Technology Council, 43

National Warning System, 12

National Weather Service (NWS), 32, 40

NECP, 7, 11

New York Times, 187

Northern Illinois University, 2

NWS, 32, 40, 44

Oppenheimer, 187
Organization for the Advancement
   of Structured Information
   Standards (OASIS), 38

Pacific Tsunami Warning Center, 24
Pager(s), 30, 47, 49–51, 71, 99, 122,
   128, 140, 150
pandemic influenza, 175–176
PandemicFlu.gov, 172
Participation barriers, 59
Paul Davidson, 47
Pepperdine University, 103
PepsiCo, 189
Personal digital assistant (PDA), 25,
   99, 122
Planned message maps, 171
Post-crisis (communication), 97, 178,
   183
Pre-crisis (communication), 157, 172,
   178, 182, 183
Pre-mediated Emergency
   Notification Messages, 169–170
Preparation for using a message
   map, 185
Private Sector Integrated
   (All-Hazards) Emergency
   Notification Systems, 50–51
product recall, 177–178, 181
Public Law (PL) 110–53 [Title IX], 7

Recovery Challenges, 76; Community
   Feelings, 76; Victim's Feelings, 76;
   Divisiveness, 76
Recovery Phase, 107, 116–117, 181
Resolution, 106–07, 115–118, 125,
   142, 163, 181
Response Phase,
Response Time, 108, 120, 125, 152,
   177, 182–183
Rich Media, 24, 34, 93, 98, 121
Risk assessment, 106–107, 111–112,
   118
Rumors and misinformation, 94, 118,
   122
Russell Lewis, 187

Short Message Service (SMS), 24,
   29–30, 33, 35–36, 51–52, 70, 128,
   140, 145, 162
SILVER Alert, 46
Six Phases of Emergencies,
   106–119
SMS and Text Messaging, 29–30
Social Media, 37
Social, Networking Services, 36
Software-as-a-Service (Saas), 52–53,
   133–134, 142–143, 151
Specific Area Message Encoding
   (SAME), 41
Stages of a crisis, 75, 180
Stock Message Templates, 162, 169,
   173
Stop, Drop and Roll, 171

Targeted Notification Systems, 47
Tavares (Lake County), Florida, 1
Technology, 71–73
Telephones, 25; Calling Trees,
   25–26; Reverse 911, 26–27;
   Hotlines and Call Centers, 27;
   In Case of Emergency (ICE),
   27–28
Testing and Validity, 103–104, 167
The Warning, Alert, and Response
   Network Act (WARN Act), 12
Three Tiers for an Alerting Message,
   184
Three-tier messages, 159
Tim Doke, 187
Total Cost of Ownership (TCO), 52;
   Next-generation interactive
   automated notification systems, 52
Twitter, 36–39, 139
Tylenol, 165, 183
Types of notifications, 88–89, 163

WARN Act, 12, 140, 141
Warning Phase, 108–113, 155, 181
Web Page, 34–36
Web-Native Application Service
   Provider, 125
Word Choice, 180–182

ABOUT THE AUTHOR

ROBERT C. CHANDLER (PhD University of Kansas; MA Wake Forest University; BA Harding College) is Professor of Communication and Director of the Nicholson School of Communication at the University of Central Florida. He is the former Chair of the Communication Division at the Center for Communication and Business at Pepperdine University. Dr. Chandler is also an adjunct Professor of Communication and Conflict Management in the Straus Institute of Dispute Resolution at the Pepperdine University School of Law. He is a member of the International Communication Association, National Communication Association, Life Member of American Forensic Association, National Board Member of the Center for the Public Trust, and was selected for membership in the American Academy of Experts in Traumatic Stress (in collaboration with the National Center for Crisis Management).

Dr. Chandler is an internationally recognized researcher and scholar with more than 100 academic and professional papers, including widely circulated white papers on emergency and crisis communication. He has previously authored more than 50 academic and professional publications, and he is the author of several books including his most recent *Surviving the Pandemic: A Communication Management Guide for Business*. His previously authored and co-authored books include *Managing the Risks for Corporate Integrity: How to Survive an Ethical Misconduct Disaster*, *Pandemic: Business Continuity Planning Priorities for the Coming Outbreak*, *Media Relations: Disaster Recovery and the News Media*, and *Crisis and Emergency Communication*.

Dr. Chandler is a recognized expert in organizational and business communication with a specialty in organizational crisis communication including communication during emergencies, crises, and disasters; emergency notification communication; crisis leaderships crisis teams; and audience analysis for message comprehension and response. Dr. Chandler is also a subject matter expert in areas such as communication and conflict management, organizational communication priorities for pandemics and other public health crises, risk communication, behavioral and psychometric assessment and appraisal, leadership, teamwork, multicultural and intercultural diversity, organizational integrity, employee ethical conduct, and business ethics. He has addressed attentive audiences around the globe ranging from Warsaw to Sydney and Seoul to St. Petersburg.

Dr. Chandler has provided communication expertise and service to the higher education community including several colleges/universities, for the National Student's Safety and Security Conference, University Risk Management Association, and National Association of College Auxiliary Services. He has also provided subject matter expertise and service to numerous businesses, companies, and agencies, including the Federal Aviation Administration, Federal Reserve Board, IBM, Verizon, State Farm Insurance Company, U.S. Customs and U.S. Border Patrol, Delta Airlines, Northwest Airlines, American Airlines, New South Wales (Australia) Food Authority, Department of Defense (CATTS), Hospital Association of Southern California, State of Montana Safety Council, State of Minnesota, Hill & Knowlton Company International, Resolutions Strategies Group, Greater Orlando Airport Authority, American Red Cross, United Way, and TANDBERG. Dr. Chandler has effectively presented and led successful training seminars for a wide range of associations and sponsoring bodies including DRJ's Spring and Fall World Conferences on Disaster Recovery, The Conference Board, International Security Conference, RSA-Europe, Association of Contingency Planners, Government Technology Conference, Joint Commission Resources, ConnecTexas, American Public Works Association, and ConSec.